Animal
Tracks
2ND EDITION

OF THE MIDWEST

by Jonathan Poppele

Adventure Publications
Cambridge, Minnesota

Acknowledgments

Wildlife tracking can sometimes look like a solitary endeavor—the lone naturalist in the field, studying tracks and sign. It is true that to get good at tracking one needs to spend considerable time in the field, often alone. But to get *really* good at tracking, one needs to learn together with others. Like all sciences, wildlife tracking is a collective enterprise, even when it appears individual. As Dr. Mark Elbroch likes to say, tracking takes more than a lifetime to learn.

I have done my best in this book to gather and present information that will be helpful to everyone who is interested in learning to identify and interpret animal tracks across the Midwest and beyond—but the knowledge I share here does not belong to me. It is the product of many lifetimes of work by countless biologists, naturalists, trackers, and educators, to whom I am deeply indebted. A warm thank-you to the community of instructors and evaluators at Tracker Certification North America, especially Dr. Mark Elbroch, Dr. Kersey Lawrence, Nate Harvey, Casey McFarland, David Moskowitz, Michelle Peziol, George Leoniak, and Marcus Reynerson, for their support of me in my own journey as a tracker and their tremendous contributions to the science of wildlife tracking. Thanks also to the members and supporters of the Minnesota Wildlife Tracking Project: Donnie, Kirsten, Rob, Amy, Brian, Bill, Mike, Sydney, Eric, Blake, Marty, Terry, Kathy, and so many more, who have spent years field-testing the first edition of this guide and pushing me to be a better tracker. I am grateful to the community of trackers on iNaturalist, particularly Kim Cabrera and Jonah Evans, for building a community and generously sharing their knowledge and experience. Special thanks also to colleagues Amy Beal, Jonathan Shapiro, Dr. Caitlin Potter, Nick Sharp, and Sue Mansfield; to my first tracking teachers, Tom Brown Jr. and Jon Young; to Julie Martinez and Bruce Wilson for their excellent illustrations; and to Brett Ortler and the staff at Adventure Publications.

Illustrations by Julie Martinez, Bruce Wilson, and Jonathan Poppele
Cover and book design by Jonathan Norberg
Edited by Brett Ortler and Ritchey Halphen
Photo credits on page 349

10 9 8 7 6 5 4 3 2

Animal Tracks of the Midwest: Easy-to-Use Guide with 90 Track Illustrations
First edition, 2012; second edition, 2022
Copyright © 2012 and 2022 by Jonathan Poppele
Published by Adventure Publications
An imprint of AdventureKEEN
310 Garfield Street South
Cambridge, Minnesota 55008
(800) 678-7006
www.adventurepublications.net
All rights reserved
Printed in China
ISBN 978-1-59193-574-2 (pbk.); ISBN 978-1-64755-034-9 (ebook)

Table of Contents

Acknowledgments 2
About This Guide 6
  What Is Tracking? 6
  Why Go Tracking? 6
  Species Included in This Book 7
  How This Book Is Organized 7
How to Use This Book: Becoming a Wildlife Detective 9
Getting Close: Individual Tracks 11
  Track Morphology 11
  Measuring Tracks 14
Mammal Track Group Chart 16
Stepping Back: Track Patterns & Gaits 18
  Two-Legged Track Patterns & Gaits 22
  Four-Legged Track Patterns & Gaits 23
  Symmetrical Track Patterns & Gaits: Walks & Trots 24
  Asymmetrical Track Patterns & Gaits: Gallops & Bounds 28
Putting It in Context: Habitat, Range & Time of Year 33
Interpreting Sign 34
Frequently Asked Questions 36
Photographing Tracks & Sign 38
  Tips for Photographing Tracks 38
Sample Pages 41
Track Accounts
  Aerial & Fossorial Mammals 44
    Bats 47
    Moles 51
    Pocket Gophers 55
  Shrews, Mice, Voles & Rats 58
    Shrews 61
    Harvest Mice 65
    House Mouse 67
    Deer Mice 69
    Voles & Lemmings 73
    Ord's Kangaroo Rat & Pocket Mice 77
    Jumping Mice 81
    Hispid Cotton & Marsh Rice Rats 85
    Old World Rats 89
    Woodrats 93

Squirrels..96
   Chipmunks..99
   Flying Squirrels.....................................103
   Red Squirrel...107
   Eastern Gray Squirrel & Eastern Fox Squirrel.........111
   Ground Squirrels.....................................115
   Black-Tailed Prairie Dog.............................119
   Woodchuck..123
Rabbits...126
   Eastern Cottontail & Relatives.......................129
   Snowshoe Hare..133
   Jackrabbits..137
Weasels...140
   Weasels..143
   Mink...147
   American Marten......................................151
   Fisher...153
   Northern River Otter.................................157
   American Badger......................................161
Skunks, Large Rodents, Opossums, Raccoons & Bears.........164
   Eastern Spotted Skunk................................167
   Striped Skunk..169
   Muskrat..173
   North American Porcupine.............................177
   American Beaver......................................181
   Virginia Opossum.....................................185
   Northern Raccoon.....................................189
   Black Bear...193
Cats & Dogs...196
   Domestic Cat...199
   Bobcat...203
   Lynx...207
   Cougar...211
   Swift Fox..215
   Gray Fox...219
   Red Fox..223
   Coyote...227
   Domestic Dog...231
   Gray Wolf..235
Hoofed & Hoof-Like..238
   Nine-Banded Armadillo................................241

Feral Pig. 245
Pronghorn. 247
Mountain Goat. 251
Bighorn Sheep. 253
White-Tailed Deer & Mule Deer 255
Elk 259
Moose. 263
American Bison 267
Domestic Cow 271
Wild Horse. 273
Herps. 274
Frogs & Toads. 277
Salamanders & Newts. 279
Lizards 281
Snakes 283
Turtles. 285
Birds. 286
Songbirds & Doves 289
Corvids. 291
Bald Eagles & Other Hawks & Eagles 293
Great Blue Heron & Other Herons 295
Northern Flicker & Other Woodpeckers. 297
Great Horned Owl & Other Owls. 299
Shorebirds. 301
Game Birds 303
Gulls & Terns. 305
Waterfowl 307
Track Patterns & Trail Measurements 308
Track Patterns: Shrews, Mice, Voles & Rats 310
Track Patterns: Squirrels. 314
Track Patterns: Rabbits 316
Track Patterns: Weasels. 318
Track Patterns: Flat-Footed Walkers & Armadillos 322
Track Patterns: Cats & Dogs. 328
Track Patterns: Hoofed Animals 332
Quick Reference Size Charts 336
Glossary 340
Index 345
Photo Credits 349
Additional Resources. 350
About the Author 352

About This Guide

Go for a walk in the woods, or even at a local park, and you are likely to see a tremendous variety of birds, flowering plants, and trees. Go to a lake and you may see an abundance of fish swimming in the shallows or lined up on an angler's stringer. Yet except for a few species well adapted to human development, wild mammals tend to elude us. This may lead us to think that there are few mammals around. In fact, they are quite common, but they are often inconspicuous. Unlike birds, many mammals are primarily nocturnal or crepuscular, coming out only when the light is dim. Mammals are usually shades of brown and blend in with the ground. They are generally fairly quiet, relying on scent and sign to mark territories, rather than using songs and calls. The tracks and sign they leave behind are often our only indications that they are nearby. To get to know about the mammals of your area, you almost certainly must learn something about tracks. Tracking is a window into the lives of the secretive mammals that live around us.

What Is Tracking?

Tracking is the study and interpretation of the tracks (footprints) and other sign left behind by animals as they go about their lives. Tracking does not necessarily mean following a string of footprints to locate the animal that made them. It means understanding the footprints, scrapes, chews, digs, and scat (animal waste) that we inevitably run across when we are out in nature. Tracking begins with identifying the animal that left the tracks and sign behind for us to see. Over time, it grows into an intimate understanding of that animal's life and the role it plays in the living systems of which we, too, are a part of.

Why Go Tracking?

Tracking may be the most ancient of all sciences. As a matter of survival, all of our distant ancestors learned to read animal tracks and sign. Today, tracking is a way for us to connect more deeply with nature. Tracking can help us feel that we are at home in the outdoors, and that we are part of an intimate conversation with the other animals that share our world.

It is easy to get started in tracking. Seeing a set of footprints in the snow or across a sandy beach awakens our natural curiosity. Like crime scene investigators, we try to piece together what happened from clues an animal left behind. What once looked like an empty woodlot or an abandoned streambank becomes a bustling bed of animal activity—with each crisscrossing trail telling a different animal's story. Learning just a little bit about identifying tracks brings empty landscapes to life and can lead us on endless adventures.

No one ever completely masters tracking. It is possible to learn to accurately identify every tree or wildflower or bird that you see, but no one can identify every track or interpret every trail. There may be too few clues for even the best detectives to solve a particular mystery, and each mystery we solve leads us to even more mysteries. There is always more to learn, and there are always new mysteries being created.

This book will help you get out on the trail to solve some of those mysteries, and discover even more to engage your curiosity. Tracking is your invitation to a life of adventure and wonder.

Species Included in This Book

This book includes 70 entries filled with information about the tracks and sign of the more than 124 species of mammals, plus major groups of birds, reptiles, and amphibians found in the states of Illinois, Indiana, Iowa, Kansas, Kentucky, Michigan, Minnesota, Missouri, Nebraska, North Dakota, Ohio, South Dakota, and Wisconsin.

Not every species is discussed individually in this book. While there are noteworthy ecological differences among species, the tracks and sign of some are too similar to distinguish in the field. In this guide, birds, reptiles, amphibians, and many species of mammals, particularly small mammals, have been grouped together with other, similar species. For example, the 12 different species in the family Soricidae found in our region are grouped together here under the heading "Shrews." In these cases, this book will help you identify the group of animals that could have left a particular set of tracks. Once you have identified the group to which a track belongs, you can use the detailed range, habitat, and behavioral information found in any good field guide to mammals to narrow the possibilities even further.

How This Book Is Organized

The individual accounts in this book are organized into groups based on similarities in tracks and typical track patterns. In most groups, there is a clear "family resemblance" among the tracks. Most groups mirror standard taxonomic divisions, while some include a variety of animals that are not closely related to one another. The groups are roughly organized from smaller to larger animals. Within each group, species are generally organized from smaller to larger track size.

The first group covers bats, moles, and pocket gophers—small aerial and fossorial mammals that rarely leave tracks but often leave prominent sign. Next is a group of tiny-track makers: the shrews, mice, voles, and rats. Most members of this group belong to one of four families in the order Rodentia. Shrews are members of the order Eulipotyphla, together with moles, but they leave tracks and track patterns similar to those of tiny rodents. Each of the next three groups represents a single family of mammals: squirrels, in the family

Sciuridae; rabbits and hares, in the family Leporidae; and weasels, in the family Mustelidae. Each family has both distinctive track features and distinctive track patterns that support identification. The next group is a diverse collection of medium and large mammals that share two common characteristics: they frequently walk, and they have a flat-footed, or plantigrade, posture. This group includes the skunks, which are members of the family Mephitidae and closely related to weasels; three large rodents that tend to walk rather than bound like most of their smaller kin; the Virginia Opossum, North America's only marsupial; and the Raccoon and Black Bear, which each represent their own family in the order Carnivora. Rounding out the mammals are three groups of cursorial animals—species highly adapted for running. These species all have relatively long legs, stand on their toes with their heels high off the ground, and typically travel in a smooth, efficient walk or trot. The first of these are the cats and dogs, the Canidae and Felidae families in the order Carnivora. These are followed by the hoofed animals in the orders Artiodactyla and Perissodactyla. The Nine-Banded Armadillo is grouped with the hoofed animals because, frankly, this unusual critter had to go somewhere and its front tracks sometimes resemble tiny hoofprints. Rounding out the book are brief sections covering the tracks of major groups of birds, reptiles, and amphibians.

The front-left track of a coyote in soft mud.

While this order may be unfamiliar at first, I think you will find that it works very well in the field for identifying tracks. Often, placing a track into the correct group is relatively simple, and for the times when it is not, each species account includes detailed comparisons to similar-looking tracks to guide you to other likely possibilities. To help identify the group a track belongs to and to help you find the correct section of the book, we have included a Mammal Track Group Chart on pages 16-17 that outlines identifying characteristics of the members of each track group.

How to Use This Book: Becoming a Wildlife Detective

Tracks are different from living organisms, such as birds and bees, and identifying tracks requires a different approach beginning with a different fundamental question. When we wish to identify a bird, for example, the object we are looking at is a living being that we want to classify. Our question is "who **is** this?" When we want to identify a track, the object we are looking at is not a living being. It is the ground. Ground that has been shaped by the movement of an animal. Our question is "who **did** this?" With this question in mind, the process becomes one of investigation rather than classification. Tracking, we might say, is "CSI Wildlife," and like all detective work, it can be tricky business.

The tracks and trails of animals are highly variable. Throughout this book, you will find words such as *often, usually, sometimes,* and *rarely* used to describe features of animals' tracks and trails. Correctly identifying which animal made a track requires using multi-factor analysis to build a case that goes beyond a reasonable doubt. Our goal is to find and analyze enough evidence to persuade a skeptical jury of our conclusion. In the real world, that skeptical jury may be a park naturalist, a community of trackers on the iNaturalist citizen science platform, or our hiking buddy.

This track lacks claw marks but shows the distinctive proportions of a canid, including large toes, a small triangular palm, and an X-shaped negative space.

If we approach tracking as classification, rather than as detective work, we may be tempted to look for individual features—field marks—that will identify a track. It is well known, for example, that cats have retractable claws that tend not to show in their tracks, so many people consider a lack of claws to be a "field mark" of a cat track. This can lead one to believe that a large track with no visible claw marks seen along a hiking trail must have been left by a large cat—a Cougar, for instance. A jury would have good reason to be skeptical of such a conclusion. Track features, such as a lack of claws, are not field marks but individual factors to consider in a multi-factor analysis. Cat tracks sometimes show prominent claw marks, while many canine tracks, particularly those of Domestic Dogs with trimmed nails, may lack obvious claws. Careful analysis of multiple factors, including the symmetry and proportions of the track, the pattern of tracks in the trail, the location of the observation, and the species most likely to be seen there, guides us toward the most likely answers to our mysteries. Unsurprisingly, most large tracks with no visible claw marks seen along hiking trails are left by large Domestic Dogs, not by Cougars.

When we approach tracking as solving mysteries rather than classification, it is natural to start thinking like a detective. Like any good detective, we want to consider a wide range of suspects and be wary of jumping to conclusions. We want to look for multiple lines of evidence, including both obvious and subtle clues. We want to weigh the evidence that we gather to come up with working hypotheses, then test those hypotheses against additional evidence.

When interpreting a track or trail, it is important to take in a variety of perspectives. Get close to study individual footprints; step back to see the patterns of tracks; and put it in context by considering the habitat, location, and time of year. Each of these perspectives offers a different set of clues to consider in your multi-factor analysis. While I discuss these perspectives in order here in the introduction, the process is holistic, and you will find it natural to move back and forth between the fine details and the big picture as you track.

As you examine the evidence offered by each of these perspectives, build your list of suspects. Consider every species that could plausibly have left a particular track or trail—and maybe a few not so plausible suspects, just for good measure. Many tracks get misidentified simply because the person forgot to consider the right suspect in their investigation. Here are a few tips for building your list of suspects:

- Consider which animals are found in your area. You might begin by flipping through the range maps in this guide and creating a list of your local species.

- Consider which animals are active this time of year. Some species are dormant all winter long, while others simply reduce or change their activity, making them less likely (but not implausible) suspects.

- Consider which animals leave tracks roughly this size. A good place to start is the Quick Reference Size Charts on page 336.

- Consider which animals have tracks similar to your most likely suspects. As you hone in on likely suspects, check the "Similar Tracks" found in those accounts.

- Focus your investigation on the likely suspects, but don't rule out unlikely suspects.

Use your list of suspects to help you ask additional questions, and continue to gather evidence using each of the three perspectives. One of your suspects may tend to show long, stout claws. What do the claw marks look like in the track? Another suspect may tend to travel in a bound. What is the track pattern? A third suspect may be most common near water. How close is the nearest waterway?

As you gather evidence, weigh it against each of your suspects. You want to gather enough evidence to identify three top suspects and be able to make a case for and against each one. Imagine you are preparing a brief for a prosecutor, then for a defense attorney, in three separate trials. Do your best to make each case—both for and against. If any of the cases is weak, use those weaknesses to guide you in asking additional questions and gathering additional evidence. Now let's dive into each of these perspectives in turn.

Getting Close: Individual Tracks
Track Morphology

Mammal feet are adapted to a wide variety of functions, from running and climbing to digging and catching prey. Though they show a range of shapes, all mammal feet—including our own—are a variation on the same fundamental structure. The earliest mammals had five toes on each foot and walked on the soles of their feet with their heels contacting the ground. Many mammals, including humans, retain all five toes and this **plantigrade** posture. Their tracks show five toes, often tipped with claws, a palm, and a heel. Over time, some groups of mammals have reduced the number of toes they use for support; lengthened their feet to raise their heels off the ground and assume a **digitigrade** posture; or evolved to walk on the tips of their toes in an **unguligrade** posture. Most reptiles and amphibians have foot structures similar to those of mammals, while birds show a distinct variation that is discussed in the introduction to the section on page 286.

Formally, the toes on a mammal's foot are numbered 1 through 5, beginning on the inside and counting outward. Our thumb is toe 1, our middle finger is toe 3, and our pinkie is toe 5. Some mammals have fewer toes. In mammal tracks that show only four toes, it is always the "thumb" that is reduced or absent and the remaining toes are numbered 2 through 5. In animals with cloven hooves, the cleaves are toes 3 and 4.

When looking at individual prints, systematically look for and study each of the following features of each track: **overall shape, toes, claws, palm, heel,** and **negative space.**

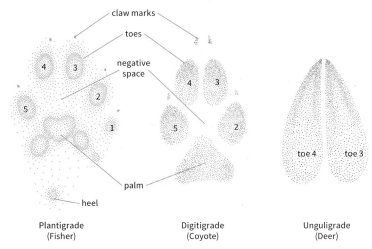

| Plantigrade
(Fisher) | Digitigrade
(Coyote) | Unguligrade
(Deer) |

Compare these left-front tracks of mammals with plantigrade, digitigrade, and unguligrade postures, showing the basic features of each track.

Compare your observations with the Mammal Track Group Chart on pages 16-17 to help identify likely suspects for your tracks.

Overall Shape

Look at the overall shape of the track. If you drew a line around the track, would it look circular, oval, egg-shaped, heart-shaped, like a mitten, or like a glove? Are the left and right sides mirror images of each other, or is the track curved, angled, or otherwise asymmetrical?

Toes

Study the shape, orientation, and number of the toes on each foot. Are the toes long and slender, like our fingers, or short and stout, like our toes? Do they connect to the palm in the track, or is there negative space in between? Do they point forward or splay to the sides? Are they arranged symmetrically or asymmetrically? How many toes are visible in each track? Be careful here: one toe may be set farther back than the others or not register clearly, and one track may register on top of another, giving the appearance of extra toes.

Claws

Most mammals have a claw on each toe, but their size and form vary widely. Skunks have long, stout claws for digging. Tree squirrels have fine, hooked claws for climbing. Beavers have wide, blunt nails on their hind feet that are often indistinguishable from the tips of their toes. Claw marks are sometimes prominent but often subtle, so look carefully. Are they long or short? Sharp or blunt? Fine or stout? Are there differences between the claws on the front and hind?

Palm

Look at the size, shape, and structure of the palm. Is it a single large pad or a group of small, individual pads? Does the palm appear behind the toes, or is it nestled between them? How large is the palm relative to other features in the track? Cats have proportionally larger palms than dogs, and both cats and dogs show proportionally larger palms in their front tracks than their hind tracks.

Heel

Is there a heel visible behind the palm? Is it made up of multiple pads? Covered with fur? Smoothly connected to the palm? Some mammals reliably show a heel, while others rarely do. All rodents other than the Porcupine have two round heel pads on their front feet that usually register. Members of the weasel family have a single heel pad on the front that often registers. Raccoons, skunks, and bears have a single, broad heel pad on their hind foot that may or may not register. Rabbits have furred heels that may look like an extension of the palm. Digitigrade animals such as cats and dogs and unguligrade animals such as deer rarely show heel marks.

Negative Space

What is the shape of the space between the toes and the palm? Is it large or small? Tall and narrow or short and wide? Could you draw an X through the center of the track, as is typical for a Coyote? Does it form a C, as it often does in cat tracks?

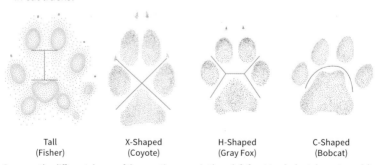

| Tall | X-Shaped | H-Shaped | C-Shaped |
| (Fisher) | (Coyote) | (Gray Fox) | (Bobcat) |

Compare the different shapes of the negative space in these left-front tracks (not shown to scale).

Measuring Tracks

Making accurate and consistent measurements of tracks takes practice, and practicing makes us better trackers. Even when I am not taking field notes, I like to measure tracks because it forces me to look more closely. It is not rare for me to spot details I missed at first glance when I am trying to decide exactly where my measurement should begin or end.

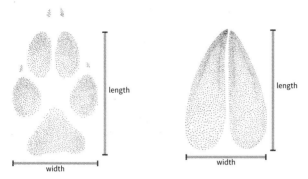

What to Measure

Measure tracks along their longest and widest points. Try to measure both the front and the hind tracks. Measure track length from the rear edge of the rearmost palm or heel pad to the front edge of the foremost toe pad. Do not include claws when measuring mammal tracks unless they are indistinguishable from the toes, and do not include the dewclaws of hoofed animals. Measure track width across the widest part of the foot, perpendicular to the length. Include all of the toes but not the claws.

The measurements in this guide represent typical ranges for each species. These ranges are based on a broad collection of data including my own field measurements, measurements of photographs taken by myself and other certified trackers, and ranges published by other professional trackers. The measurements cover the vast majority of tracks left by adults for each species in this guide, as well as some sub-adults and juveniles, but they do not include every track I or my colleagues have ever encountered. I have tried to offer ranges that are broad enough but also narrow enough to be genuinely useful. The ranges are generous, but it is possible you will encounter tracks that fall outside of these parameters. This is partly because you may find the tracks of an unusually large- or small-footed individual, and partly because making precise, reliable measurements of tracks can be quite difficult. Remember that measurements are useful but are only one factor to consider in our multi-factor analysis.

Finding the Edge of a Track

One challenge when measuring tracks is defining the exact edge. Most track compressions have a smooth, curving shape similar to a shallow bowl. The point where the bottom or "floor" of the track meets the side is subjective, but where we define that edge can make a huge difference in our final measurement. This is especially true on soft surfaces, which can spread considerably as an animal places and lifts its foot. When measuring tracks, try to identify where the relatively flat track floor meets the steep, sloping "side" of the track. Determining where the track floor ends and the side of the track begins is a matter of judgment—but that judgment improves with practice, and practicing improves our attention to track detail. Measurements of large tracks by experienced trackers usually agree within less than ⅛" (3 mm) of one another. Casual measurements by inexperienced observers sometimes vary by more than 1".

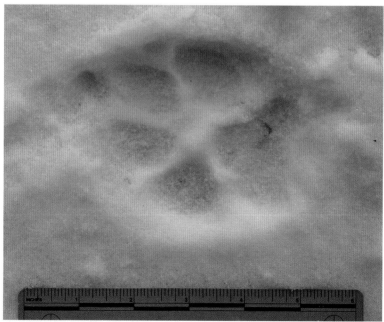

This Wolf track in snow shows how important it is to carefully identify the edge of the track. The total compression in the snow measures 5⅛" long by 3⅝" wide. The track floor—roughly the darkest part of the track—is less than three-quarters that size, measuring just 3⅜" long by 2¾" wide.

Mammal Track Group Chart

Track Group	General Description	Typical Toes	Typical Claws
Shrews, Mice, Voles & Rats	¼" to < 1"; long toes and small palms	4 or 5 front, 5 hind (1-3-1). Usually splayed.	Sharp. Tiny. May be inconspicuous.
Squirrels	Long toes. Front palm is triangular; hind palm forms an arc.	4 front (1-2-1), 5 hind (1-3-1). Long.	Stout (ground squirrels) or fine (others). Usually register.
Rabbits	Egg-shaped. Covered with dense fur.	5 front (4 distinct), 4 hind. Teardrop.	Short and blunt. May be obscured.
Weasels	Tall negative space. Chevron-shaped palm.	5 front and hind. Small ovals or teardrops.	Fine. Usually visible.
Skunks	Compact. Toes do not splay.	5 front and hind. Stubby.	Long and stout. Usually prominent.
Large Rodents	Long toes. Hind tracks usually larger than front.	4 front, 5 hind. Finger-like or indistinct.	Stout. May be indistinguishable from toes.
Five-Toe Walkers	Often resemble human hand- or footprints.	5 front and hind. Resemble human fingers or toes.	Variable. May or may not show clearly.
Cats	Round. Asymmetrical. Palm makes up most of the track.	4 front and hind. Oval or teardrop.	Sharp. Usually retracted but can be prominent.
Dogs	Oval. Symmetrical. Toes make up most of the track.	4 front and hind. Oval or slightly triangular.	Fine to stout. Usually register but can be inconspicuous.
Armadillo	Unique bird-like tracks	4 front, 2 register; 5 hind, 3 register	Stout. Prominent. Often indistinguishable from toes.
Hoofed	Round or heart-shaped hoofprints	1 (horses), 2 (others). Cleaves.	Dewclaws may show at speed or in deep substrate.

Typical Palm	Typical Heel	Typical Track Patterns	Page		
Tiny individual pads	Tiny individual pads	Scurry or bound	58		
Front: triangular Hind: arc	Front: 2 pads register Hind: may register	Bound (some ground squirrels walk or lope)	96		
Obscure	May register	Bound	126		
Lobed chevron. Usually slender.	Front: 1 pad may register	Bound or lope (Badgers walk)	140		
Wide	Broad. Sometimes registers.	Walk or lope	167		
Front: triangular Hind: broad Porcupine: fused to heel	Front: 2 pads register Hind: may register Porcupine: fused to palm	Walk	173		
Opossum: 4–5 pads Raccoon and bear: large and smooth	Broad. Sometimes registers.	Walk	185		
Trapezoidal; 3 trailing lobes	Rarely registers	Walk	199		
Triangular	Rarely registers	Trot	215		
Rarely registers	Does not register	Lope	241		
Does not register	Does not register	Walk	241		

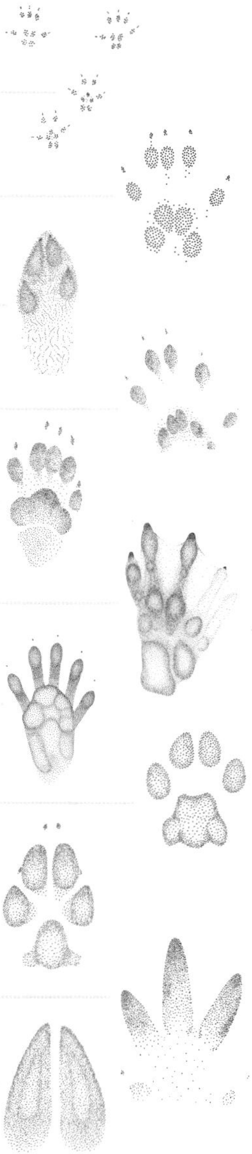

Stepping Back: Track Patterns & Gaits

A **track pattern** is an arrangement of footprints on the ground. A **gait** is the way an animal moves its body for locomotion. Animals leave different track patterns depending on the gait they use. Track patterns give us insight into gaits in much the same way that clear footprints give us insight into foot morphology. Different animals have different characteristic gaits, and animals use different gaits depending on what they are doing. Studying track patterns can help us understand if an animal was walking like a cat, loping like a Fisher, or bounding like a rabbit. It can also help us interpret if a fox, for example, was walking as it might to investigate, trotting as it typically does to travel, or galloping as it might to chase or flee. Track patterns provide valuable clues for interpreting tracks and trails, and they are an important factor in our multi-factor analysis.

The Challenge of Defining Gaits & the Value of Complexity

As with so much in nature, gaits are complex and variable, and they defy simple classification. On the one hand, individual species tend to have only a few general ways of coordinating their bodies to move—a few basic gaits. Each gait functions a bit like a gear in a car. As an animal speeds up or slows down, it "shifts" from one gait to another. We experience this in our own movement. If you gradually speed up while walking, at some point you "shift" into a run. With one stride you are walking, and with the next you are running. As you slow down again, you "shift" back into a walk. We can walk and run at a variety of speeds and with a variety of forms, but walking and running are discrete gaits in humans. Most species typically use just a few gaits that can, in principle, be distinguished just as clearly.

Different species of animals, however, have different postures, proportions, and biomechanics that affect the way they move, complicating the classification of gaits. The way we define a gait for one species may not apply well to another. Some broad categories apply clearly across species, while others do not. A Mink, with its short legs and supple spine, for example, moves quite differently than a White-Tailed Deer, with its long legs and flat back. Each animal sometimes uses a gait that can be called a bound, but these two bounding gaits leave completely different track patterns. Indeed, some authors reasonably refer to the Mink's bound as a lope and the White-Tailed Deer's bound as a gallop. These are not errors in classification, but rather the inevitable shortcoming of grouping anything as variable as animal movement into a few simple categories.

Dramatically different track patterns left by a bounding Mink (top) and a bounding White-Tailed Deer (bottom)

Though challenging for classification, this variability is often helpful for us as trackers. Raccoons, for example, have a walking gait so different from other mammals that their common track pattern is diagnostic for the species. Rabbits and squirrels both typically travel in a bound, but they too bound in different ways, leaving different track patterns.

The track patterns of bounding rabbits and squirrels are often distinctive enough to identify at a glance.

Naming and categorizing gaits can help us in identifying and interpreting tracks and trails as long as we recognize the limitations of our system of classification and don't apply our terms too rigidly. Our purpose, after all, is not to classify track patterns but to understand how an animal was moving as it left tracks on the ground. This section outlines the fundamentals of track patterns and gaits using a system of categories and terms that have been widely adopted by wildlife trackers in North America—a system that has proved useful for both learning and communicating with other trackers.

Learning Track Patterns & Gaits

One of the best ways to learn the relationship between animal movement and track patterns is to simply watch animals move. Watch wildlife films. Watch clips on YouTube. Watch your pet. Where conditions allow for it, watch an animal move, then immediately go look at the tracks it created. A nearby beach where people play with their dogs may be perfect for this. And to fully experience how an animal creates a particular track pattern, try making it yourself. Get down on all fours and figure out how to move your own body to reproduce a track pattern. Or watch an animal and practice copying its movement. This kind of whole-body engagement speeds up the learning process and is a whole lot of fun. When I go out in the field with other trackers, we usually end up on the ground at some point, trying to reproduce a track pattern that we've run across.

Wildlife biologist Kurt Rinehart role-plays an animal to understand the relationship between gaits and track patterns.

Describing Track Patterns & Gaits

Some basic terms and broad distinctions will help us begin to describe track patterns and the gaits that produce them. First, recall that a **gait** is the way an animal moves its body for locomotion. A **track pattern** is the arrangement of footprints left on the ground by an animal moving in some particular gait. Gaits, and therefore track patterns, can be broadly divided into two categories, *symmetrical* and *asymmetrical,* and defined in part based on *stride, step, trail,* and *group.*

Symmetrical: Symmetrical gaits have a steady rhythm, such as the "clip-clop, clip-clop, clip-clop, clip-clop" of a walking Horse. Our own walking and running gaits are symmetrical. In symmetrical gaits, the right and left footfalls of each front or hind pair are spaced evenly (symmetrically) in time. Symmetrical gaits produce symmetrical track patterns. Since the right and left hind *footfalls* are spaced evenly in time, right and left hind *tracks* are spaced evenly on the ground. Likewise for the fronts. In quadrupeds, symmetrical gaits produce patterns of evenly spaced track pairs. Symmetrical gaits include walks and trots.

Asymmetrical: Asymmetrical gaits have an interrupted rhythm like the three beat "co-co-nut, co-co-nut, co-co-nut, co-co-nut" of a loping Horse (known in English riding as *cantering*). In asymmetrical gaits, the body flexes and extends, while each front or hind pair of limbs move as a coordinated pair. Footfalls are grouped together in time, and tracks are grouped together on the ground. In quadrupeds, asymmetrical gaits produce repeating patterns of four tracks. Asymmetrical gaits include bounds and gallops.

Stride: A stride is the basic repeating unit of an animal's gait. It is a complete sequence of footfalls, from one foot contacting the ground until that same foot contacts the ground again. A stride is therefore also the basic repeating unit of a track pattern. The length of a stride is the distance from any track in a sequence to the next track made by the same foot.

Step: A step is half of a stride in a symmetrical gait. It is the movement from one foot contacting the ground until the opposite foot from the same pair contacts the ground. Step length is the distance from one hind track to the next hind track on the opposite side of the body. Symmetrical gaits, by definition, are made up of a repeating series of steps. Asymmetrical gaits are not made up of steps. *Note:* Fitbit users, many runners, and some wildlife trackers use the word *stride* to refer to what I am calling a *step* when discussing symmetrical gaits and track patterns. I prefer to use the word *stride* to refer to a full gait cycle, because that definition applies to all symmetrical and asymmetrical gaits and track patterns of both bipeds and quadrupeds; I find this easier. If you consult different references, which is always a good idea, be sure to check how different authors define their terms.

Trail width: The distance between the outer edge of the tracks on one side of the trail and the outer edge of the tracks on the other side of the trail is called the trail width. Trail width often varies between different gaits, and with the speed of some gaits.

Track group: The visual grouping of four tracks left by a single stride of an asymmetrical gait is called the track group. Although a group always includes four tracks, hind tracks may land on top of fronts producing groups with only two or three distinct footprints.

Intergroup: The distance between groups in an asymmetrical gait is the intergroup distance. The length of the track group plus the intergroup distance equals the stride. *Note:* Some wildlife trackers use the word *stride* to refer to only the intergroup distance when discussing asymmetrical gaits and track patterns.

A wolf direct-register trotting gait showing stride and trail width

A Woodchuck bounding gait showing group length, intergroup distance, stride, and trail width

Two-Legged Track Patterns & Gaits

The easiest place to start learning the relationship between gaits and track patterns is with bipedal movement. Once we understand how two-legged gaits leave particular track patterns, it is easier to understand many of the complexities of four-legged locomotion. And, being bipeds ourselves, two-legged gaits come quite naturally to us, especially the symmetrical bipedal gaits of walking and running.

Walking & Running

The symmetrical two-legged gaits of walking and running are made up of alternating right and left steps with a consistent rhythm. A gait is considered a walk if there is always at least one foot on the ground; it is considered a run if there is a moment of suspension when both feet are off the ground. Put another way, a gait is a walk if each foot is on the ground for more than half of the stride cycle and a run if each foot is on the ground for less than half of the stride cycle. The track patterns left by both walks and runs are zigzagging strings of evenly spaced tracks. Human beings, large birds, and some smaller birds that spend a good deal of time on the ground usually walk or run.

Track patterns of a Wild Turkey walking (top) and an American Robin running (bottom). Note the proportionally longer stride and narrower trail of the robin's running trail.

In general, walks show shorter strides and wider trails than runs, but there is considerable variation, and it is not always possible to distinguish the gait based on track pattern alone. There is more variation among different walks than there is between the most extended walks and the most compressed runs. Stride length, however, is constrained in a walk. Since one foot is always on the ground when an animal is walking, a stride length much more than one-and-a-half times the animal's leg length is likely from a run, and a stride length double the leg length must be from a run.

Hopping & Skipping

Asymmetrical bipedal gaits, called *skips* and *hops,* are made up of a series of leaps. The gait is called a hop when the animal jumps with both feet together, leaving side-by-side tracks. It's called a skip when the footfalls are staggered, like a child "galloping" on a hobby horse, resulting in offset pairs of tracks.

Many perching birds typically hop or skip on the ground. One mammal in our region, Ord's Kangaroo Rat, regularly travels in a bipedal hop or skip.

Track patterns of a Northern Flicker hopping (top) and an American Crow skipping (bottom).

Four-Legged Track Patterns & Gaits

With the exception of humans and Ord's Kangaroo Rat, all Midwestern mammals are *quadrupedal,* meaning that they travel on four feet. Four-legged movement is more complicated than the two-legged movement used by us bipeds, and it produces more-complicated track patterns. To interpret quadrupedal track patterns, it is sometimes easiest to think of them as two overlapping bipedal track patterns—like the tracks left by two people wearing a horse costume.

The first thing to determine is if the tracks were produced by a symmetrical gait or an asymmetrical one. Symmetrical gaits leave evenly spaced pairs of tracks, while asymmetrical gaits leave repeating patterns of four tracks. Many patterns can be distinguished at a glance, but some can be deceptive. Even difficult patterns, however, can be reliably identified by looking at only the hind tracks. If the distance between each hind track in a pattern is consistent—that is, if the hind tracks alone look like a walk—then the track pattern is symmetrical and was left by a symmetrical gait. If the distance between the hind tracks alternates short, long, short, long, then the track pattern is the product of an asymmetrical gait.

These track patterns left by a Striped Skunk walking (top) and loping (bottom) look similar, but note the different spacing of the hind tracks. When the skunk is walking, the distances between right and left hind tracks are symmetrical. When the skunk is loping, the distances are asymmetrical.

Symmetrical Track Patterns & Gaits: Walks & Trots

As with bipeds, symmetrical quadruped gaits are divided based the amount of time each foot is on the ground. If each foot is on the ground for more than half of the stride, the gait is called a *walk*. If each foot is on the ground for less than half of the stride, the gait is called a *trot, pace,* or *amble,* depending on how the front and hind legs are coordinated. Of these, the trot is by far the most common and is the only "running" gait regularly observed in medium- to large-sized wild mammals in the Midwest.

Walks

Animals walking on four legs move like two people walking together in a horse costume: the front and hind legs move independently, but they need to coordinate so the hind feet don't kick the front as they swing forward. The most common way for animals to do this is to step with the hind foot and then the front on one side of the body, followed by the hind foot and then the front on the other side. Animals may also move both legs on the same side of the body at nearly the same time, which is typical for Raccoon; diagonal opposite legs at nearly the same time, which is typical for Opossum; or anything in between.

Depending on an animal's posture, leg length, and how it coordinates its front and hind steps, there are four different positions the hind track can appear in relative to the front track in a track pattern.

Direct Register: Each hind track is superimposed on top of the front track from the previous step. Only hind tracks are clearly visible, and the track pattern appears nearly identical to the pattern left by a bipedal walk. Deer often leave direct-register track patterns when they walk.

The direct-register track pattern left by a walking White-Tailed Deer

Indirect Register: Each hind track appears partially overlapping or next to the front track from the previous step. This sometimes produces confusing tracks showing features of both front and hind tracks or "extra" toes. It is a matter of judgment whether to call a track pattern a direct register or an indirect register. Generally, if features of the front track are clearly visible, the pattern is called an indirect register. Opossums and large rodents often leave indirect-register track patterns when they walk.

The indirect-register track pattern of a walking Opossum, traveling left to right. Note the jumble of toes created by each indirect register.

Understep: Each hind track appears behind the front track from the previous step. Front tracks lead hinds in the track pattern. Bison often leave an understep track pattern when they walk.

The understep track pattern of a walking Bison, traveling left to right. The lead (forwardmost) track in each pair is the front track.

Overstep: Each hind track appears in front of the front track from the previous step. Hind tracks lead fronts in the track pattern. Bears, skunks, cats, Coyotes, and Pronghorn often leave overstep track patterns when they walk.

The overstep track pattern of a walking Black Bear, traveling left to right. The lead (forwardmost) track in each pair is the hind track.

Raccoon Walk

Raccoons have a unique walking gait that leaves one of the most distinctive track patterns in the Midwest. In what could be described as an extreme overstep, they place each hind foot on the ground next to the opposite front, leaving an alternating paired track pattern. The hind tracks may register even with, slightly ahead of, or slightly behind the fronts.

The distinctive paired track pattern of a walking Raccoon. Front and hind tracks appear side-by-side, appearing on alternate sides of the trail with each step. This pattern can resemble the side-trot pattern of a canid (page 328) or a bounding weasel (page 320), but the angle of each pair alternates.

Trots

An animal running on four legs is a bit like two people running in a horse costume. The front and hind legs need to by carefully coordinated to avoid interference and maintain a fluid stride. The most common way to do this is with a trot.

In a trot, diagonally opposite legs move at the same time, or nearly so, and there is a split second when the animal has all four feet off the ground. The difference between a walk and a trot is analogous to the difference between a bipedal walk and run. In fact, the diagonal coordination of front and hind legs in a trot is the same as the diagonal coordination of our arms and legs when we run upright—we drive forward with our right hand and left leg at the same time. Trots are the most common gaits for members of the dog family, and many animals that typically walk may speed up into a trot. The slight bounce created by a trot can be easily seen in the stride of a Domestic Dog.

The direct-register track pattern of a trotting Coyote

Similar to walks, trots can leave either direct-register or overstep track patterns. For a trot to produce an overstep, the animal needs to adjust its posture. Think about our two people in the horse costume: the person in back needs to shift to one side or widen their stance so they don't kick their partner in the heels as they run. Animals do something similar. Most canids shift their hips slightly to one side to extend their trotting stride. The resulting track pattern is called a *side-trot* and is nearly unique to the canid family. In a side-trot, all of the front tracks appear on one side of the trail, and all of the hind track appear on the other, a little ahead of the fronts.

The side-trot pattern left by a fox. The smaller hind tracks lead the larger front tracks.

This track pattern can resemble the patterns left by a walking Raccoon (page 322) or a bounding weasel (page 320). In the Raccoon's walk pattern, the angle between the two tracks alternates with each step. In one step, the track on the right is farther forward, and in the next the track on the left is farther forward. In the side-trot, the angle between the two tracks remains the same. The tracks on one side of the trail are consistently ahead of the tracks on the other side of the trail. In the weasel's 2x2 bound, each group is made up of four tracks, rather than two.

Animals may also produce an overstep trot by spreading their hind legs apart to straddle their fronts. The resulting track pattern shows a nearly straight line of front tracks with hind tracks out to the sides. This track pattern is often seen in the trotting trails of Elk and Gray Foxes.

The straddle-trot pattern of an Elk traveling left to right. The smaller hind tracks lead and straddle the fronts.

Distinguishing Walks & Trots

While walks and trots can produce similar-looking track patterns, they can usually be distinguished by stride and trail width. Walks nearly always show shorter strides and wider trails than trots. For most larger animals that typically either walk or trot, such as felids, canids, and ungulates, stride length roughly corresponds to the animal's size as follows:

In a direct-register track pattern left by a walk, the stride is a bit more than the length of the animal's body, from shoulder to rump. This is also a bit more than the height of the animal's back.

In a direct-register track pattern left by a trot, the stride is approximately double the length of the body from hip to shoulder. This also means that the step length (half-stride) is roughly equal to the animal's height.

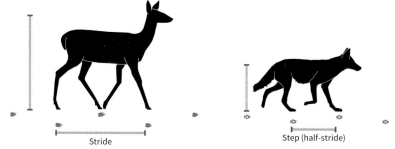

Stride

Step (half-stride)

Deer Walking and Coyote Trotting

In the field, you can use these guidelines to compare the size of a track pattern to the size of the animal that left it. Stretch your arms out to cover a single stride (two steps). Does that look like about the length of the animal's body? Put your hand that same distance above the ground. Does that look like about the height of the animal's back? If so, it was likely walking. Next, stretch your hands out over a single step (half a stride) and ask the same questions. Does that look closer to the size of the animal? If so, the animal was likely trotting. This technique can both help distinguish walks from trots and also help you visualize the animal you are tracking.

Other Symmetrical Gaits: Paces, Ambles & Scurries

In addition to trots, there are three other ways a four-legged animal might coordinate its legs to run. One is to move both legs on the same side of the body at nearly the same time; this is called a *pace.* The other two ways involve moving the legs out of phase—halfway between a trot and a pace. These are called *ambles.* Elephants can run in an amble. Camels run in a pace, as can a few breeds of Domestic Dogs. Some well-trained horses can perform one of more of these gaits, which have specialized names in different equestrian traditions. But these gaits are rarely used by medium- to large-sized wild mammals in the Midwest except as brief transitions between typical gaits.

The story is less clear for our smallest mammals, whose gaits are exceptionally difficult to study in detail. Some gaits used by shrews, mice, and voles blur the lines between walks, trots, and ambles. For this reason, I refer to the symmetrical gaits of many tiny mammals using the catch-all term *scurry*.

Asymmetrical Track Patterns & Gaits: Gallops & Bounds

Asymmetrical gaits involve an animal flexing and extending its body while using its front and hind limbs as coordinated pairs. They have an interrupted rhythm rather than a continuous one, and they produce groups of four tracks rather than the strings of regularly spaced track pairs left by symmetrical gaits.

Wild mammals display a tremendous diversity of asymmetrical gaits. Various species demonstrate everything from slow, gentle lopes in which there is always at least one foot on the ground to blazing gallops in which the animal spends more time airborne that it does touching the earth. Asymmetrical gaits include the fastest modes of locomotion for four-legged mammals, and all quadrupedal mammals may use asymmetrical gaits when top speed is required. For some animals, including many small rodents, most squirrels, rabbits, and smaller weasels, asymmetrical gaits are the norm, even when they move slowly.

Asymmetrical gaits and track patterns are broadly divided into two categories based on how the hind limbs are coordinated. Gaits in which each foot lands independently are called *gallops* and *lopes*. Gaits in which the hind feet land at nearly the same time are called *bounds*.

Each asymmetrical gait has a moment of **suspension** when all four feet are off the ground, or at least bearing very little weight. The suspension is the pause in the audible rhythm of the animal's footfalls. It is the "comma" that punctuates the loping Horse's "co-co-nut, co-co-nut, co-co-nut" rhythm. Some asymmetrical gaits have two (or rarely three) suspensions, with one being longest. Bounds are typically dominated by an **extended suspension**—the animal is airborne (or nearly so) when its body is in an extended posture after pushing off with its hind feet. Gallops and lopes are more variable. Many lopes and some gallops, including those of Horses, are characterized by a **gathered suspension**—the animal is airborne (or nearly so) when its legs are gathered underneath its body after pushing off with its front feet. Other gallops are dominated by the extended suspension, similar to most bounds.

A bounding rabbit (left) in an extended suspension and a loping Coyote (right) in a gathered suspension

Gallops & Lopes

Gallops are asymmetrical gaits in which each hind foot lands and pushes off independently as the animal flexes and extends its body. Such gaits include the stiff-legged "rocking horse" gaits often seen in dogs playing; the fluid "Slinky-like" gaits used by weasels; and the dramatic whole-body contracting and extending gaits of cats or Greyhounds in all-out sprints.

The track patterns left by all but the fastest gallops are made up of visual groups of four tracks that begin with a front track and end with a hind track. Since gaits are cyclic, we could begin and end the group anywhere, but the most natural *visual* grouping begins with a front track. In some track patterns, the groups are easy to define. In others, the intergroup distance may not be much different than the largest gaps between tracks within the group. When identifying the track group for a gallop, keep two things in mind. The track group begins with a front track and ends with a hind track. If one front and one hind track are close together or overlapping, they are the middle tracks in the group. In some of the fastest gallops, tracks can be almost evenly spaced on the ground. In these cases, there may be little value in defining a visual group of four.

The clearly defined track groups left by a loping skunk (top) and the less-well-defined track groups left by a loping deer (bottom). The two overlapping tracks in the deer's trail are the middle tracks in the group.

Lopes are a subset of gallops. A lope is any slow, gentle gallop that can be sustained for long periods of time. Lopes may be used for travel. In the first edition of this book, I offered a narrower definition of a lope. But along with most other definitions, it failed to distinguish at least some gaits that we generally recognize as lopes from others that we would like to call gallops. What we consider a lope is inherently subjective, and it is not always possible to distinguish a lope from a gallop when watching an animal move, let alone from the track pattern it leaves behind.

Although the distinction between lopes and other gallops is subjective, we might reasonably consider a gait to be a lope if the track groups are compact and the intergroup distance is short, *or* if the track group shows one hind foot behind or beside one of the front tracks. If both hind tracks land beyond both front tracks *and* the track groups are stretched out, the gait was likely not a lope.

The track pattern of a loping River Otter. The order of the footfalls in each group is right front, right hind, left front, left hind.

The track pattern of a galloping Red Fox. Note the order of the prints in this single, elongated track group: left front, right front, right hind, left hind.

Note that in gathered-suspension gallops, which include most lopes, the visual grouping of tracks in the pattern is different from the rhythmic groupings of footfalls in time. Recall that the rhythm of the Horse's lope (a.k.a. its canter) is the three-beat "co-co-nut, co-co-nut, co-co-nut." The

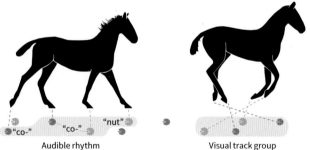

Audible rhythm   Visual track group

A loping Horse shown above the resulting track pattern. The image on the left shows the horse immediately after the final footfall in the audible rhythm of the gait. The image on the right shows the horse in gathered suspension above the visual track group. The front feet have just pushed off, leaving the two initial tracks in the pattern. The hind feet are moving forward to land, at which time they will leave the final two tracks in the pattern.

footfall sequence is hind ("co"), front–hind pair ("co"), and front ("nut"), followed by a gathered suspension (the "comma"). The track pattern left by this gait, by contrast, shows visual groupings of front–hind/front–hind. Additionally, the front and hind tracks that appear side-by-side on the ground are not made by the two feet that land at the same time. Instead, they are made by the first and last footfalls in the three-beat rhythm. The gathered suspension occurs in the middle of the track pattern.

Transverse & Rotary Patterns

Gallops and their resulting track patterns can be described as either transverse or rotary, depending on the sequence of the animal's footfalls and which tracks "lead" in the resulting track pattern. A track is said to **lead** another when it appears farther forward in the track pattern. If the right-front track appears in front of the left-front track, the right front leads the left. In gallops, one track of each front or hind pair always leads the other. When front and hind leads match—when, for example, the right front and right hind are both ahead of the corresponding left tracks—we call the track pattern and the gait that produced it a **transverse gallop.** When front and hind leads differ, we call it a **rotary gallop.** The track groups produced by a transverse gallop show four tracks in a zigzag or a diagonal line. The track groups produced by a rotary gallop show four tracks arranged in a curve.

Compare the C-shaped track pattern of a Marten in a rotary lope (top) with the zigzagging or diagonal line of tracks left by a Fisher in a transverse lope.

Animals may switch leads at any time for a variety of reasons, but many species tend to prefer either a transverse or rotary sequence when moving in particular gaits. These tendencies can help us with identification. Marten, for example, almost always use a rotary lope. Fisher and Mink, which are closely related to Marten and leave similar tracks and trails, use a mixture of transverse and rotary lopes.

Rotary gallops may have either gathered or extended suspensions. Transverse gallops tend to have only a gathered suspension.

Bounds & Hops

Bounds are similar to gallops except the hind feet push off and land together. The resulting track patterns show hind tracks side-by-side, or nearly so. Most bounds are dominated by an extended suspension. Bounds typically produce relatively compact, well-defined track groups with distinct gaps between the groups. Bounds are the most common gaits for rabbits, tree squirrels, many tiny mammals, and smaller weasels. Many mammals bound when jumping over obstacles, moving over rough terrain, or traveling through deep snow.

The track pattern of a bounding Gray Squirrel. Note that the front tracks appear side-by-side behind the hind tracks in each group.

Animals that spend a large portion of their time in trees, such as Gray Squirrels, tend to place their front feet side-by-side when they bound. Animals that do not climb, such as rabbits, more often bound with one front foot leading the other.

The track pattern of a bounding Eastern Cottontail. Here the front tracks land one in front of the other behind the hind tracks.

The distinction between bounds and gallops is subjective. Hind feet rarely land at exactly the same time, and one hind track usually leads the other by at least a tiny amount. Some gaits that we call bounds are nearly identical to gaits we call gallops—particularly some rotary gallops with an extended suspension. If an offset between the hind tracks is large enough, we may choose to interpret a track pattern as a gallop rather than a bound.

This track pattern left by a Black-Tailed Jackrabbit could be reasonably described as either a bound or a gallop.

Bounding animals' hind feet usually straddle their front feet, causing hind tracks to register wider. To conserve energy in deeper snow, many animals switch to a 2x2 bound in which their hind feet land directly in the front tracks. Tracks may appear side-by-side or, as is common for many members of the weasel family, one side may lead. The resulting track patterns can closely resemble those left by the Raccoon walk and the canid side-trot. In the case of the 2x2 bound, each compression is both a front and a hind track, and each group contains all four tracks, registering in just two spots.

The 2x2 track pattern of a bounding Mink. While the pattern resembles that left by a walking Raccoon or trotting canid, each compression is made by two overlapping prints.

A **hop** is a term of convenience to distinguish bounding patterns where one or both front track appear in front of both hind tracks in the track pattern.

This track pattern was left by a Meadow Vole. We can call this pattern a hop since a front track leads in each group.

Putting It in Context: Habitat, Range & Time of Year

While it is easy to focus on individual footprints, it is important to put what we are seeing in context by considering habitat, range, and time of year. I sometimes do this by drawing freehand maps of the trails, terrain, and features of the areas I tracked. Most often these days, I take photographs with my phone and upload them to iNaturalist—a citizen science website that automatically maps my observations. I can then view my observations on either a map or a satellite photo.

Taking a "bird's-eye" perspective helps us to make connections that we can easily miss when our focus is on the individual tracks. I learned a great lesson in the power of this perspective some years ago when I gave a presentation on Wolf tracking to a group of Environmental Studies majors at a local university. None of the students had ever been tracking, and most had little or no knowledge about Wolves. After a 10-minute introduction to Wolf ecology and behavior, I showed the students a map from a tracking expedition in which our team had used CyberTracker software to plot our data in the field. The first map showed all of our data about Elk, the Wolves' primary food in that area; Coyotes, which tend to steer clear of Wolves; and human traffic, which the Wolves tend to avoid. The map covered some 300 square miles of rugged wilderness. I asked the students where they would go to look for Wolf sign. Seeing the big picture, the students quickly identified the exact locations where we found the most Wolf activity. When we put everything in context, even a little bit of knowledge can go a long way.

Even while you are still out in the field, as you examine a track or analyze a track pattern, it's helpful to look around at the context: the animal's habitat and range. Our region is broadly divided into three major biomes: grasslands, eastern broadleaf forests, and northern boreal forests. Within and across these major biomes, there are wetlands, lakes and riverways, developed lands, and transitional areas. Some species are habitat generalists, while others have fairly specific habitat requirements. Similarly, some species are found across the Midwest, while others are generally limited to one small part of our region. Finally, some animals are active all year, while others may change or reduce their activity in winter. Most accounts in this book include maps showing the typical known range for each animal, along with information about preferred habitats and patterns of activity.

While range maps are useful, they are an imperfect source of information. Mammals are well equipped with feet, and many have a habit of wandering far away from the areas where they are "supposed" to be—it is not uncommon to find a lone individual hundreds of miles outside of its known range, particularly for larger species. Moose from northern Minnesota sometimes wander as far south as Iowa, and Cougars from the western Dakotas sometimes show up in Wisconsin. In addition, range maps will often include many places that are completely unsuitable to a particular species. River Otters, Muskrat, and Beavers, for example, have extensive ranges but are usually found only near open bodies of water. For this reason, it is important to use range maps and habitat preferences together, and to weight them as evidence in our multi-factor analysis. Additionally, you don't need to rule out a suspect just because you are outside of that animal's known range or typical habitat. But to build a compelling case for such a suspect, your other evidence must be that much stronger.

Interpreting Sign

Sign are any clues left behind by animals other than footprints. Sign can include scat (animal droppings), digs, chews, nests, and much more. These sign can help reveal the presence of an animal when there are no tracks visible at all, and they can give us additional insight into the lives of these animals. This book focuses on animal tracks, but most accounts also include a brief description of each animal's scat and notes about other common sign. Sign are even more diverse and variable than tracks, but we go about interpreting them in much the same way. Like crime scene investigators, we want to create a list of suspects and build a case for and against each one based on multiple lines of evidence. Like a prosecutor going before a jury, we want to weave this evidence together into a cohesive narrative. Our narrative should consider who had the means, the motive, and the opportunity to create the sign we are studying.

Antler rub of a White-Tailed Deer. The shredded appearance of the bark at both the top and the bottom indicates that this was done by antler tines scraping both up and down rather than incisors scraping up.

Getting Close: Means

Study the individual sign. Whether it is scat, a dig, a chew, or a scrape, we want to ask which specific animal has the means to create the specific sign. Many animals feed on acorns in the fall, for example, but they have different means, so their feeding sign will look different. Rodents gnaw with sharp incisors, deer grind with flat molars, and bears crush with pointed carnassials. Senior tracker Dave Moskowitz invites us to imagine that we had a toolbox with us in the field and ask what tools we would use to reproduce the sign we find. Then ask which animals have these tools. Which animals have the means to create this sign? Scat is a little different. With scat, the size, content, shape, and structure all give us insight into who had the means.

Stepping Back: Motive

Study how and where the sign was placed. Animals leave sign for some reason. They have motives. These motives are often expressed in exactly how and where the sign is left. Red Foxes often deposit scat on top of a rock along the side of a trail as a marker. Gray Squirrels form vertical stripes of gnawed bark on the leeward side of large trees, so their scent is not washed away by the rain. Mice tend to feed under cover for protection, while chipmunks typically feed on raised surfaces so they have a view of their surroundings. How and where a sign is placed gives us insight into who had the motive.

Putting It in Context: Opportunity

Just as with tracks, take the habitat and location into consideration when you interpret sign. Also consider the time of year—not just whether the species is active, but what particular activities it is engaged in. Deer only create antler rubs on small trees at the start of the breeding season, but they will scrape bark with their incisors to feed on cambium during the winter. These sign can look similar, but are made at different times. Habitat, range, and time of year give us insight into who had the opportunity.

Frequently Asked Questions

What is tracking?

Tracking is the art of interpreting the tracks and other sign left behind by animals to answer questions about the natural world. These questions may be simple, such as "Who walked through the snow in front of my house before I got up today?" or quite involved, such as "What caused this rabbit to suddenly stop feeding and dart into those bushes?" Tracking includes the skills of identification (who made these tracks?), interpretation (what was the animal doing?), aging (when did the animal pass?), and trailing (where is the animal now?). This guide focuses on identification.

Is it hard to identify animal tracks?

No. Except when it is. With a little practice, you will find that it is quite easy to identify the clear tracks of many species with confidence. Most of the tracks you will encounter in the field, however, will not be clear prints. It can take many years of practice to identify these with confidence.

Is it always possible to identify what made a track?

No. Even the best trackers can't always make a correct identification. In fact, many footprints by themselves are too faint, too worn, or too distorted to allow for positive identification. Using all of the available clues, an experienced tracker will often be able to identify an animal from surprisingly subtle tracks and sign. But often there are simply not enough clues to give positive identification. Plus, mammals are highly adaptable and creative creatures and can often surprise us. Part of the joy of tracking is that no matter how good we get, we never run out of mysteries.

What is the best place to look for tracks?

Tracks can be found nearly anywhere. While it is easy to think that we need to get deep into the woods to find mammals, I have tracked White-Tailed Deer, Red Fox, and Striped Skunk through urban backyards; Mink, River Otters, Beavers, and Coyotes along urban waterways; and Cougars across suburban parklands. Look for natural "track traps" near your home—places that combine regular animal activity with substrate such as dust, mud, or damp sand that reliably captures clear footprints. Some of the best spots include riverbanks, muddy ATV trails, sand pits, and dusty ground under bridges. Some dirt roads, sand traps on golf courses, and dusty corners of city lots are also excellent. And of course, fresh snow is a tracker's delight!

Do animals always leave tracks?

Yes, but most of the tracks they leave behind are too subtle for us to see. Only in substrates such as mud, snow, dust, soft dirt, or damp sand do animals leave tracks that we can easily study.

If it is so hard to find clear footprints, how do trackers follow a trail?

Trackers use a large number of clues from the environment to follow a trail, including partial footprints, disturbed vegetation, and a sophisticated knowledge of the habits of the animal being followed. For an excellent treatise on following animal trails in the field, check out *Practical Tracking: A Guide to Following Footprints and Finding Animals,* by Mark Elbroch, Louis Liebenberg, and Adriaan Louw.

Do I need any special equipment to track?

No. All you need are your own two eyes and a curiosity about the natural world around you. If you want to record your observations, you will want to carry a ruler or tape measure and a camera, smartphone, or small notepad and pencil. And of course, remember to bring this book!

How can I share my observations?

Phone cameras and social media have revolutionized the way trackers share observations. At the turn of the century, only a few specialists regularly photographed animal tracks. Clear photos were difficult to come by, and it was hard for most individuals to share their findings beyond a small circle of friends or colleagues. Today there are public databases with tens of thousands of photographs of tracks, many taken by enthusiasts just like you, identified and verified by communities of certified wildlife trackers. There are a number of social media groups and citizen science projects dedicated to wildlife tracks and sign. Posting photographs to these groups is a great way to share what you find and get help with identification from some of the most skilled trackers in the country. Two of the best sites are iNaturalist's **North American Animal Tracks Database,** where I participate regularly, and Facebook's **Animals Don't Cover Their Tracks: Animal Track Identification Help Group.** There are also some excellent local and regional groups on these and other platforms. Both you and others will get the most out of your posts if you have a good photographic record of your observation. On the following pages are some tips for recording and documenting what you find.

Photographing Tracks & Sign

A good photographic record allows others to see and interpret what you observed, as if they were standing beside you in the field. When we interpret tracks and sign, we use clues at multiple spatial scales—getting close, stepping back, and putting it in context. The best records have images and information at each of these scales, including multiple, clear, in-focus photographs of the following:

- Individual tracks (including a ruler for scale)
- Groups of tracks, showing the track pattern
- The surrounding habitat and the animal's view of the landscape
- The exact location of the observation. Most smartphones can geotag photos. For rare or endangered species, you may not want to share an exact location online. In this case, a clear description of the habitat and biome may be best. iNaturalist allows users to obscure the coordinates of an observation.
- The date of the observation.
- Notes to help others interpret your photographs. These could include your own measurements of tracks or track patterns, along with local knowledge about species presence or behavior.

Tips for Photographing Tracks

- **Include a scale:** Whenever possible, include a ruler in your photos. Make sure the ruler is flat on the ground and the same distance from the camera as the track. If you don't have a ruler, use a penny or other coin. Pocketknives, lighters, hands, and shoes come in many sizes and are of little use as scales.

- **Pay attention to lighting:** Make sure the outline of the track is clearly visible. In bright or dappled sunlight, your photos will usually look better when the track is shaded. On an overcast day, it may help to sidelight the track—the flashlight on your friend's phone should do the trick. Try different lighting conditions. You can delete the poor photos later once you see how things look on a full-size screen.

- **Take photos straight down:** Even a slight angle can distort features and apparent size.

A Muskrat trail showing track patterns of less common, fast gaits. Began in a trot (stride 17 ¼"; trail width 3 ¼"), then shifted into a lope (stride 16 ¼", trial width 4 ¼", group length 6 ¾"). Observed at Fort Snelling State Park, Minneapolis–St. Paul metro area, on May 16, 2020. Uploaded to iNaturalist (observation 46264651).

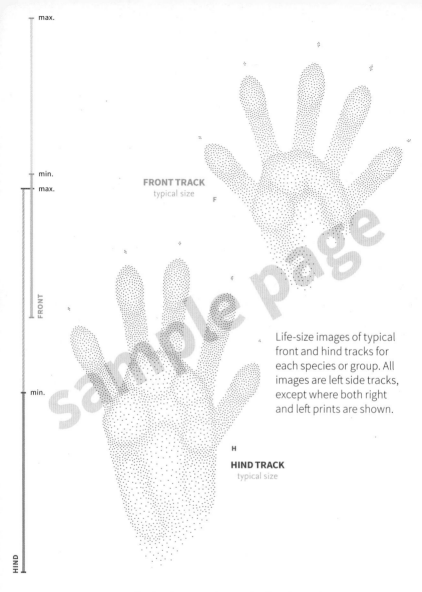

max.

min.
max.

FRONT

min.

HIND

FRONT TRACK
typical size

F

Life-size images of typical
front and hind tracks for
each species or group. All
images are left side tracks,
except where both right
and left prints are shown.

H

HIND TRACK
typical size

(See "Track Patterns: Flat-Footed Walkers & Armadillos" on pages 322 & 324.)

QUICK ID TIPS

• Key points to help you identify this species' or group's tracks.

Species (or group) common name
Scientific name

TRACKS
- A detailed description of the tracks shown in the facing illustration. Descriptions include notes about the overall shape, toe pads, claw marks, palm pads, heel marks, and negative space as appropriate. Use the descriptions together with the illustrations to learn the distinguishing features of each track. Some fine details described here will be visible only in exceptionally clear tracks in excellent substrate, such as fine mud or dust.

- A further description of details specific to the front and hind tracks of the species or group, including typical measurements.

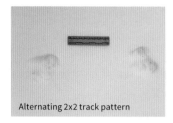
Alternating 2x2 track pattern

TRACK PATTERNS & GAITS

A short description of the typical gaits used by the species or group, along with the track patterns they leave behind. For additional information about the track patterns left by each species or group, see the "Track Patterns & Trail Measurements" section (page 308).

HABITAT

Short notes about the environments where the species or group is typically found. This may include information about vegetation cover, proximity to water, or tolerance for human development.

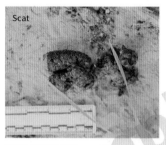
Scat

OTHER SIGN

Notes about scat and other clues, such as nests, burrows, and feeding sign, commonly left by members of this species or group.

ACTIVITY

The times of year and times of day you can expect members of this species to be most active.

SIMILAR TRACKS

Information about other species or groups that leave similar tracks, along with tips for distinguishing them.

NOTES

Detailed notes about the species or group that may be of particular interest to trackers.

Wildlife biologist Dr. Caitlin Potter and certified tracker Kirsten Welge help run a wildlife-tracking survey at the University of Minnesota's Cedar Creek Ecosystem Science Reserve.

Bats, moles, and pocket gophers rarely leave tracks but are often easy to detect by the conspicuous sign they leave behind. As we find these animals by observing their distinctive sign, we may occasionally find their tracks as well.

TRACKS

The tracks of each of these groups of mammals are both unusual and distinctive. Only those of pocket gophers risk being mistaken for the tracks of other mammals; mole and bat tracks are most likely to be confused with the tracks of small reptiles or amphibians. Pocket gopher tracks can resemble those of other rodents, particularly small ground squirrels. Ground squirrels have only four well-developed toes on their front feet, while pocket gophers have five. The three middle toes (toes 2–4) on ground squirrel hind feet are nearly the same length and register parallel to each other, giving the leading edge of the track a flat profile. The middle toe (toe 3) on pocket gopher hind tracks is the longest, and their toes tend to splay more, giving the leading edge of the track a pointed or rounded profile.

TRACK PATTERNS

Bats and moles walk leaving distinctive understep track patterns similar to those of those of a small turtle. Pocket gophers scurry almost exclusively, leaving track patterns similar to those of voles.

SIGN

Bats have established roosts they return to each day. Entrances to roosts can become stained from body oils and white streaks of uric acid. Scat often accumulates below roosts. Bat scat is similar in size and shape to mouse scat but made entirely of insect remains.

Pocket gophers and moles leave conspicuous signs of their subterranean tunneling. Moles push up ridges in the soil as they forage just below the sod layer, while both moles and gophers eject mounds of dirt onto the surface.

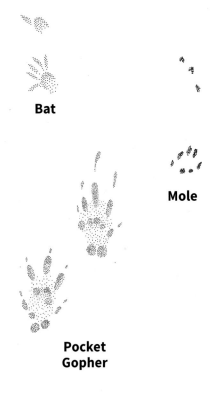

Bat

Mole

**Pocket
Gopher**

QUICK ID TIPS

- Distinctive tracks are exceptionally rare.

- Common sign include scat and urine stains near roosts and resting places.

- Often seen foraging for insects in flight on warm summer evenings.

Bats

Order Chiroptera: *Tadarida brasiliensis*, and Family Vespertilionidae

TRACKS

With their front limbs adapted for flight and their hind limbs adapted for hanging from perches and scooping up insects in flight, bats have tracks that are as unusual as they are rare. With their long front fingers tucked back, bats walk on the wrists of their forelimbs, while their hind feet point to the sides or even backward. These tiny tracks measure about ¼" or less.

- Front tracks are small, round indents left by the wrists. The thumb (toe 1) may also register. The forelimbs typically register wider than the hind feet.

- Hind tracks show five slender toes extending from a blocky palm pad. Bats' hind limbs are turned backward at the hip so their knees point up when they are on the ground, rather than forward, and their feet point backward or out to the sides.

TRACK PATTERNS & GAITS

Bats walk in a slow understep pattern similar to that of a turtle. All four limbs extend out to the sides, with their long forelimbs registering wider than their hind feet. Trails meander side-to-side and usually show drag marks from the claws, wings, and body.

HABITAT

Found in every Midwestern habitat but most abundant where there are good roosts and significant insect activity. Most species prefer to be near water and are most active in edge habitats.

OTHER SIGN

Uric acid streaks

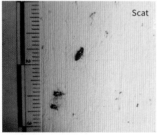

Scat

Scat: Similar in size and shape to mouse scat but made entirely of insect remains. Irregular, roughly cylindrical with pointed ends, scat measures about ¼" long and ¹⁄₁₆" in diameter. Most often found under bridges or below daytime roosts.

Daytime Roosts: Bats have established roosts they return to each day. Colonial roosts may house dozens or even thousands of individuals. Large colonies of Brazilian Free-Tailed Bats (*Tadarida brasiliensis*) number into the millions. Entrances to roosts become stained from body oils, and scat often accumulates underneath. White streaks of uric acid may also form below roosts.

ACTIVITY

Active from spring to fall, migrating or hibernating from November to April. Nocturnal; usually most active for 1–2 hours after sunset. Returns to daytime roosts before sunrise. Occasionally active during the day, especially during migration.

SIMILAR TRACKS

Tracks and trails, while rare, are unique. They may be mystifying but are unlikely to be confused with those of any other animal. Scat can appear similar to that of other insectivorous species, but placement is often distinctive.

Bats make up the second-largest order of mammals after rodents, with about 1,100 species. Most bats are tropical, but more than 20 species live in the Midwest. Except for the Brazilian Free-Tailed Bat, all are members of the family Vespertilionidae, the diminutive evening bats. Though their wings stretch 8"–16" across, the bodies of Midwestern bats range from the size of a small shrew to that of a large mouse and weigh between 4 grams (less than a nickel) and just over an ounce.

All Midwestern bats are insectivorous. Efficient hunters, they can consume half their body weight in insects in just 1–2 hours each evening and provide an important control of agricultural pests, mosquitoes, and other nuisance insects. Our bats usually capture insects in flight but occasionally glean them from foliage or off the ground.

To conserve energy, bats seek cool shelters to roost, including caves, rock crevices, trees, and human structures. They have strict needs for hibernation sites, including stable temperatures and high humidity. Well-suited caves, storm sewers, or other structures will be used for generations, and individuals may migrate hundreds of miles to reach them.

About 1% of Midwestern bats carry rabies. Only one to three people contract rabies in the U.S. each year, but most who do get it from a bat. Avoid direct contact with bats, and seek guidance from your doctor or local public health department if you have had an encounter.

Many bat populations are in decline. Most Midwestern bats live 10–20 years and have just one or two pups each year. Their long lives and slow reproduction make them vulnerable to habitat disturbance. Though I have watched a house cat catch a bat in flight and I have found bat skulls in owl pellets, bats' aerial lifestyle and secluded roosts make them less susceptible to predation than other small mammals. Major threats to these important animals are pesticides, disturbance of caves, and white-nose syndrome—a fungal infection that wakes bats up from hibernation. It is best to leave bat caves undisturbed.

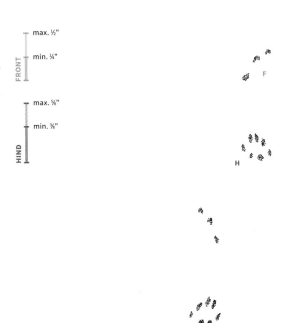

FRONT
max. ½"
min. ¼"

HIND
max. ⅝"
min. ⅜"

F

H

QUICK ID TIPS

• Usually only claw marks show in tracks.

• Typically three deep claw marks show in each front track, five in each hind.

• Runways and molehills are the most common signs.

Moles

Family Talpidae: *Scalopus aquaticus, Condylura cristata,*
and *Parascalops breweri*

TRACKS

Moles have five toes with stout claws on both front and hind feet, and often only the claws register. The nails on the front feet are extremely long and robust, creating a distinctive curved line in the tracks that is more likely to be confused with a turtle or toad than with any mammal.

- Moles' shoulders and forelimbs are built so that their large, spade-like front feet face forward for digging rather than down for walking. With this unusual posture, the front feet register only as an angled line of three or four pronounced claw marks. The nails often rake forward out of the tracks, leaving conspicuous drag marks. Front nail marks measure ⅜"–⅝".

- Hind tracks typically show five claws in a fairly symmetrical arc. The three middle toes (toes 2–4) are similar in length and may register in a nearly straight line, like a rodent. The narrow palm and even narrower heel occasionally register as well. Hind tracks measure ¼"–½" long x ¼"–½" wide.

TRACK PATTERNS & GAITS

Moles travel on the surface by twisting and wiggling their body as they scurry, producing understep track patterns similar to those of turtles. Often, the hind foot registers next to the front track from the opposite side of the body.

HABITAT

Meadows, fields, lawns, streambanks, and open woods with soft soils. Eastern and Star-Nosed Moles avoid gravelly soils. Eastern and Hairy-Tailed Moles prefer well-drained soil with enough moisture to hold its form. The Star-Nosed Mole tolerates mucky, waterlogged soils and may live in swamps or marshes. All moles avoid heavy clay and arid landscapes.

OTHER SIGN

Scat: Moles usually deposit scat underground but will sometimes form latrines next to burrow entrances underneath a log or similar cover. Scat shows varying amounts of structure depending on diet. When well formed, scat is cord-like and twisted, measuring about ⅛" in diameter and ½"–1" in length.

Molehill

Molehills: As moles excavate, they may push soil up to the surface through vertical tunnels, forming small mounds. These small, symmetrical molehills are not burrow entrances and show no evidence of an opening. They appear most often in the fall as moles excavate deeper tunnels for winter. Some individual moles rarely make molehills while others often do. Eastern Moles form fewer molehills in the southern parts of their range than in the north. Hairy-Tailed Moles make molehills the most often.

Runway

Runways: Moles often forage by tunneling just beneath the surface, pushing up a ridge of soil as they go. Runways are travel routes, and often temporary. They are sometimes backfilled with dirt excavated from the permanent burrow system, which is deeper underground. Eastern Moles create prominent runways. Hairy-Tailed Mole runways are often less conspicuous.

ACTIVITY

Active year-round and at all times of the day and night. Dig most actively on damp, cloudy days in the spring and fall. Do little digging in the winter.

SIMILAR TRACKS

Toads and hatchling turtles may leave superficially similar tracks or trails. Turtles take shorter strides, and their hind feet show just four claws. Toad trails are generally wider, and they have completely different foot morphology. Pocket gopher mounds are generally larger and fan-shaped, and they have a plugged entrance at one edge. Pocket gopher eskers are solid cords of earth on top of undisturbed ground.

NOTES

There are three species of moles in the Midwest. The Eastern Mole (*Scalopus aquaticus*) is the largest and most widespread. It is the strongest digger and the most fossorial of the three, often living its entire life underground. The Star-Nosed Mole (*Condylura cristata*), found in our region's northern and eastern states, prefers wet habitats, is encountered the least often, and is the least likely to leave prominent signs of digging. The Hairy-Tailed Mole (*Parascalops breweri*), limited to the easternmost parts of our region, is the most active aboveground.

Moles are highly adapted for fossorial (burrowing) life. They have tiny eyes, no external ears, and velvety fur that can flow in either direction, allowing them to back up in their tunnels with ease. Although they spend most of their lives underground, some venture out frequently. Hairy-Tailed Moles often forage in leaf litter at night and are the most likely to leave tracks that we can find. Star-Nosed Moles spend a great deal of time hunting in the water and may burrow under the snow in the winter. Moles of any species may come to the surface to avoid saturated soils after flooding or heavy rains.

Moles are predators, feeding primarily on earthworms, grubs, adult insects, and other invertebrates. They will also eat some vegetable matter, subterranean fungi, and carrion. Most moles are solitary and do not tolerate other moles in their tunnel systems outside of breeding season and raising young. Star-Nosed Moles are more social and may share tunnel systems. Mole tunnels are also used by shrews, voles, lemmings, mice, salamanders, and toads. Many of these animals are more abundant in mole tunnels than moles themselves.

max. 1½"

min. ¾"

FRONT

F

max. 1¼"

min. ⅝"

HIND

H

(See "Track Patterns: Shrews, Mice, Voles & Rats" on pages 310 & 312.)

QUICK ID TIPS

- Digging sign is usually conspicuous, but tracks are uncommon.
- Five slender toes on each foot with long, prominent claws.
- Scurries almost exclusively, usually leaving irregular track patterns.

Pocket Gophers

Family Geomyidae: *Geomys bursarius, Thomomys talpoides,* and *Cratogeomys castanops*

TRACKS

Highly adapted for digging, pocket gophers have a distinctive foot structure. Each foot has five slender toes tipped with stout claws. The toes appear thin, without bulbous tips, and connect to the palms in the tracks. Palm pads are small and generally indistinct.

- Front tracks are long and narrow, with prominent claws. The middle toe (toe 3) is the longest and set the farthest forward. The pinkie (toe 5) and thumb (toe 1) are set the farthest back. The thumb (toe 1) is more developed than in most rodents and is usually clear in the track. Two heel pads usually register. Narrower and longer than hind tracks. Front tracks measure ¾"–1½" long x ⅜"–⅞" wide, including claws.

- Hind toes generally splay more widely than front. As with the front foot, the middle toe (toe 3) is set the farthest forward and the outer toes (1 and 5) are set the farthest back. Claws are prominent but roughly half the length of the front claws. The heel sometimes registers. Hind tracks measure ⅝"–1¼" long x ⅜"–1" wide, including claws.

TRACK PATTERNS & GAITS

Scurries almost exclusively. Trails show a variety of understep, indirect-register, and overstep patterns and often have an irregular appearance. Pocket gophers can scurry equally well forward and backward—ideal for life in underground tunnels. They occasionally bound in the open.

HABITAT

Prairies, meadows, brushland, agricultural fields, disturbed forests, and roadsides. Gophers prefer loose, well-drained, sandy or loamy soil but tolerate gravel and easily excavate stones up to 1". Most common in relatively arid landscapes but surprisingly well adapted to wet conditions and may survive seasonal flooding. Northern Pocket Gophers tolerate a wider range of soil conditions than other species.

OTHER SIGN

Scat: Usually deposited in underground latrines. In winter, latrines may form under the snowpack and be visible after spring thaw. The typical form of the scat is a smooth, oval pellet with rounded ends measuring about ¼"–½" in length.

Mounds: As pocket gophers dig their extensive burrows, they push excavated earth out into fan-shaped mounds on the surface. Each mound has a tunnel entrance at its narrow end. These entrances are usually plugged from the inside and are often difficult to locate. The tunnels slope down from the entrance, in the opposite direction of the dirt mound. In arid landscapes, mound production tends to peak after rainfalls.

Eskers/Soil Castings: In winter, pocket gophers tunnel under snow to forage and gather nesting material. They may fill some of these tunnels with soil excavated from their burrow network. When the snow melts, these cords of excavated soil are exposed. Eskers measure 2"–3" in diameter and look like a jumble of thick rope.

Active year-round and at all times of day and night.

Other small rodents have smaller claws and four clawed toes on their front feet, and the middle three toes (toes 2–4) on their hind feet are more equal in length. **Molehills** are generally smaller and more symmetrical than pocket gopher mounds, and lack a tunnel entrance. Mole runways are created when soil is pushed up from under the surface and cover a tunnel. Pocket gopher eskers are solid and sit on top of undisturbed ground.

Pocket gophers are among the most fossorial mammals in North America. They excavate large, elaborate burrows where they spend the majority of their lives. They occasionally travel aboveground, but it is signs of their digging, rather than their tracks, that we see most often.

There are three species of pocket gopher in the Midwest. The Plains Pocket Gopher (*Geomys bursarius*) lives in the central and southwestern parts of our region, the Northern Pocket Gopher (*Thomomys talpoides*) spans the Dakotas, and the Yellow-Faced Pocket Gopher (*Cratogeomys castanops*) lives in parts of western Kansas. Where their ranges overlap, the species tend to segregate into areas with different soil types.

All three species are well adapted to a fossorial lifestyle with long claws, powerful front legs. and small eyes and ears. Their lips close behind their incisors, allowing them to use their front teeth to dig without getting dirt in their mouth. Their short, velvety fur allows them to move in tunnels with ease.

Pocket gophers are herbivores and eat a variety of roots, tubers, grasses, and forbs. They forage in their tunnels, dragging green plants underground by their roots. They can do damage to crops and gardens, but they also turn, aerate, and fertilize the soil, and some native plants depend on pocket gophers for survival.

Each pocket gopher maintains its own burrow system and defends it against other gophers. Other small animals are usually tolerated; other rodents, amphibians, and reptiles make use of gopher tunnels. Burrow systems are mostly excavated within a foot of the surface and include deeper nesting, food-cache and latrine chambers, and a shallower network of tunnels for foraging. Despite being primarily fossorial, gophers fall prey to many predators. Weasels and snakes can enter burrows to hunt; Badgers, Red Fox, and Coyotes dig them out; and hawks and owls frequently take gophers as they are pushing soil out of their burrows.

Shrews, voles, and mice are among the most common mammals in many Midwestern habitats, but they often go unnoticed. Tiny and secretive, they spend most of their time under cover. Learning the tracks and sign of these small mammals gives us a window into their hidden lives. There are nearly 40 species of shrews, mice, voles, and lemmings in the Midwest that can leave tracks less than ½" across. Another nine species of rats leave similar-looking tracks that are only a bit larger. While some of these species are uncommon or have limited ranges, many are widespread and abundant. Tiny tracks can lack detail, so we often need to consider track patterns, habitat, behavior, and associated sign. Even then, identifying tracks to species may not be possible, but we can usually narrow down to just a few possibilities in any given location. In the following accounts, species are grouped together with those that leave similar tracks and sign. Shrews are considered as a group, as are voles and lemmings. Mice and rats get a little more differentiation. The Least Weasel, which also leaves tiny tracks, is discussed in the weasel section.

TRACKS

All of these tiny-track makers have five toes on their hind feet. Shrews and weasels also have five fully developed toes on their front feet, while most rodents have four. When tracks lack detail, look at the overall shape. Shrews' and weasels' front and hind tracks are nearly the same size, while most rodent front tracks are smaller than hinds. Deer mouse tracks look round, while vole, House Mouse, and harvest mouse tracks appear more elongated.

TRACK PATTERNS & GAITS

Most mice travel in a bound. They also walk and trot while foraging and when under cover, but we are less likely to see these trails. Long-Tailed Shrews often bound as well, leaving track patterns tiny enough to rule out most other mammals. Voles and the larger Short-Tailed Shrews leave a wider variety of track patterns. They generally walk or trot, but also they lope and occasionally bound. Bounding track patterns tend to be irregular and are used only for short stretches. Least Weasels typically lope or bound, often leaving a 2x2 track pattern. Their strides are much longer than those of voles, which may leave similar-looking track groups. When looking at tiny track patterns, also consider small reptiles and amphibians, which may leave similar trails.

SHREWS, MICE, VOLES & RATS

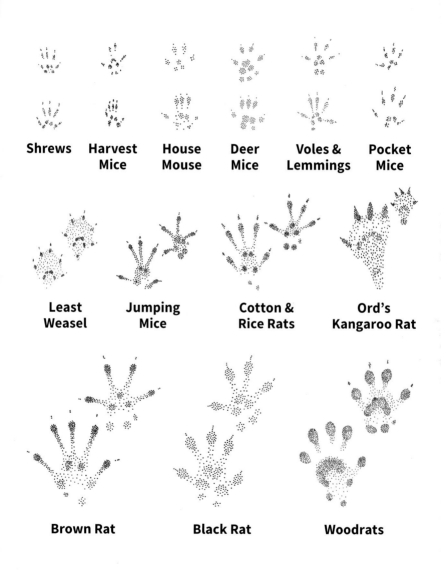

Shrews   **Harvest Mice**   **House Mouse**   **Deer Mice**   **Voles & Lemmings**   **Pocket Mice**

Least Weasel   **Jumping Mice**   **Cotton & Rice Rats**   **Ord's Kangaroo Rat**

Brown Rat   **Black Rat**   **Woodrats**

(See "Track Patterns: Shrews, Mice, Voles & Rats" on pages 310 & 312.)

FRONT

max. ⅜"

min. ³⁄₁₆"

F

HIND

max. ⅜"

min. ³⁄₁₆"

H

(See "Track Patterns: Shrews, Mice, Voles & Rats" on pages 310 & 312.)

QUICK ID TIPS

- Five long toes and numerous palm pads on each tiny foot.
- Tiny tracks range from mouse-size down to the smallest of all mammal tracks.
- Front and hind tracks appear more similar than in other tiny mammals.

Shrews

Family Soricidae: *Sorex* spp., *Blarina* spp., and *Cryptotis* parva

TRACKS

Shrews have five fully developed toes on each foot, each tipped with a sharp claw. Each foot has several small palm pads, with the exact number and placement varying among species. There are one or two heel pads on each foot that occasionally register as well. Front and hind tracks are similar in size and appearance.

- Front tracks are slightly smaller than hind, but the difference is subtle. The middle toe (toe 3) is the longest, and the tips of the three middle toes (toes 2–4) typically form an arc. Small heel pads may also register. ³⁄₁₆"–³⁄₈" long; ³⁄₁₆"–³⁄₈" wide.

- On the hind track, the three middle toes (toes 2–4) are nearly the same length. They typically splay less than in front tracks, and their tips often form a straight line, similar to the tracks of many rodents. Often slightly longer than wide. ³⁄₁₆"–³⁄₈" long; ³⁄₁₆"–³⁄₈" wide.

TRACK PATTERNS & GAITS

Shrews generally travel in a trot (scurry), slow to a walk when investigating, and bound when crossing open areas. Bounding track patterns are more variable than in mice. Front feet generally register wider apart, giving trails a more boxy appearance; hind feet may be offset, creating a lope-like pattern; group lengths may be very short—similar to a 2x2 bound; and they may hop, with the hind feet landing behind the front. Long-Tailed *(Sorex)* Shrews generally switch to a 2x2 bound in deeper snow. Short-Tailed *(Blarina)* Shrews generally continue to trot in snow but may also switch to a 2x2 bound. Trails in the snow are usually short and end at a tunnel or other access to the subnivean layer.

HABITAT

Most species prefer moist habitats with a debris layer on the ground but may be found nearly anywhere with cover and with invertebrates for food.

OTHER SIGN

Scat

Scat: Shrews drop scat at random along travel routes and near their burrows. The structure of the scat varies with diet and ranges from formless to tiny capsules, depending on how many hard-bodied insects the shrew has eaten. Scat typically measures less than ½" and is often less than ¼" in length.

Tunnels: Shrews follow the tunnels of other small mammals in addition to digging their own. Tunnel entrances are most prominent in snow. Short-Tailed *(Blarina)* Shrew tunnels are similar in size to those of mice and voles, about 1" across. Long-Tailed *(Sorex)* Shrew tunnels are about the size of a penny (¾") but may be much smaller—hardly more than pencil-width.

ACTIVITY

Active year-round, though some species become torpid (inactive) in extremely cold weather. Most active at night, especially aboveground, but are in nearly constant search of food and rest less than most other mammals.

SIMILAR TRACKS

Rodent front tracks are generally smaller than their hinds and show only four fully developed toes. **Mice** bound with a more consistent track pattern, and their front feet are usually closer together. **Vole** trails are generally larger, but there is overlap in size. Both voles and shrews use a variety of gaits and use the same networks of trails. Distinguishing these trails is not always possible. **Least Weasel** 2x2 bound patterns show much longer strides.

NOTES

Shrews are renowned for their voracious appetites and high-strung personalities. The smallest shrews approach the lower size limit for a warm-blooded animal and need to feed almost constantly to maintain their body temperature. Shrews typically eat more than their body weight in food each day and may starve to death in as little as 4 hours. Almost constantly foraging, shrews rest less than most mammals, and some enter into torpor when not feeding.

The shrew family, Soricidae, includes the smallest mammals in the Midwest. There are 12 species of shrews in our region, grouped into three genera: tiny Long-Tailed Shrews in the genus *Sorex*, which can weigh as little as 2 grams; larger Short-Tailed Shrews in the genus *Blarina*, which are about the size of mice; and the Least Shrew (*Cryptotis parva*), which is similar in size and behavior to the smallest long-tailed shrews.

Shrews eat mostly slugs, worms, insects, and other invertebrates. They spend most of their time foraging in networks of tunnels, under the leaf litter, under the snow (the subnivean layer), and underground. They dig some of their own tunnels and also follow the tunnels and trails made by moles, voles, and other small mammals.

Shrews are common and abundant in most areas with sufficient ground cover, but they are often elusive, and population estimates for most species are inconclusive. Shrews are frequently killed by predators, and their skulls are common in owl pellets in many areas. These skulls can be distinguished from those of small rodents by their narrow profile; lack of cheekbones (zygomatic arches); and sharp, carnivore-like teeth with dark-red tips. Curiously, many mammalian carnivores often kill shrews and then discard them uneaten, perhaps because of a musky odor the shrews produce.

Shrews are so light that their tracks will not show on many surfaces. Their tiny tracks are easiest to find in snow but also appear in fine mud or in dust under logs and other woody debris.

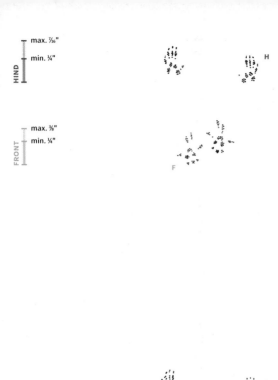

HIND max. ⁷⁄₁₆"
min. ¼"

FRONT max. ⅜"
min. ¼"

H

F

(For details on sign and behavior, see "Deer Mice" on page 70.
For details on track patterns, see "Track Patterns: Shrews, Mice, Voles & Rats" on pages 310 & 312.)

QUICK ID TIPS

- Smallest mouse tracks in the Midwest.

- Toes are longer and less bulbous than in deer mice.

- Distinctive hind track resembles a tiny human hand or Opossum hind print.

Harvest Mice
Reithrodontomys spp.

TRACKS

Harvest mouse tracks appear smaller, more delicate, and less symmetrical than those of most other mice. Toes are long and slim, and they usually connect to the palm in the tracks. Small claws often register in clear prints. Unlike in pocket mice and house mice, front and hind tracks are nearly the same size.

- Front tracks show typical rodent structure, with four toes arranged in a 1-2-1 pattern. The middle toe (toe 3) registers the farthest forward. Three palm pads form a small triangle, and two tiny heel pads often register. Front tracks measure ¼"–⅜" long x ¼"–⅜" wide.

- Hind tracks show five toes in a variation on the typical 1-3-1 rodent pattern. The middle three toes (toes 2–4) are parallel and point forward. The pinkie (toe 5) may not splay much and often registers close to the middle toes. The thumb (toe 1) is longer and set farther back than in other mice. The overall effect is a track that often looks similar to a tiny human hand or Opossum hind print. Four palm pads are arranged in a rough trapezoid. Hind tracks measure ¼"–⁷⁄₁₆" long x ¼"–⅜" wide.

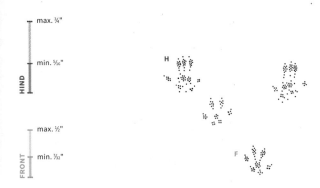

max. ¾"

min. ⁵⁄₁₆"

HIND

max. ½"

min. ⁷⁄₃₂"

FRONT

H

F

(For details on scat and some sign, see "Deer Mice," page 70. For details on behavior, see "Old World Rats," page 91. For details on track patterns, see "Track Patterns: Shrews, Mice, Voles & Rats" on pages 310 & 312.)

QUICK ID TIPS

- Closely associated with people; almost always found in or near buildings.

- Shows greater size difference between front and hind tracks than most native mice.

- More elongated than deer mouse tracks, with longer toes and narrower palms.

House Mouse
Mus musculus

TRACKS

House Mice have a classic rodent foot structure, with four toes on the front and five on the larger hind. The size difference between front and hind tracks is more pronounced than in most native mice. Their long toes have slightly bulbous tips that usually register separate from the palm. Tiny claws often show but may be indistinguishable from the toes. The tracks appear more elongated than those of deer mice, with longer, less bulbous toes and narrower palms that make up less of the total area of each track.

- The front shows four toes in the typical 1-2-1 rodent pattern. The tiny thumb may register in good substrate. Three small palm pads form a triangle. Two heel pads sometimes show, but less clearly than in most deer mouse tracks. Front tracks measure 7/32"–1/2" long x 9/32"–3/8" wide.

- Hind tracks show five toes arranged 1-3-1, with the middle toes (toes 2–4) usually registering tightly together. Unlike in harvest mice, the outer toes (toes 1 and 5) are both set far back on the palm and splay widely. Four palm pads are arranged in a rectangle that is taller than it is wide—contrasting with deer mice, where the palm is wider than tall. The naked heel sometimes registers. Hind tracks measure 5/16"–3/4" long x 5/16"–7/16" wide.

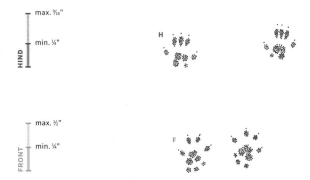

(See "Track Patterns: Shrews, Mice, Voles & Rats" on pages 310 & 312.)

QUICK ID TIPS

- Bulbous toe and palm pads. Tracks often look like a collection of dots.

- Prints appear round—roughly as long as they are wide.

- The most common tiny mammal tracks in many habitats.

Deer Mice
Peromyscus spp.

TRACKS

Deer mouse tracks show a classic rodent structure, with four toes on the front foot and five on the hind. Tracks are nearly round, with short toes and proportionally large, broad palms. Pads are bulbous. Toe pads typically register separate from the palm, and tracks often look like a collection of dots. Tiny claws often show but may be indistinguishable from the toes. Prints are often wider than long, while other mouse and vole tracks are usually longer than wide.

• Front tracks show four toes in the 1-2-1 rodent pattern. Three palm pads are arranged in a broad, rounded triangle. Two heel pads may also register. The tiny thumb (toe 1) has a claw and sometimes registers. Slightly smaller than the hind track, front tracks measure ¼"–½" long x ¼"–⁷⁄₁₆" wide.

• Hind tracks show five toes in a 1-3-1 pattern. The thumb (toe 1) is the smallest and set the farthest back. Four palm pads are arranged in a rectangle. Three pads usually fuse together into a plump right-angle (¬) shape. The remaining pad, located at the base of the thumb (toe 1), registers more lightly and marks the fourth corner of the rectangle. Two tiny heel pads are sometimes visible. Hind tracks measure ¼"–⁹⁄₁₆" long x ⁵⁄₁₆"–½" wide.

TRACK PATTERNS & GAITS

Deer mice bound almost exclusively, usually leaving consistent, even track patterns. Their long tails may register in softer substrates. Deer mice travel on top of the snow more often than most tiny mammals, where their prints may merge into an H-shaped 2x2 pattern. They sometimes walk sort distances. Harvest mice usually bound when traveling, leaving less regular track patterns. They often scurry when in cover, leaving an indirect register. House Mice usually bound in the open, leaving patterns similar to deer mice, and often scurry when close to cover.

HABITAT

At least one species of deer mouse is common in nearly every habitat in the Midwest. Harvest mice prefer open, grassy, and brushy areas, including prairies, grasslands, fields, briar patches, and forest clearings. House mice are always close to human habitation.

OTHER SIGN

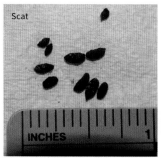

Scat

Scat: Mice leave tiny, irregularly shaped scat wherever they roam. Droppings tend to accumulate along well-used trails and at feeding sites. Scat has a wrinkled appearance and typically measures 1⁄16" or less in diameter and less than 1⁄4" in length.

Feeding Sign: Look for the remains of chewed nuts and seeds underneath rocks and logs. Squirrels and birds typically leave feeding remains on top of exposed surfaces.

Nest

Nests: Mice build small, spherical nests of woven grasses and other plant fibers in trees, shrubs, and sometimes in tall grass. Deer mice also build nests under logs, in abandoned burrows, or in woodrat stick houses. Nests measure 3"–6" in diameter, with a small, round opening on the side.

ACTIVITY

Active year-round but may hole up or retreat into buildings during bad weather. Primarily nocturnal but occasionally active during the day.

SIMILAR TRACKS

Shrew tracks and trails are generally smaller. Front and hind tracks each have five toes and are similar in size and appearance. **Vole** tracks look "fingery," with long claws and slender, widely splayed toes usually connecting to a smaller palm. Their front and hind tracks are similar in size. Voles usually scurry or lope rather than bound. **Pocket mice** and **jumping mice** show more difference in size between their front and hind feet. Their bounds are often irregular and their front feet usually register turned out (duck-footed). Pocket mice have longer claws and show four toes in their hind tracks.

NOTES

Deer mice, members of the genus *Peromyscus*, are believed to be the most abundant wild mammals in North America. Highly adaptable, they are found in nearly every habitat on the continent. The two most common and wide-spread species are the North American Deer Mouse (*Peromyscus maniculatus*), and the White-Footed Mouse (*Peromyscus leucopus*). Four other species range into at least one corner of our region. Although deer mice are nocturnal and generally inconspicuous, their sign are common and easy to find. The Midwest is also home to three species of harvest mice *(Reithrodontomys* spp.), which are smaller than deer mice but similar in appearance and behavior.

These mice are adept climbers and may leave signs of their presence at every level of vegetation from the ground to the canopy. They form well-worn runs between regular nesting and feeding locations, and also make use of existing vole trails. They will even venture underground, using burrows and tunnels excavated by other small mammals. Most species are capable swimmers as well. Nests may be built in tree cavities, in vegetation, on the ground, or underground.

Harvest mice eat mostly the seeds of various grasses and herbs, supplemented with leaves and insects, particularly caterpillars. Deer mice are quite omnivorous, eating a wide variety of seeds, berries, nuts, vegetation, invertebrates, and fungi. Many species cache large amounts of food for the winter, storing it in places ranging from tree cavities, hollow logs, and rock crevices to bird nests, abandoned burrows, and buildings.

As they are so common, deer mice are a dietary mainstay for many small and medium-size predators. They are an important food source for weasels, foxes, Bobcats, hawks, owls, and many snakes. They are also preyed on by larger carnivores, such as Coyotes and even Wolves.

Two other comparably rare and elusive species of mice are found in the Midwest: the carnivorous Northern Grasshopper Mouse (*Onychomys leucogaster*) of the western prairies and the arboreal Golden Mouse *(Ochrotomys nuttalli),* found in the southeastern parts of our region. Little is known about the tracks or trails of either, but they are believed to be similar to those of deer mice.

FRONT

max. ½"

min. ¼"

F

HIND

max. ⅝"

min. ¼"

H

(See "Track Patterns: Shrews, Mice, Voles & Rats" on pages 310 & 312.)

QUICK ID TIPS

- "Fingery" appearance with slender, widely splayed toes radiating out from tiny palms.

- Typically walk or trot, rather than bound.

- Maintain runways through tall grasses, under leaf litter, and under snowpack.

Voles & Lemmings

Microtus spp., *Myodes gapperi,* and *Synaptomys cooperi*

TRACKS

Typical rodent form with four toes on the front feet, five toes on the hind. The toes splay widely and the outer toes may point straight to the sides. The toes appear slender and are often connected to the palm in the track. Palms are relatively small. Claws are long and often conspicuous.

- Front shows four toes in a 1-2-1 pattern. The middle toes (toes 3 and 4) usually splay, forming a V at the front of the track (think *V* for "vole"). Three small palm pads are arranged in a tight triangle. Two small heel pads sometimes register. The tiny thumb (toe 1) occasionally registers. Front tracks are slightly smaller than hinds and measure ¼"–½" long x ¼"–½" wide.

- Hind tracks show five toes, arranged 1-3-1. The middle toes (toes 2–4) may splay or register nearly parallel. The outer toes (toes 1 and 5) don't always register clearly. There are four palm pads. The pad at the base of the thumb (toe 1) is the smallest and registers the lightest. The other three pads often form a thick L-shape, defining the palm. The palm, and typically the entire track, appears longer than wide. Two small heel pads occasionally register. Hind tracks measure ¼"–⅝" long x ¼"–½" wide.

TRACK PATTERNS & GAITS

Voles usually scurry (walk or trot), leaving a variety of understep, direct-register, and overstep patterns. They may speed up into a lope, hop, or occasionally a bound when exposed. These asymmetric patterns tend to be less consistent than similarly sized mouse or shrew trails. Scurrying trails are common in light snow. As snow deepens, they may switch to a 2x2 bound, but generally tunnel under it.

HABITAT

Found in nearly every habitat with some sort of ground cover. In arid regions, they are most common along riverways.

OTHER SIGN

Scat

Runway

Scat: Typically a smooth, capsule-shaped pellet with rounded ends ⅛" or less in diameter and about ¼" long. Color ranges from dark brown to bright green. Drops some scat at random along travel routes, but also forms latrines.

Runways: Most species create well-traveled networks of runways through thick vegetation or under leaf litter. Runways measure 1"–2½" across and often connect to subterranean tunnels. Runways through grass are usually kept "mowed," and some runways are "paved" with dirt excavated from tunnels. Under snowpack, some runways get filled with dirt, grass clippings, or scat, leaving behind eskers similar to those made by pocket gophers.

Nests: Voles typically build nests in thick cover or in underground burrows. Sometimes they also construct nests under deep snowpack, which may be exposed in the spring. Nests are fully enclosed, woven of grasses, and measure about 3"–5" across.

ACTIVITY

Active year-round, living predominantly under the snowpack during northern winters. May be active at any time of day or night.

   Shrew front and hind tracks are closer in size and have five toes each. Shrew scurrying (walk/trot) trails tend to be narrower, and their bounding trails tend to be more regular. **Cotton** and **rice rat** tracks are larger. **Mice** bound more often and for longer stretches. Deer mice have bulbous toes that do not usually connect to the palm in the track. Their tracks appear round and are often wider than long. **Harvest mice** splay their toes less, and their hind tracks are distinctly asymmetrical.

NOTES
   Together with Muskrat, voles and lemmings make up the rodent subfamily Arvicolinae. All are similar in appearance, with blunt snouts, small eyes and ears, and a tubular body. There are five widespread species in the Midwest, plus another four with limited ranges at the fringes of our region. They can be found everywhere there is fresh vegetation and sufficient cover and are the most abundant mammal in many habitats.

Voles are perhaps best known for their dramatic population cycles. Most voles live less than a year but are highly prolific, capable of producing a litter of pups every month. When food is abundant, populations can explode. Swelling populations may deplete local food resources, causing a crash. Some species go through boom-and-bust cycles every year, while others follow three- to four-year cycles of growth and decline.

Midwestern voles are terrestrial and semi-fossorial. They dig tunnels, follow the tunnels made by other small mammals, and spend considerable time underground. They sometimes venture into low shrubs but generally do not climb. They stay under cover when traveling, forming well-worn runs, which are often the most obvious sign of their presence. When snow accumulates, voles create runways under the snowpack.

Voles eat primarily green vegetation, supplemented with roots, tubers, seeds, and fungi, and spend a great deal of time foraging both day and night. When green vegetation is sparse, many voles will gnaw on the inner bark of trees, sometimes girdling and killing them. Voles are a mainstay in the diet of many predators, including weasels, foxes, Bobcats, Coyotes, snakes, hawks, and owls, whose scat and pellets often contain vole remains. Where predators rely heavily on voles for food, their populations often end up following the boom-and-bust cycles of their prey.

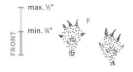

FRONT

max. ½"

min. ¼"

F

ORD'S KANGAROO RAT

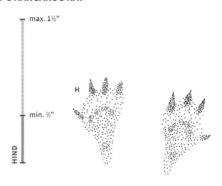

max. 1½"

min. ½"

HIND

H

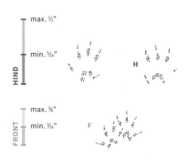

HIND

max. ½"

min. 5⁄16"

H

FRONT

max. 3⁄8"

min. 3⁄16"

F

POCKET MOUSE

(See "Track Patterns: Shrews, Mice, Voles & Rats" on pages 310 & 312.)

QUICK ID TIPS

- Hind feet are much larger than front.
- Unlike most rodents, hind feet show only four fully developed toes.
- Kangaroo rat's bipedal bound is distinctive.

Ord's Kangaroo Rat & Pocket Mice

Family Heteromyidae: *Dipodomys ordii, Chaetodipus hispidus,*
and *Perognathus* spp.

Ord's Kangaroo Rat ◼

TRACKS

Pocket mice and kangaroo rats typically show four toes in their hind tracks and may show five in their fronts, unlike most rodents. Long, slender toes are tipped with prominent claws. Palm pads sometimes register clearly but are often obscured by fur. Hind tracks are much larger than fronts.

• Front tracks typically show four widely splayed toes. The thumb (toe 1) is more developed than in most small rodents and sometimes shows. Claws are long and pronounced. Small palm pads form an arc behind the toes, and two heel pads sometimes register. Kangaroo rat front feet rarely register. Pocket mouse front tracks measure ³⁄₁₆"–³⁄₈" long x ⅛"–³⁄₈" wide.

• Hind tracks show only four well-developed toes. Unlike most rodents, the thumb (toe 1) is greatly reduced and rarely registers. The middle toes (toes 2–4) point forward, and the pinkie (toe 5) is set farther back and points to the side. There is often a large negative space between the toes and palm. The long, narrow heel rarely registers in pocket mice, but often shows in kangaroo rat tracks, giving many an "ice cream cone" shape. Pocket mouse hind tracks measure ⁵⁄₁₆"–½" long x ³⁄₁₆"–³⁄₈" wide; Ord's Kangaroo Rat hind tracks measure ½"–1½" long x ³⁄₈"–1" wide.

TRACK PATTERNS & GAITS

Pocket mice travel in a bound. Their front tracks often register duck-footed (turned out) and overlapping. Ord's Kangaroo Rats travel in a distinctive bipedal hop or skip. They occasionally bound on all four feet when foraging, creating trails similar to those of pocket mice.

HABITAT

Arid and semiarid grasslands and shrublands with sandy soils. The Hispid Pocket Mouse (*Chaetodipus hispidus*) tolerates high levels of clay and gravel, while the Plains Pocket Mouse (*Perognathus flavescens*) prefers soft soils.

OTHER SIGN

Kangaroo rat scat

Scat: Dry, hard pellets with round or pointed ends. Sometimes linked together in short chains. Often deposited underground but sometimes found near burrow entrances or foraging sites. Ranges from less than ¼" to ½" long.

Runs: Pocket mice and kangaroo rats create established runs between their burrows and foraging sites. Following runs is often the easiest way to locate clear tracks, burrows, and other sign.

Dust Baths: Shallow depressions in the sand are used for hygiene and play a role in communication. They are often located along well-established runs.

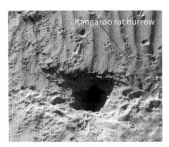

Kangaroo rat burrow

Burrows: Ord's Kangaroo Rats create burrows in the open and at the base of shrubs and logs. Burrow entrances are usually 2"–3" and may be taller than they are wide. Pocket mouse burrows are often concealed under shrubs, logs, or rocks. Entrances are about 1" in diameter.

ACTIVITY

Reduces activity in cold and inclement weather. Some species hibernate intermittently through the winter, waking periodically to feed. Highly nocturnal. Rarely active during the day and may even avoid moonlit nights.

SIMILAR TRACKS

Jumping mouse tracks are larger than those of pocket mice. Their long toes usually connect to the palm in the tracks and often appear curved. **Other mice** show less difference in size between front and hind tracks and show five fully developed toes on their hind feet. The bipedal track patterns of kangaroo rats are unique among Midwestern mammals. Under some conditions, pocket mouse and kangaroo rat tracks can resemble those of **songbirds.**

NOTES

Pocket mice and kangaroo rats belong to the family Heteromyidae, a nocturnal, semi-fossorial group of New World rodents adapted for life in arid landscapes. Heteromyids' front feet are built for digging, while their large hind legs are specialized for leaping. They are such strong jumpers that some have adopted a bipedal lifestyle. When moving at any speed, kangaroo rats hop on their hind feet with their forefeet and tails aloft, like their Australian namesake.

Predominantly desert dwellers, this large family has only five species represented in the Midwest: Ord's Kangaroo Rat (*Dipodomys ordii*), the relatively large Hispid Pocket Mouse (*Chaetodipus hispidus*), and three small species in the genus *Perognathus*—Wyoming, Silky, and Plains Pocket Mice—which leave some of the smallest mammal tracks in our region. Most are found only in the westernmost parts of the Midwest, but the Plains Pocket Mouse ranges as far east as the Mississippi River in Iowa and Minnesota.

Heteromyids are granivores, feeding primarily on seeds. Though they eat some seeds while foraging, they carry most back to their burrows in the large cheek pouches from which pocket mice get their name. Stored underground, these seeds absorb moisture from damp burrow walls, providing a modest source of water in arid environments. Masters of water conservation, pocket mice and kangaroo rats can get all the water they need from their food. They plug their burrow entrances to keep moisture in, stay underground whenever the sun is up, have a specialized metabolism that produces extra water from the starches in their food, and produce highly concentrated urine and bone-dry scat.

max. ⅞"

min. ½"

HIND

max. ½"

min. ⁵⁄₁₆"

FRONT

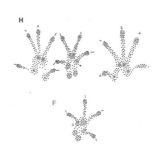

H

F

(See "Track Patterns: Shrews, Mice, Voles & Rats" on pages 310 & 312.)

QUICK ID TIPS

- Extremely long, slender toes, especially the middle three toes of the hind foot.
- Compact track patterns usually show the front feet turned strongly outward.
- Hind tracks can resemble those of a small songbird.

Jumping Mice

Subfamily Zapodini: *Zapus hudsonius*, *Zapus princeps*,
and *Napaeozapus insignis*

TRACKS

Jumping mouse tracks show a variation on the typical rodent form. They
have extremely long, slender toes that nearly always connect to the palm in
the track. The toes splay widely, with the outermost toes typically pointing
straight to the sides or even curved slightly backward. Claws generally
register. Hind tracks are much larger than front tracks.

- Front tracks show four toes, which frequently appear slightly curved in the
  track. The palm is compact, with three palm pads forming a small triangle
  and two round heel pads tucked closely behind. The tiny, vestigial thumb
  (toe 1) is sometimes visible as well. Front tracks measure 5/16"–1/2" long x
  3/8"–1/2" wide.

- Hind tracks are long and narrow, with extremely long toes. The middle three
  toes (toes 2–4) are grouped together, while the outer toes (toes 1 and 5) are
  set far back on the long, narrow palm. There are four small pads on the palm.
  A long, slender heel rarely registers. Often only the middle three toes (toes
  2–4) and the forward portion of the palm register clearly, giving the tracks a
  bird-like appearance. Hind tracks measure 1/2"–7/8" long x 3/8"–5/8" wide.

Jumping mouse tracks

TRACK PATTERNS & GAITS
Bound almost exclusively, leaving irregular, compact groups of tracks. Front tracks usually register turned out (duck-footed) and often offset from one another and may appear behind, between, or in front of the hinds. Usually takes short strides of less than 10" but capable of leaping 8' or more.

HABITAT
Damp areas with thick ground cover, especially along waterways. Meadow and western jumping mice prefer open, grassy habitats, or woodland edges. Woodland jumping mice are most common in dense, mature conifer or mixed forests.

OTHER SIGN
Scat: As far as I know, no one in the tracking community has identified jumping mouse scat in the field. Scat of captive jumping mice appears twisted with tapered ends and measures ¹⁄₁₆"–½" in length.

Feeding Sign: Jumping mice often clip grass and herbaceous plant stems into short lengths when feeding. These 1"–2" long clippings may accumulate in small piles.

Nests: Like other mice and voles, jumping mice build globular nests of tightly woven grasses and leaves. Nests may be on the ground, in shallow burrows, in tree cavities, or suspended in vegetation and measure 4"–6" in diameter. Compared with vole nests, jumping mouse nests are usually more spherical, more tightly woven, and lack clear trails leading from them.

ACTIVITY
Deep hibernators, jumping mice are inactive from mid-fall until mid-spring. Primarily nocturnal but sometimes active on overcast days.

SIMILAR TRACKS
Other small mammals show less difference in size between the front and hind tracks and show shorter, straighter toes. **Voles** usually trot. **Deer mice** have bulbous toe tips and leave more regular bounding patterns. **Pocket mice** often overlap their front feet when bounding. Jumping mouse hind tracks can resemble **songbird** tracks when only the middle toes (toes 2–4) register clearly. Look for evidence of additional toes—the outer toes in jumping mice and the rear-facing hallux in songbirds—and for evidence of front tracks. The outward-turned front tracks of jumping mice can resemble the inward-turned front tracks of **frogs,** but hind tracks look quite different.

NOTES

There are three species of jumping mouse in the Midwest. The widespread Meadow Jumping Mouse (*Zapus hudsonius*) lives in every state in the region. The Woodland Jumping Mouse (*Napaeozapus insignis*) is found in the northern forests of Minnesota, Wisconsin, and Michigan, and the Western Jumping Mouse (*Zapus princeps*) ranges into the far western Dakotas.

Jumping mice are not closely related to other North American mice but are closer kin to the bipedal jerboas of North Africa and Asia. As their name suggests, jumping mice's bodies are specialized for making powerful leaps. In addition to their large hind feet and strong legs, they have extremely long tails, which are often 1½ times the length of the rest of their body and act as a stabilizer in the air. While they usually travel in short bounds of 1"–6", they are capable of leaping 6'–8'. When startled, they usually take several long, frog-like jumps, then duck into cover, remaining motionless. Shy creatures, they are rarely seen by people.

Jumping mice are the smallest rodents in the Midwest that hibernate through the winter. They hibernate in small nests, buried underground, with the entrances filled in and sealed. They store no food but rely on fat reserves to sustain them for over half a year of torpor—typically from September to May. Most do not survive. Rare individuals have been known to avoid hibernation by moving into human homes for the winter and returning outdoors in the spring. Either way, jumping mice do not leave tracks in the colder months of the year.

Jumping mice are good swimmers and capable divers. They readily take to water and may dive into the water to flee. Jumping mice are omnivorous, eating seeds, berries, insects, and fungi. As jumping mice recover from hibernation, insects are an important part of their spring diet. Subterranean fungi in the genus *Endogone* make up a substantial fraction of the diet of many jumping mice, and these fungi may actually depend on jumping mice and other small mammals to complete their life cycle. Not only do jumping mice disperse the fungi's spores, but there is also evidence that the spores require exposure to a mammal's digestive system to germinate.

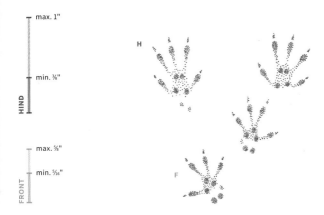

max. 1"

min. ⅜"

HIND

max. ⅝"

min. ⁵⁄₁₆"

FRONT

H

F

(See "Track Patterns: Shrews, Mice, Voles & Rats" on pages 310 & 312.)

QUICK ID TIPS

- Wide-splaying toes in a typical rodent arrangement.

- Long, slender toes usually connect to the palm.

- Similar to vole tracks, but larger.

Hispid Cotton & Marsh Rice Rats

Subfamily Sigmodontinae: *Sigmodon hispidus* and
Oryzomys palustris

TRACKS

Cotton and rice rats have long, slender toes that usually connect to the palm in the track. Toes often splay wide and are arranged in a typical rodent structure, with the middle toes pointing more forward and the outer toes angling to the sides. Palm pads are small and may not register clearly. Claws usually register. Hind tracks are larger than front tracks. Rice rat tracks are less symmetrical than cotton rat tracks, but the differences are subtle.

- Front tracks show three palm pads forming a small triangle. The tiny, vestigial thumb (toe 1) is sometimes visible. Two heel pads occasionally register close behind the palm. Front claws tend to be pronounced in rice rat tracks. Front tracks measure 5/16"–5/8" long x 3/8"–5/8" wide.

- Hind feet are long, but often only the front portions register clearly. The outermost toes (1 and 5) are set far back on the palm. The tips of these toes may register even with or even behind the leading edge of the palm. The palm is long and narrow, with four small pads arranged in a tall rectangle, but the rearmost pads don't register reliably. The heel occasionally registers. Hind tracks measure 3/8"–1" long x 3/8"–3/4" wide.

TRACK PATTERNS & GAITS

Usually scurry like voles rather than bound like mice. Typically walk when foraging and trot across open ground. Like voles, they may also bound when exposed or threatened. Bounding patterns tend to be irregular, with the hind feet landing behind, beside, or ahead of the fronts.

HABITAT

Found in diverse habitats across their range. Most common in areas with thick, dense ground cover such as meadows, roadsides, and the borders of cultivated fields. Rice rats prefer wet environments and are unaffected by periodic flooding. They are most common in marshes along the Gulf and Atlantic Coasts. In the Midwest, they inhabit inland marshes, river- and streambanks, and wet meadows.

OTHER SIGN

Scat: Small pellets measuring about ⅛" in diameter and ¼"–½" long. Appearance may vary seasonally with diet. During the growing season, scat tends to resemble that of voles—small green, yellow, or tan capsules. Deposited along runs and near nests.

Cotton rat with nesting material

Runs: These rats build extensive networks of runways similar to those of voles but on a larger scale, measuring 2"–4" across. Many runways are "mowed" and grass clippings are heaped in small piles. Runways may connect to underground tunnels measuring 1"–2" across.

Nests: Cotton and rice rats build spherical nests of grass and plant fibers. In dry habitats, nests may be underground or located under rocks, logs, or other cover. In wet habitats, rice rats will sometimes build nests suspended in vegetation. Nests can range from 6" to more than 12" and tend to be larger in the Midwest than in the southern parts of these animals' range.

ACTIVITY

Active year-round. Predominantly nocturnal or crepuscular but may be active any time of the day or night. Rice rats are more nocturnal than cotton rats.

SIMILAR TRACKS

Brown Rat tracks are typically larger but can look nearly identical. Habitat and behavior are important clues to consider. Brown rats' front claws are shorter, and their toes and palms are proportionally wider. **Black Rat** tracks have more-bulbous pads, particularly palm pads. The palm pads on Black

Rat tracks will generally fill the entire palm, while the palm pads of cotton and rice tracks often appear as small dimples within the palm. **Vole** tracks are smaller and show less difference in size between the front and the hind. **Chipmunks** have more bulbous pads on their feet, and their toes splay less.

NOTES

The Hispid Cotton Rat and Marsh Rice Rat are the two most northern-ranging species in the rodent subfamily Sigmodontinae, and the only two that extend into the Midwest. In their core ranges across the southern and southeastern U.S., these small rats are the most abundant mammals in many habitats. Found in some of the southernmost parts of the Midwest, they occupy niches similar to those of voles and lemmings in most of our region, and they leave similar-looking tracks and sign. As with voles, we are more likely to find the well-worn runs of these small rats than their clear tracks.

Even where they are abundant, these rats may often go unseen. They are primarily nocturnal and generally shy, and they live in areas with thick, herbaceous ground cover. Rice rats are the more elusive of the two, being semi-aquatic and more strictly nocturnal than cotton rats.

The diets of cotton and rice rats vary seasonally, ranging from almost entirely green plants in the growing season to mostly seeds and invertebrates in the winter. They also consume a variety of berries, roots, tubers, fungi, and small vertebrates. They do not appear to cache food. In some locations, they can do considerable damage to crops, eating newly planted seeds and seedlings.

These small rats are common prey animals. Within their ranges, they make up a large fraction of the diet of many predators, especially raptors.

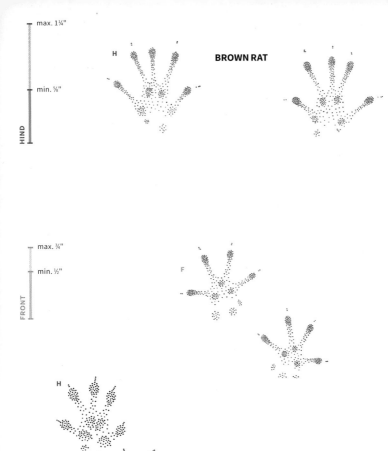

max. 1¼"

min. ⅝"

HIND

H

BROWN RAT

max. ¾"

min. ½"

FRONT

F

H

F

BLACK RAT

(See "Track Patterns: Shrews, Mice, Voles & Rats" on pages 310 & 312.)

QUICK ID TIPS

- Tracks have a mouse-like appearance, but are much larger.
- Toes splay more widely than in most similarly sized native rodents.
- Most common around buildings and rarely far from human habitation.

Old World Rats

Brown Rat (*Rattus norvegicus*)
and Black Rat *(Rattus rattus)*

Black Rat

TRACKS

Old World rat tracks show typical rodent structure. The middle toes point forward, and the outer toes splay widely to the sides—wider than in our native rats. The tips of the outer toes often fall behind the leading edge of the palm. Brown Rats have slender toes and small palm pads. Black Rats have more bulbous toes and pads—midway between those of Brown Rats and the plump pads of woodrats. Toes often connect to the palm, especially in Brown Rats. Fine claws typically show. Hind tracks are larger than fronts.

- Front tracks show four widely splayed toes. Three individual palm pads form a small triangle. Two heel pads and the tiny, vestigial thumb (toe 1) often show as well. Front tracks measure ½"–¾" long x ½"–¾" wide.

- Hind tracks have five toes arranged in the typical 1-3-1 rodent pattern. The outer toes (toes 1 and 5) are set far behind the middle three (toes 2–4) and often splay 180° to the sides. The thumb (toe 1) is the smallest and set the farthest back. Four individual palm pads form a trapezoid. Two small heel pads occasionally register. Hind tracks measure ⅝"–1¼" long x ⅝"–1" wide.

TRACK PATTERNS & GAITS

Commonly scurries (walk or trots) when foraging and traveling along cover. Bounds to cross open areas. Scurrying trails usually leave indirect-register track patterns. When bounding, the front feet are offset.

HABITAT

Anywhere people reside. Closely associated with urban and rural human development. Found in and around buildings as well as grain fields in agricultural areas and garbage dumps. Sometimes ranges into adjacent waste areas such as weedy roadsides and fencerows.

OTHER SIGN

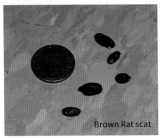

Brown Rat scat

Scat: Deposited at random wherever they go. Size, color, and consistency vary with these animals' wide-ranging diets. The typical form is a pellet measuring ⅛"–¼" in diameter and ¼"–⅞" long.

Holes & Other Damage: Gnaw through walls, make holes in insulation, chew on wires, and nibble through food containers. Make use of all manner of crevices, passageways, and holes in walls and other structures. These openings usually develop dirty smudges around them. Brown rats may also dig burrows, which usually connect to buildings. Burrow entrances measure 2"–3" in diameter.

Nests: Build nests of shredded fiber, similar to nests of other small rodents. Nests are commonly made of paper, fabric, and other synthetic materials rather than grass or leaves. Nests are built in or under cover and may be located in walls, building foundations, storage boxes, or under rubbish piles.

ACTIVITY

Active year-round though may reduce activity in cold weather. Primarily nocturnal but may be active at any time.

SIMILAR TRACKS

Cotton and rice rat tracks can closely resemble BrownRat tracks. They are smaller and appear less substantial, with proportionally longer claws and longer, narrower palms, particularly on the hind foot. **Chipmunk and other squirrel** front and hind tracks are more similar in size, and their toes usually splay less. The palm pads on their hind feet register as a wide arch rather than as a tall trapezoid, and their front heel pads are larger. **Woodrat** tracks can be difficult to distinguish from black rat tracks in the field. Their toe and palm pads are even more bulbous and appear more fully fused. Their toes splay less, and the tips of the outer toes are not set as far back in the track.

NOTES

Together with their close relative the House Mouse, these cosmopolitan rats are completely adapted to life among people. Natives of Asia, they have been introduced worldwide and are now found nearly everywhere people reside. They live primarily in and around human structures and spread into nearby grain fields, waste areas, and riverways in agricultural regions. They are prolific breeders, and their populations can grow very quickly. They are more social than our native rats and mice and can tolerate much higher population densities. Brown Rats and House Mice are found across the Midwest, but Black Rats appear to be established only in and around Chicago, St. Louis, and Kansas City.

Highly omnivorous, these rodents will eat nearly anything they can gnaw through, including grain and other vegetable matter, animals alive and dead, and all manner of human garbage. Brown Rats *(Rattus norvegicus)* are particularly carnivorous and will raid bird nests and kill rabbits, chickens, mice, and even other rats. House Mice eat mostly vegetable matter but also consume invertebrates and some carrion.

These rodents are primarily terrestrial but are capable climbers and good swimmers. Black Rats *(Rattus rattus)* are especially adept climbers and typically nest in the upper stories of buildings. Brown Rats prefer damp habitats and generally nest in basements, along foundations, or in sewer systems. House Mice are well adapted to arid environments and can live in buildings that offer food and shelter but little available water.

Being so well adapted to living beside people, these rodents are considered the most serious pests of all mammals. They can spread disease, foul food stores, and put holes in everything from furniture, clothing, and books to walls, pipes, and building foundations. Rats have been known to start fires by stripping electrical wiring and trigger floods by burrowing through dams and gnawing through pipes. At the same time, Brown Rats and House Mice are the source of laboratory rats and mice, which have led to immeasurable advances in science and medicine.

(See "Track Patterns: Shrews, Mice, Voles & Rats" on pages 310 & 312.)

max. 1"

min. ½"

HIND

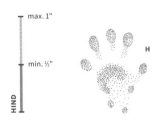

H

max. ⅞"

min. ⅜"

FRONT

F

QUICK ID TIPS

- Pudgy-looking tracks with short, bulbous toes and robust palms.

- Resemble deer mouse tracks, but much larger.

- Distinctive nests are usually prominent and close by.

Woodrats
Neotoma spp.

TRACKS

Woodrat tracks have a pudgy look, with short, bulbous toes and robust palms. The plump toe pads usually appear separate from the palm. Small claws sometimes register close to the toe pads. Front tracks are slightly smaller than hinds. The tracks resemble those of deer mice, but on a larger scale.

- Front tracks show four bulbous toes in a typical 1-2-1 rodent pattern. Three palm pads form a large, plump triangle. Two small heel pads often show, registering narrower than the palm. The tiny, clawless thumb (toe 1) shows in clear tracks. Front tracks measure ⅜"–⅞" long x ⁷⁄₁₆"–⅞" wide.

- Hind tracks have five toes arranged 1-3-1. The thumb (toe 1) is the smallest and set the farthest back. Three palm pads are partially fused and form a plump arc or L-shape in the track. A fourth, smaller palm pad registers at the base of the thumb (toe 1). The heel rarely registers when the animal is walking but may show when bounding. There are two small heel pads, which form a small triangle with the pad at the base of the thumb. Hind tracks measure ½"–1" long x ½"–1" wide.

TRACK PATTERNS & GAITS

Usually walks in or near cover but often bounds when in the open. Generally bounds with its front feet set one in front of the other.

HABITAT

Found in a variety of habitats including woods, swamps, rocky outcroppings, and arid scrub. Least likely to live in marshes or lush grasslands. Allegheny Woodrats prefer rocky, timbered regions. Southern Plains Woodrats prefer open habitats with abundant cactus. Bushy-Tailed Woodrats are most common in arid, rocky regions.

OTHER SIGN

Scat

Scat: Woodrats deposit scat along travel routes and in and around nests, often forming large latrines. Droppings are capsule-shaped pellets ranging from ¼" to ½" long and a little over ⅛" in diameter. Some woodrats also deposit a soft, formless scat that they appear to use to scent-mark travel routes. This tar-like excrement can build up in large quantities over time.

Stick house

Houses: Most woodrats construct large houses of sticks and other local debris. Houses are often several feet across, have a jumbled appearance, and are adorned with odd items. They are often built in a rock crevice but may also be in a tree, thicket, briar patch, or outbuilding; under the hood of a car; or in a variety of other locations.

Runs: Woodrats maintain travel routes connecting nests and foraging areas. Trails measure 2½"–4" wide and often make use of existing cover. They are usually kept free of debris, but scat often accumulates.

ACTIVITY

Active year-round but may hole up during bad weather. Generally nocturnal and most active during the crescent moon.

SIMILAR TRACKS

Chipmunks, squirrels, and **Old World rats** have longer, less bulbous toes and less robust palms. The heel pads in chipmunk and squirrel front tracks register as wide as the palm. **Chipmunks** bound almost exclusively, usually placing their front feet side-by-side. **Ground squirrels** have long, prominent front claws. **Old World rats** splay their toes more widely, and their individual palm pads appear more separate and distinct. **Black Rat** tracks can look similar, so examine carefully where ranges overlap. **Brown Rats** have much more slender toes.

NOTES

Woodrats, also known as pack rats, are best known for their habit of collecting odd objects such as bones, pieces of scat, tin cans, coins, gun casings, and even small mammal traps set out by researchers. They seem to have a particular fondness for shiny objects, and many lifelong campers have a story about a woodrat disappearing with a set of keys, pocketknife, or other equipment— sometimes snatched right from the person's hand.

Most species of woodrat also build large houses out of sticks and other plant debris, which are then adorned with these odd objects. Some houses are elaborate structures with multiple chambers for nesting, food storage, and defecation. Others are little more than a pile of debris across the entrance to a rock crevice or underground burrow. Each woodrat may maintain multiple houses. They continually add to these structures, and large houses can represent the work of many generations of these short-lived rodents. Houses also provide shelter for other small animals, including mice, snakes, lizards, rabbits, and even skunks. Woodrats are competent climbers, readily scale shrubs and trees to forage, and may build nests in trees. Capable diggers, they may also excavate sizable burrows, either beneath a stick house or in place of one.

Four species of woodrat range into the southern and westernmost parts of our region. The Allegheny Woodrat (*Neotoma magister*) lives in rocky habitats of greater Appalachia. Unlike our other woodrats, it does not construct enclosed stick houses but builds its cup-shaped nests in rock crevices or on cliff ledges. Populations of this species are in decline throughout their range. Eastern Woodrats (*Neotoma floridana*) are found across the southeastern U.S. and occupy the broadest range of habitats. They are most common along limestone outcroppings but are also found in forests, swamps, and grasslands. They are the most likely to build large free-standing houses. Southern Plains Woodrats (*Neotoma micropus*) range into southwestern Kansas. They are strongly associated with prickly pear cactus, often nesting in prickly pear patches and using the cactus pads to build their houses. They appear to be unaffected by cactus spines. Bushy-Tailed Woodrats (*Neotoma cinerea*) are found in the western Dakotas and Nebraska. They usually build their houses in rock crevices, caves, or abandoned mines and rarely build free-standing houses. All species of woodrats eat mostly green plants, supplemented with nuts, seeds, fungi, and occasional animal matter. They cache large amounts of food, both in their houses and in large piles in the open.

FAMILY SCIURIDAE

The squirrel family includes many of the most conspicuous and familiar wild mammals in the Midwest. Though neither particularly large nor especially numerous, most squirrels are diurnal, tolerant of people, and adapt well to human-transformed landscapes. The 14 species of squirrels in the Midwest can be broadly divided into two groups: the semi-fossorial ground squirrels and the highly arboreal tree squirrels. Ground squirrels, which include chipmunks, prairie dogs, and Woodchucks, dig extensive burrows where they spend a large portion of their lives. Tree squirrels, which include flying squirrels, Red Squirrels, and Gray Squirrels, are at home in the canopy and often travel by leaping from tree to tree. All spend a good deal of time foraging on the ground.

TRACKS

Squirrel tracks show the typical rodent structure of four fully developed toes on the front foot and five on the hind. The middle toes point forward, while the outer toes are set farther back and splay to the sides. Toes tend to splay less than in many rats and mice. The middle three toes on the hind foot are nearly the same length and usually register close together, giving the track a flat leading edge. The outer toes rarely splay more than 45°. The front palm pads form a triangle, as is typical for rodents. Hind palm pads are generally arranged in a broad arc, contrasting with the tall, narrow hind palms of many rats and mice. Front heel pads are fairly large and prominently define the trailing edge of the track when they register clearly. With the exception of chipmunks, ground squirrel tracks tend to be less symmetrical than tree squirrel tracks and often appear to angle or curve to the inside.

TRACK PATTERNS & GAITS

Squirrels typically move in a walk or a bound. Tree squirrels and chipmunks bound almost exclusively, usually placing their front feet side-by-side when they do. Other ground squirrels walk frequently. When they do bound, they are more likely to place one front foot ahead of the other, as is typical for members of the rabbit family.

SQUIRRELS

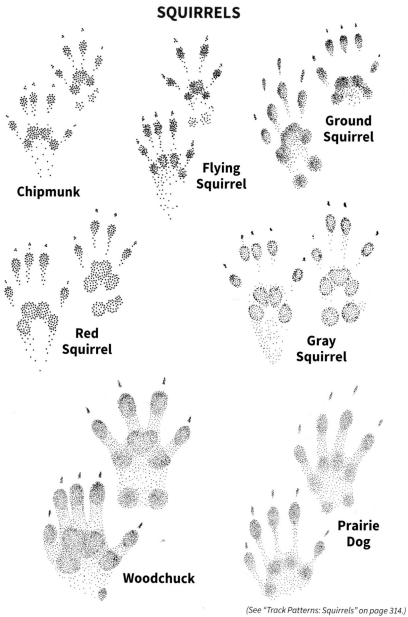

Chipmunk

Flying Squirrel

Ground Squirrel

Red Squirrel

Gray Squirrel

Woodchuck

Prairie Dog

(See "Track Patterns: Squirrels" on page 314.)

max. 1⅛"

min. ½"

HIND

max. ⅞"

min. ½"

FRONT

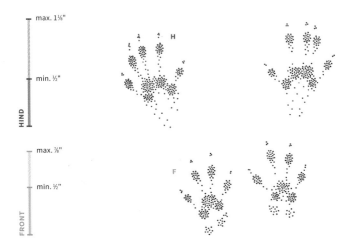

H

F

(See "Track Patterns: Squirrels" on page 314.)

QUICK ID TIPS

- Tracks and trails resemble those of a giant deer mouse or a miniature tree squirrel.
- Bounds almost exclusively.
- Hibernates in winter but may venture out on warmer days.

Chipmunks

Tamias striatus and *Tamias minimus*

TRACKS

Chipmunk tracks show the classic squirrel foot structure, with four toes on the front foot and five on the hind. The middle toes point forward, while the outer toes angle outward. Toe pads are somewhat bulbous and typically register separate from the palm. The negative space is free of fur, and pads register crisply. Tracks often appear blocky and compact compared with those of tree squirrels. The fine claws usually register.

- Front tracks show three palm pads arranged in a compact triangle. Two heel pads, which often register, are proportionally smaller and closer to the palm than in tree squirrels. The tiny, vestigial thumb (toe 1) rarely registers. Front tracks measure ½"–⅞" long x ⅜"–⅞" wide.

- Hind tracks are slightly larger than fronts, but measurements are similar. Toes may curve slightly to the inside. The pinkie (toe 5) is set slightly farther forward than the thumb (toe 1). Four palm pads are fused into a C-shaped arc. Claws are slightly smaller than on the front. The heel, which is covered with fur, rarely registers. Hind tracks measure ½"–1⅛" long x ½"–⅞" wide.

TRACK PATTERNS

Bounds almost exclusively, leaving track patterns that resemble those of giant deer mice or miniature tree squirrels. Occasionally hops or walks near its burrow or while foraging. May leave a single body print while bounding in deeper snow.

HABITAT

Eastern Chipmunks are most abundant in deciduous forests. They are also common in rural, suburban, and urban parks and residential areas with trees and ground cover. Least Chipmunks are a boreal species, partial to open, dry coniferous forests. Both are generally found above the floodplain or on well-drained slopes.

OTHER SIGN

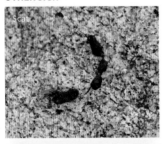
Scat

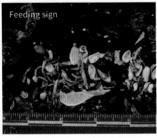
Feeding sign

Scat: Appearance varies with diet but tends to be more spherical than that of other squirrels. Round-to-oblong pellets measure about ⅛"–¼" and may clump.

Feeding Sign: Chipmunks usually feed on elevated perches such as logs, stumps, or large rocks. Look for small accumulations of scraps and scat. Chipmunks rotate feeding locations more frequently than Red Squirrels, so less sign accumulates. On logs, sign is often spread along the length rather than concentrated in one spot. Mice, rats, and voles usually feed under some kind of cover.

Burrows: Though frequently hidden under some kind of cover and difficult to locate, chipmunk burrow entrances are distinctive. A 1¼"–2" entry hole descends vertically for at least 4" before sloping down at an angle. There is no throw mound, and the entry is kept free of debris. Burrows may be near dead trees, where the chipmunk can take advantage of natural root cavities.

ACTIVITY

Diurnal. Especially active mid-morning and late afternoon. Hibernates in the winter, waking every few days to feed. May come above ground to forage on warmer winter days.

Flying squirrel tracks usually appear less robust, with longer toes and smaller palm pads. Front heel pads are set farther behind the palm. The palm pads on the hind track form a shallower arc, and the pinkie (toe 5) is longer and set higher on the foot. Flying squirrels hop more often, and their track patterns often have a more "boxy" appearance, with the hind feet turned out less and the front feet set wider apart. **Red Squirrel** tracks are larger and more elongated, and they have less-bulbous toes. The heel pads on their front track are larger and set farther back. The palm pads on the hind track usually form a shallower arc. **Rats** splay their toes more and show more difference in size between front and hind tracks. **Cotton rats, rice rats,** and **Brown Rats** have more slender toes. **Woodrats** and **Black Rats** have more-bulbous toes. **Mouse** tracks are smaller, though large mouse tracks can approach the size of Least Chipmunk tracks. **Ground squirrel** tracks are more strongly curved, have shorter toes and longer claws. Ground squirrels walk more frequently, and usually stagger their front feet when they bound.

NOTES

Small, attractive members of the squirrel family, chipmunks share characteristics with both tree squirrels and ground squirrels. They forage above ground and climb into trees, but they also dig burrows and hibernate in the winter. Territorial, vocal, and strictly diurnal, they can often be seen foraging not only in the woods but also around picnic tables and bird feeders.

Chipmunks may be best known for their large, fur-lined cheek pouches, which they use for gathering food and nesting materials. Chipmunks do not hibernate as deeply as ground squirrels. Instead of storing body fat to last them through winter, they amass large food stores and wake from hibernation every few days to feed. Though they generally remain in their burrows during winter, they may emerge on warm days to forage, especially if there is a reliable concentration of food such as a bird feeder.

Generally tolerant of people, chipmunks are easy to observe. Though they appear rather cute and charming to us, they are among the most aggressive and anti-social rodents. They are also more omnivorous than most squirrels, supplementing their diet of nuts and seeds with fungi, green plants, fruits, berries, insects, and small vertebrates. When nuts are in season, they may make continuous trips from tree to burrow, hoarding a bushel of nuts over a few days. Competent climbers, chipmunks readily venture into shrubs and trees but do not jump from branch to branch like tree squirrels. They are vulnerable to predation from weasels, hawks, Bobcats, foxes, and snakes and, when startled, give a distinctive "chip!" call as they retreat to cover.

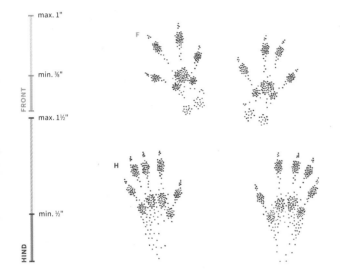

max. 1"

min. ⅜"

FRONT

max. 1½"

min. ½"

HIND

F

H

(See "Track Patterns: Squirrels" on page 314.)

QUICK ID TIPS

- Leaves "boxy" track patterns and hops more often than other squirrels.

- Tracks often appear less crisp than those of other squirrels.

- The pinkie (toe 5) on the hind foot is set far forward.

Flying Squirrels
Glaucomys sabrinus and *Glaucomys volans*

TRACKS

Flying squirrel tracks show typical squirrel morphology, with four toes on the front foot arranged 1-2-1 and five on the hind with a slight variation on the 1-3-1 pattern. Toes are long and thin, with bulbous tips that do not usually connect to the palm. Toe and heel pads often appear smaller and less distinct than those of other squirrels. Claws often register but are shorter and more arched than in other similar sized squirrels.

- The front track has three palm pads arranged in a small triangle. Two heel pads usually register and are set farther back from the palm than in chipmunk tracks. The tiny thumb (toe 1) rarely registers. Front tracks measure ⅜"–1" long x ⅜"–¾" wide.

- The hind track has thinner palm pads that form a shallower arc than in other squirrels. The thumb (toe 1) is set the farthest back. The pinkie (toe 5) is relatively long, sits farther forward on the foot, and splays relatively little. As a result, it often registers close to the line formed by the middle toes (2–4), creating a variation on the standard 1-3-1 toe pattern. The fur-covered heel sometimes registers. Hind tracks measure ½"–1½" long x ⅜"–1" wide.

TRACK PATTERNS & GAITS

Flying squirrels bound but also hop much more often than other squirrels. Front feet may register in front of, between, or behind the hind feet. Their front feet usually register wider apart than in other squirrels, and their hind feet tend to angle out less, giving their track patterns a "boxy" appearance. They may leave a 2x2 pattern in deeper snow.

HABITAT

Mature forests, especially where old trees and snags are riddled with woodpecker holes. Also found in parks, woodlots, and residential areas. Southern Flying Squirrels prefer deciduous woods, especially oak, hickory, and beech, located close to water. Northern Flying Squirrels favor coniferous and mixed forests, but they also do well in deciduous woods where Southern Flying Squirrels are absent.

OTHER SIGN

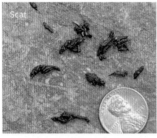

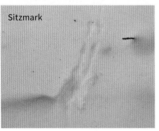

Scat: Usually deposited in tree cavities. Accumulated scat, often mixed with flecks of decaying wood, may flow out of these cavities and build up on the ground. The basic form of the scat is a tiny, oval pellet about ¼" long.

Sitzmark: Flying squirrels usually climb to the ground and glide from tree to tree. Occasionally, however, one will glide to the ground, leaving a whole-body "sitzmark" where it lands.

Feeding Sign: Southern Flying Squirrels carve distinctive carrying notches into the ends of hickory nuts, then chew smooth, circular holes in the shells. Red Squirrels make a rough opening, larger squirrels crush the nut, and mice make 2–3 rougher openings.

ACTIVITY

Active year-round. Southern Flying Squirrels may become torpid during cold winter weather but do not hibernate. Nocturnal and rarely seen, even where common. Most active for a few hours after sunset and before dawn.

SIMILAR TRACKS

Chipmunk and **Red Squirrel** tracks tend to appear more crisp, with larger, more clearly defined pads. The palm pads on their hind feet form a stronger arc, and the pinkie (toe 5) is set farther back. They also hop much less often, usually register their front feet closer together, and angle their hind feet out more. Red Squirrel tracks are larger and have longer toes. Chipmunk tracks tend to look more stout, and the heel pads on their front track register closer to the palm. **Rats** splay their toes more and show a greater difference in size between front and hind tracks. **Cotton rats, rice rats,** and **Brown Rats** have more slender toes. **Woodrats** and **Black Rats** have more bulbous toes.

NOTES

The only nocturnal tree squirrels, flying squirrels are rarely seen even where they are quite common. They are primarily arboreal and sometimes avoid the ground entirely by gliding from tree to tree. When they do come to the ground, it is often to a forest floor where their tracks can easily go undetectable in the leaf litter. We most often encounter flying squirrel tracks in the snow.

Flying squirrels do not truly fly but glide on folds of skin stretched between their legs that act as a cross between a parachute and a glider wing. They are quite agile in the air, able to make sharp turns and to pull up for four-point landings on tree trunks.

Flying squirrels are generally solitary in summer but may den communally in winter. They den mostly in cavities, especially "abandoned" woodpecker holes with openings 1½"–2" in diameter located 8'–20' up in a standing dead tree. They may also build leaf nests or occupy leaf nests made by other squirrels, particularly in the summer. As with other tree squirrels, flying squirrels maintain multiple nests and use various cavities and dreys for sleeping, for caching food, and as latrines.

Less is known about the diet of flying squirrels than about those of other tree squirrels. They appear to be quite omnivorous, eating tree nuts, seeds, buds, berries, sap, fungi and lichens, bird eggs, nestlings, insects, and carrion. Southern Flying Squirrels appear to feed largely on acorns, hickory nuts, and beech nuts. Northern Flying Squirrels in the Pacific Northwest depend heavily on subterranean fungi (truffles), but it is not clear if these are a substantial part of their diet in the Midwest. Like other tree squirrels, they cache nuts in the fall to feed on through the winter. Nuts are usually cached in tree cavities, but some are also buried.

Where their ranges overlap, the smaller Southern Flying Squirrel tends to displace its larger Northern Flying Squirrel cousin. Where this happens, Southern Flying Squirrels are more likely to be found in hardwood and mixed-forest stands, while Northern Flying Squirrels are likely to live only in pure conifer stands.

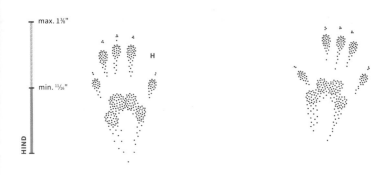

max. 1⅜"

min. ¹¹⁄₁₆"

H

HIND

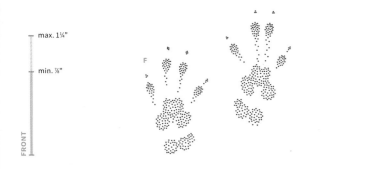

max. 1¼"

min. ⅞"

F

FRONT

(See "Track Patterns: Squirrels" on page 314.)

QUICK ID TIPS

- Distinctive squirrel track and trail patterns.

- Tracks usually appear more delicate, elongated, and "fingery" than those of other squirrels.

- Vocal and active during the day, Red Squirrels are often seen and heard when present.

Red Squirrel
Tamiasciurus hudsonicus

TRACKS

Red Squirrels show the typical squirrel track form. with their middle toes pointing forward and outer toes angling the sides. Their toes are long and slender, often connecting to the palm in the track. With little fur on the bottom of the foot, pads tend to register crisply. Fine claws usually register.

- Front tracks show four toes in the typical 1-2-1 squirrel pattern. Three palm pads form a small triangle behind the toes. Two large heel pads sometimes register, as does the tiny vestigial thumb (toe 1). The heel pads are proportionally larger than in both chipmunks and larger tree squirrels. Tracks sometimes appear slightly curved. Front tracks measure ⅞"–1¼" long x ⁹⁄₁₆"–⅞" wide.

- Hind tracks have five toes in the 1-3-1 squirrel pattern. The middle toes (toes 2–4) are parallel and equal in length, giving the leading edge of the track a flat profile. The thumb (toe 1) is the smallest and set slightly farther back than the pinkie (toe 5). Four palm pads form a broad arc behind the toes. The furred heel sometimes registers, especially in snow. Hind tracks measure ¹¹⁄₁₆"–1⅜" long x ⁹⁄₁₆"–1" wide.

TRACK PATTERNS & GAITS

Travels in a bound. Group length varies considerably but is elongated more often than in other tree squirrels. Front feet are generally side-by-side but are sometimes offset. In deep snow, the group length may shorten to leave an H-shaped 2x2 bound pattern. Will also tunnel under deep snow. Walks when exploring, leaving an indirect register pattern.

HABITAT

Most common in coniferous forests. Also found in mixed forests, hardwood forests (especially maple, basswood, birch, and aspen), old orchards, parks, suburbs, and farmstead shelterbelts. Prefers mature tree stands with a connected canopy, tree cavities, and loose soil.

OTHER SIGN

Scat

Feeding sign

Scat: Typically an oval pellet with round or pointed ends, ¼"–½" long. Deposited at constricted points along travel routes and dropped at random. May accumulate under feeding posts.

Feeding Sign: Usually on an elevated perch such as a branch, stump, or log. Large quantities of food remnants, called *middens,* collect under regular perches. Red Squirrels also nip twigs to harvest buds or small conifer cones from the tips of skinny branches. The nipped twigs fall to the ground, where they may accumulate.

Bite Marks on Trees: In the spring, Red Squirrels "tap" the small, vertical trunks and branches of maple trees for sugar. They turn their heads sideways, anchor their top incisors, and scrape with their lower incisors, leaving a diagonal "dot and dash" bite mark. When the sap flows, they leave it to dry into a natural maple syrup before returning to feed. Red Squirrels also leave bite marks as part of communication behavior. These marks are usually on the lower, horizontal branches of a dominant tree in their territory. Red Squirrels will strip patches of bark to harvest cambium for food and nesting material. The damage can look similar to Porcupine sign but with smaller incisor marks.

Active year-round. Diurnal. May reduce activity in inclement weather.

SIMILAR TRACKS

Red Squirrel tracks typically appear more delicate, elongated and "fingery" than those of other squirrels. **Chipmunk** tracks are smaller with shorter toes and a more compact appearance. Their bounding trails are narrower, nearly always under 3". **Flying squirrel** tracks are generally smaller. Their hind palm pads usually form a shallower and more slender arc. Their hind pinkie (toe 5) usually splays less and is set higher on the foot. Their bounding track patterns appear more boxy and they are more likely to hop. **Gray Squirrel** tracks are larger, but measurements overlap. They typically appear more robust, with thicker pads and proportionally shorter toes. Their front heel pads are proportionally smaller, and their front thumb (toe 1) rarely registers. **Weasel** and **Mink** hind tracks can resemble squirrel front tracks, while their front tracks can resemble squirrel hinds. Study the track pattern to distinguish fronts from hinds.

NOTES

Conspicuous and noisy forest dwellers, Red Squirrels are highly territorial and known for their habit of energetically scolding intruders. They feed primarily on conifer seeds, tree nuts, and fungi, storing large quantities for the winter. In the Midwest, they typically store about half their cache in one to four large larders and scatter the rest across their territory. Their large larders, which are more vulnerable than scattered caches, drive their territorial behavior.

Primarily arboreal, Red Squirrels prefer to nest in tree cavities but also make use of fallen logs, leaf nests, and underground burrows. Not well adapted for digging, they tend to use existing burrows or root tangles with natural air pockets. They create larders in similar locations and occasionally nest in with a larder. Nests may be difficult to find, but middens usually accumulate near larders.

Red Squirrels supplement their diet with a wide variety of foods, including tree buds, sap, fruit, berries, bark, insects, bird eggs, and hatchlings. They are known to eat Amanita mushrooms, which are deadly to humans, and cache them on exposed tree branches to dry.

Only a few predators are routinely successful at hunting these vigilant and vocal forest denizens. Red Squirrels are uncommon prey for Bobcats, Lynx, foxes, Mink, and weasels but make up a large fraction of the diet of many goshawks, Marten, and Fisher.

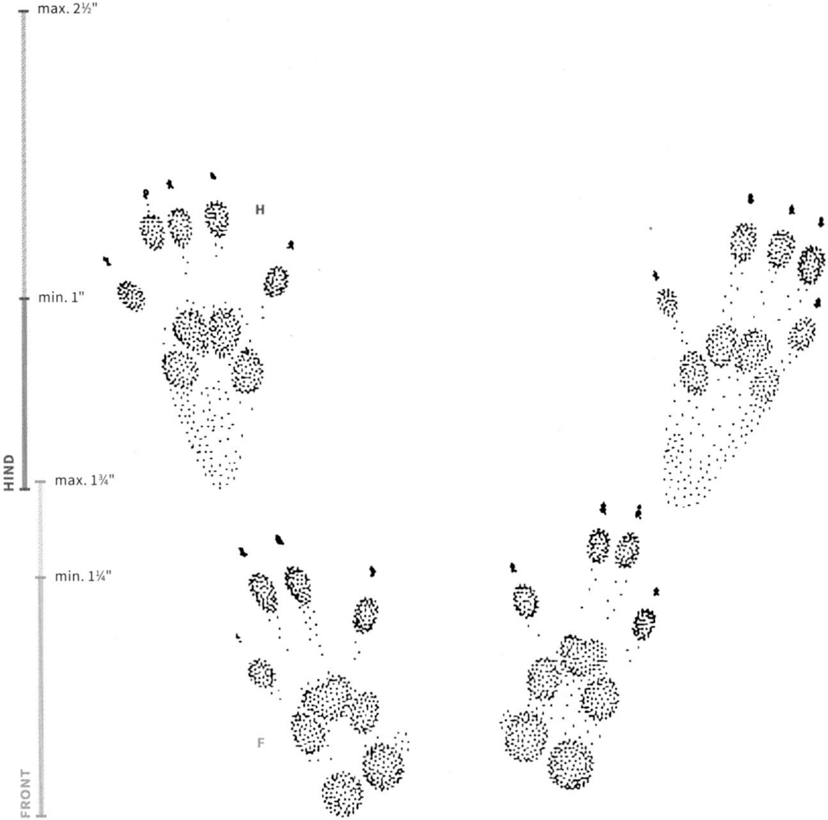

max. 2½"

min. 1"

H

HIND

max. 1¾"

min. 1¼"

F

FRONT

(See "Track Patterns: Squirrels" on page 314.)

QUICK ID TIPS

• Distinctive squirrel track and trail patterns.

• Toe and palm pads are usually clear and crisp, as if made by a stamp.

• Leading edge of the hind track is flat, not curved or pointed.

Eastern Gray Squirrel & Eastern Fox Squirrel

Sciurus carolinensis and *Sciurus niger*

TRACKS

Fox and Gray Squirrels leave typical squirrel tracks, with middle toes pointing forward and outer toes angling to the sides. Toes usually register separately from the palm but may connect. Palm pads are well developed and hairless, and usually register crisply. Sharp claws usually register. Fox Squirrels are larger than Grays, but there is considerable overlap in track and trail size.

- Front tracks show four toes in the 1-2-1 squirrel pattern. Three palm pads form a triangle, and two heel pads often register. The tiny vestigial thumb (toe 1) is rarely visible. The ring toe (toe 4) is slightly longer than the middle toe (toe 3). Front claws are longer than hind and register more reliably. Front tracks measure 1¼"–1¾" long x ¾"–1⅛" wide.

- Hind tracks show five toes in the 1-3-1 squirrel pattern. The middle toes (toes 2–4) are parallel and equal in length, giving the leading edge of the track a flat profile. The thumb (toe 1) is smaller and set slightly farther back than the pinkie (toe 5). Four palm pads form a broad arc behind the toes. The heel, which is furred in the winter, may register. Hind tracks measure 1"–2½" long x ⅞"–1½" wide.

TRACK PATTERNS & GAITS

Generally travels in a bound, leaving a distinctive squirrel track pattern. Most often, front feet register side-by-side with a bit of space between them. Hind feet register wider, ahead of the fronts, and slightly turned out. In deep snow, the group length may shorten into a 2x2 bound. The feet tend to drag along the outside of the trail as they enter and exit the snow, creating an H-shaped imprint. Sometimes walks while foraging. Fox Squirrels walk more often and for longer distances than Grays.

HABITAT

Hardwood and mixed forests with nut-bearing trees, especially oak and hickory. Also common in parks, suburbs, and cities with scattered large trees. Gray Squirrels tend to be more common in wetter habitats and more mature forests with dense underbrush. Fox Squirrels are better adapted to drier, younger, more open, and more isolated woodlots with less ground cover. In many areas, both species are common.

OTHER SIGN

Scat: Deposited at random and may be seen anywhere along travel routes. Scat is typically a small pellet about ¼"–⅞₆" long with round or pointed ends. It is difficult to distinguish from other squirrel scat. In winter, fresh scat often "dissolves" on snow, leaving a small brown patch.

Feeding Sign: Look for the gnawed shells of acorns, hickory nuts, walnuts, beechnuts, or pecans. Gray and Fox Squirrels have powerful jaws and break shells into smaller pieces than other squirrels do.

Vertical stripe

Vertical Stripes: Tree squirrels gnaw and rub their cheek glands on bark as a form of communication. They create individual marks, similar to Red Squirrels, as well as communal "message boards" low on the trunks of large trees with furrowed bark. Marks accumulate into vertical stripes and are usually on the lee side of a leaning tree or sheltered from rain by a large branch or other overhang.

Digs: Tree squirrels leave small, shallow holes in snow or earth where they retrieve cached nuts during winter and spring.

Nests: Gray and Fox Squirrels keep multiple nests and change nests frequently. They prefer natural cavities in large trees such as oaks, elms, sycamores, or maples, especially in the winter. Openings are typically 2"–3" in diameter and 25'–40' off the ground. Gray Squirrels regularly build leaf nests, woven together with twigs, high in the branches of similar large trees. Nests are 12"–24" in diameter, quite sturdy, and often difficult to see in summer but obvious after autumn leaf fall. Fox, Red, and flying squirrels also build leaf nests, but less often.

ACTIVITY

Active year-round but may hole up for days in inclement weather. Diurnal. Gray Squirrels are most active in the early morning and late afternoon. Fox Squirrels rise later and are more active midday. Activity peaks in the fall when harvesting and caching nuts.

SIMILAR TRACKS

Red Squirrel tracks appear more delicate and "fingery," with proportionally longer toes. Their front tracks appear more elongated, show larger heel pads, are more likely to appear curved, and are more likely to show the tiny thumb (toe 1). **Mink** hind tracks can closely resemble squirrel front tracks, while Mink front tracks can resemble squirrel hinds. Study the track pattern to distinguish fronts from hinds. Mink front tracks will have splayed rather than parallel toes and a curved rather than flat leading edge. Mink palm pads are more slender.
Cottontails leave a more triangular-shaped track pattern, with their front tracks touching or one in front of the other. Their hind tracks point straight ahead, and the leading edge of the tracks is round or pointed rather than flat. In deep snow, their feet drag down the middle of the trail, rather than to the outsides.

NOTES

Common and widespread, Fox and Gray Squirrels have adapted extremely well to human development and are common in parks even in our largest cities. Primarily arboreal, they spend the majority of their lives in trees, but they come to the ground frequently to forage. They are most active on the ground in fall when caching nuts, and in winter when retrieving caches.

Gray and Fox Squirrel diets are dominated by hardwood-tree nuts, especially acorns, hickory nuts, walnuts, and pecans. Most squirrels rely on cached nuts to sustain them through winter and bury individual nuts in shallow depressions throughout the fall. Nuts are usually cached 50'–100' from where they were harvested. While most nuts are recovered, enough viable seeds remain to be an important source of new tree plantings. In addition to nuts, Gray and Fox Squirrels eat buds, flowers, bark, and occasionally insects, bird eggs, or nestlings. Both will feed on corn, but Fox Squirrels are more likely to make it a significant part of their diet. They sometimes nip twigs and tap branches for sap, though less often than Red Squirrels. Frequent visitors to bird feeders, they can work around nearly any form of "squirrel proofing."

Though generally solitary, Gray and Fox Squirrels often congregate at good feeding locations and may den communally in winter.

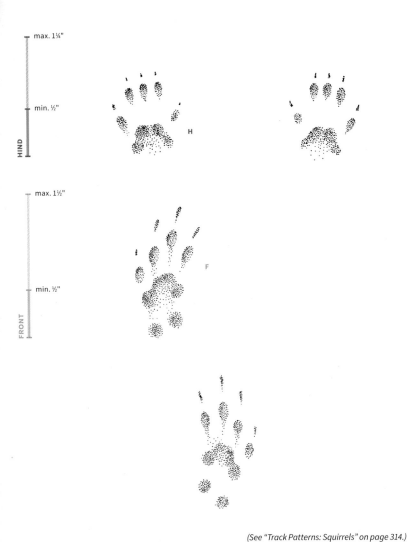

HIND

max. 1¼"

min. ½"

H

FRONT

max. 1½"

min. ½"

F

(See "Track Patterns: Squirrels" on page 314.)

QUICK ID TIPS

- Front tracks are asymmetrical and have long, prominent claws.
- Hind tracks often look squat and may be as wide as they are long.
- Usually bounds with one front foot ahead of the other.

Ground Squirrels

Ictidomys tridecemlineatus, Poliocitellus franklinii,
Urocitellus richardsonii, and *Xerospermophilus spilosoma*

TRACKS

Ground squirrel tracks show a variation on the typical squirrel pattern.

- Front tracks are distinctly asymmetrical and have long, prominent claws. The middle toe (toe 3) is set the farthest forward, the index and ring toes (2 and 4) are on about the same level, and the pinkie (toe 5) is set farthest back. Three palm pads form a lopsided triangle, and two heel pads sometimes register. Front tracks show little splay and are usually narrower than hinds. Front tracks of small ground squirrels are ½"–⅞" long x ½"–¾" wide. Those of large ground squirrels are ⅝"–1½" long x ⅝"–1¼" wide.

- Hind tracks show more typical squirrel form. The middle three toes (2–4) are nearly parallel and on the same level, while the outer toes (1 and 5) are set farther back and angle out. Toes are shorter than in tree squirrels. Tracks often look squat and may be as wide as they are long. Four palm pads are arranged in an arc behind the toes. The heel sometimes registers. Claws may register but are much smaller than on the front. Hind tracks of small ground squirrels measure ½"–1" long x ½"–⅞" wide. Those of large ground squirrels measure ⅝"–1¼" long x ⅝"–1⅜" wide.

TRACK PATTERNS & GAITS

Generally travels in a bound. Often walks while foraging and scurries around burrows. Typically bounds with one front foot in front of the other, though occasionally front feet land side-by-side.

HABITAT

Prairies and prairie borderlands. Thirteen-Lined Ground Squirrels prefer flat, open grasslands with short cover, making them well adapted to the mowed lawns of golf courses, cemeteries, schools, parks, and roadsides. Franklin's Ground Squirrels prefer medium-to-tall grass that borders woods. They are common along fencerows, wooded banks, railroad lines, and roadsides, as well as in many campgrounds and state parks.

OTHER SIGN

Scat

Burrow entrance

Scat: The basic form of the scat is a pellet, ¼"–¾" long, pointed on one end and flat on the other. Succulent browse can lead to softer, twisted scat with two tapered ends or scat that is clumped together. Often found around the entrances to burrows.

Burrows: Entrances measure 2"–4" in diameter and typically have a clear throw-mound of dirt. Conspicuous trails may radiate from a burrow location.

ACTIVITY

Long period of winter hibernation may last six months or more in northern climates. In hot, dry regions, many species also estivate (become dormant) through much of summer. Diurnal. Most active on sunny days and may remain underground on gray or rainy days.

SIMILAR TRACKS

Chipmunks and **tree squirrels** leave front tracks that are more symmetrical with shorter claws, and they usually place their front feet side-by-side when bounding. **Chipmunk** tracks are usually smaller. **Gray** and **Fox Squirrel** tracks are usually larger. **Prairie dogs** leave larger tracks and walk much more often. **Pocket gophers** have five well-developed toes on their front feet. The middle three toes (toes 2–4) on their hind feet are less equal in length and tend to splay more, giving the rear track a pointed or rounded, rather than flat, leading edge.

NOTES

There are four species of ground squirrel in our region. The smaller Thirteen-Lined Ground Squirrel *(Ictidomys tridecemlineatus)* and Spotted Ground Squirrel *(Xerospermophilus spilosoma)* are a bit larger than chipmunks. The larger Richardson's Ground Squirrel *(Urocitellus richardsonii)* and Franklin's Ground Squirrel *(Poliocitellus franklinii)* are a bit smaller than Gray Squirrels. All four species leave similar tracks and sign. All ground squirrels are semi-fossorial, digging burrows where they spend a significant part of their lives. Midwestern ground squirrels are deep hibernators, and some are active for only a few months each spring and summer. They spend late summer and early fall putting on a heavy layer of fat before retreating to their burrows for much of the year.

Ground squirrels eat mostly seeds and green vegetation. They supplement their diet with berries, insects, and whatever meat they can find, including bird eggs, nestlings, and the occasional mouse, vole, or young rabbit. While they rely on fat to sustain them through the winter, they may hoard seeds in their burrows to eat when they come out of hibernation.

Thirteen-Lined Ground Squirrels tend to be colonial, while Richardson's, Franklin's, and Spotted Ground Squirrels are more solitary. All are quite defensive of their burrows. Though burrows may be close together, males are fiercely territorial with one another. They regularly fight for access to females in the spring after emerging from hibernation and are often injured.

Being diurnal and residing in open habitats, ground squirrels are highly susceptible to predation by hawks, snakes, and mammalian predators. They are somewhat skittish and quickly dart to their burrows, which are always nearby, when they detect danger. But they are also curious animals. They often stay just inside their burrow entrance, retreating deeper if the threat remains but otherwise venturing back out. They are generally tolerant of people and relatively easy to approach and observe.

max. 1¼"

min. ⅞"

FRONT

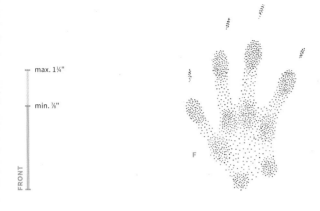

F

max. 1¾"

min. ⅞"

HIND

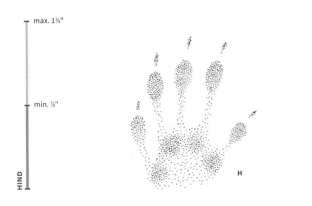

H

(See "Track Patterns: Squirrels" on page 314.)

QUICK ID TIPS

- Asymmetrical, curved, yet distinctly squirrel-like track.
- Long, stout claws are prominent in the front tracks.
- Lives in enormous "towns" made up of prominent burrows.

Black-Tailed Prairie Dog

Cynomys ludovicianus

TRACKS

Prairie dog tracks show typical squirrel family traits, with four toes on the front foot and five on the hind. The middle toes point forward, and the outer toes angle to the sides. Tracks are asymmetrical, curving to the inside. Toes are relatively short and palms broad, giving tracks a chunky appearance. Toes generally register separately from the palm, which are free of fur and register cleanly. Front and hind tracks are similar in size.

- Front track show long, stout, prominent claws. Toes are arranged in the 1-2-1 squirrel pattern, but because of the asymmetry the middle toe (toe 3) often appears to lead. The pinkie (toe 5) is set the farthest back. The tips of the other three toes (2–4) may form a pointed leading edge to the track. Three palm pads form a triangle or trapezoid. The diminutive thumb (toe 1) has a claw and occasionally registers. Two large heel pads often register. Front tracks measure ⅞"–1¼" long x ¾"–1" wide.

- Hind tracks show five toes arranged in the 1-3-1 squirrel pattern. The pinkie (toe 5) often curves inward. Four large palm pads form a thick arch. Hind claws are much smaller than front and may not show clearly. The furred heel rarely registers. Hind tracks measure ⅞"–1¾" long x ¾"–1½" wide.

TRACK PATTERNS & GAITS

Walks most of the time, leaving an indirect register pattern. May lope when covering open ground and bound when fleeing.

HABITAT

Shortgrass prairies, mixed-grass prairie, desert grassland, and well-grazed rangeland.

OTHER SIGN

Scat

Town

Scat: Basic form of the scat is a pellet about ¼"–½" in diameter and ½"–2" long. Softer scat may clump or string together, sometimes forming long chains. Scat is dropped near burrow entrances and accumulates throughout towns.

Towns: Prairie dogs live in unmistakable collections of colonial burrows called *towns.* Some burrow entrances are flush to the ground, but others have a large mound of excavated dirt around them and look like tiny volcanoes. In the Midwest, such "rim crater" burrows are unique to Black-Tailed Prairie Dogs. Burrow entrances typically measure 4"–6" across.

ACTIVITY

Active year-round but may hole up in their burrows for many days during inclement weather. Primarily diurnal. Most active in the morning and evening during hot weather. Active all day during cooler weather.

SIMILAR TRACKS

Richardson's and **Franklin's Ground Squirrel** tracks are smaller and appear less robust, with proportionally longer toes. These squirrels' front tracks appear narrower, and they bound more often. **Marmot** tracks (see "Woodchuck," page 123) are larger, with more-robust palm pads and less-prominent claws.

The signs of this highly communal ground squirrel are unmistakable. Prairie dogs live in large colonial burrow systems called *towns* that may contain several thousand individuals and cover more than 100 acres. Each town is made up of *wards,* and each ward is further made up of *coteries,* or family groups. Coteries include a male, one to four females, pups, and yearlings. Members of a ward collectively care for burrow systems, groom each other, and "kiss" one another in greeting, touching noses, then incisors, together.

Prairie dogs are semi-fossorial, spending much of their lives underground. They rarely stray far from their burrows, which provide protection from the elements and predators. For added safety, they clear the area around their burrows of vegetation for an unobstructed view of the surroundings. Highly vocal, they have a well-developed system of alarms to warn each other of danger.

Prairie dogs eat the roots and leaves of green plants, especially grasses, which they can consume in great quantities. Though they do not hibernate, they put on large stores of fat in the fall to sustain them through the lean winter. Their voracious appetite for grass and their habit of clearing away vegetation has put them at odds with ranchers. Prairie dog populations spiked in the 1800s after Bison were removed from the plains. As competition with cattle grew, prairie dogs also became the targets of extermination campaigns. Populations declined more than 90 percent, nearly leading to the extinction of their traditional predator, the Black-Footed Ferret. Today, Black-Tailed Prairie Dogs inhabit only a few percent of their historic range.

Some ranchers still poison prairie dogs, but most now protect prairie dog towns, recognizing that moderate populations enhance rangeland. With the ferret all but gone, the prairie dog's primary predators are Coyotes, Bobcats, eagles, hawks, snakes, and Badgers.

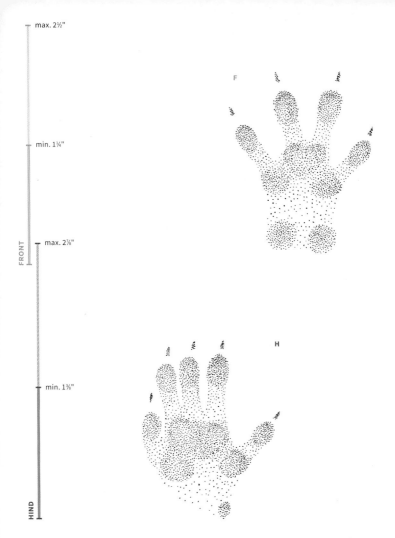

max. 2½"

min. 1¼"

F

max. 2⅞"

min. 1⅜"

H

FRONT

HIND

(See "Track Patterns: Squirrels" on page 314.)

QUICK ID TIPS

- Largest squirrel family track in our region shows four toes front and five toes hind.

- Tracks appear stocky, with large palm pad and short toes.

- Somewhat-asymmetrical tracks usually angle or curve to the inside.

Woodchuck
Marmota monax

TRACKS

Woodchuck tracks show distinctive squirrel-family traits, with the middle toes pointing forward and the outer toes set farther back and splayed. Tracks are somewhat asymmetrical, angling or curving inward. Toes are relatively short, and toe pads usually register separate from the palm. Palm pads are large, register cleanly, and often appear wider and more fused than in other squirrels. Claws are often prominent. Front and hind tracks are similar in size.

• Front tracks show four toes in the distinctive 1-2-1 squirrel pattern. Three palm pads form a broad, rounded trapezoid. The central palm pad is roughly heart-shaped and sometimes looks like two separate pads. The middle toe (toe 3) is slightly longer than the ring toe (toe 4). The tiny thumb (toe 1) rarely shows. Two large heel pads often register close behind the palm. Claws are longer than on the hind. Front tracks measure 1¼"–2½" long x 1"–2" wide.

• Hind tracks show five toes arranged in the 1-3-1 squirrel pattern. The pinkie (toe 5) is the smallest and often curves inward. Four large palm pads form a thick arch. The trailing edge of the palm may be indistinct. The heel rarely registers. Hind tracks measure 1⅜"–2⅞" long x 1¼"–1⅞" wide.

TRACK PATTERNS & GAITS

Usually walks leaving an indirect-register track pattern. May trot or lope across open ground and bound when fleeing.

HABITAT

Woodchucks live at the boundary between fields and woods. They have adapted well to human-transformed landscapes and are most common along the wooded edges of meadows, pastures, cropland, parks, suburban yards, golf courses, and highways. They prefer well-drained, slightly rocky soils.

OTHER SIGN

Scat

Scat: Rarely encountered. Usually deposited in an underground latrine or buried in the throw-mound of the burrow. Varies in size, consistency, and color depending on diet, but the typical form is a cylinder ½"–¾" in diameter and 1½"–2½" long.

Burrow

Burrows: Main burrow entrances measure up to about 12" across and usually have large, conspicuous throw mounds. The tunnel slopes gently down from the entrance, narrowing to about 6" in diameter. Active burrows usually have fresh dirt on the throw mounds. Burrow openings used primarily for escape are often inconspicuous. Some "plunge holes" may drop 3' before leveling off into a tunnel or chamber. Burrows are most common in rocky soil on sloping ground near the edge of the woods.

Runs: Well-used runs connect foraging sites and burrows. Trails measure 5"–9" wide.

ACTIVITY

Hibernates from mid-autumn until late winter or early spring, often emerging while there is still snow on the ground. Increases activity as green vegetation emerges. Most active from June to September. Diurnal, with peak activity in the afternoon.

SIMILAR TRACKS

Raccoon hind tracks may appear similar, as can their bounding gait pattern. Raccoons have five toes on their front feet, their palm pads are less distinctly lobed, the tips of their toes are less bulbous, and their claws are smaller.

Opossum indirect registers often look like a jumble of pads. Their front toes splay more, their hind tracks have a distinctive thumb (toe 1), and their claws are smaller. **Other squirrel** tracks are smaller.

NOTES

Whether you call it a Groundhog, a Woodchuck, or a Subterranean Whistlepig, this large ground squirrel has a prominent place in popular culture. Despite the popular tongue-twister, the name Woodchuck has nothing to do with either wood or chucking, but is a transliteration of *Wuchak,* an Algonquin Indian name for the animal. Woodchucks are herbivores and feed primarily on lush green grasses and herbs, such as clover, alfalfa, and common plantain. They are good swimmers and capable climbers, and they often venture into shrubs or trees to forage or view their surroundings.

Semi-fossorial, Woodchucks dig extensive burrows for sleeping, safety, raising young, and hibernation. Main burrow systems are large and complex, with multiple entrances and exits, while some smaller burrows are used only for escape or hibernation. Outside of hibernation, Woodchucks use multiple burrows and rotate among them frequently. Burrows are continually maintained, and active burrows usually have fresh dirt on the throw mound. Summertime burrows may be located in fields but are most common along a wooded edge. Hibernation burrows are often farther into the trees and high above the floodplain.

Woodchucks never stray far from a burrow entrance. They know all the burrows in their home range and will use one another's burrows for escape. Though not strongly territorial, they do not generally share burrows for sleeping or nesting, and males do not usually overlap their home ranges. Burrows may be reused by generations of Woodchucks and are often shared or taken over by other animals.

Yellow-Bellied Marmots, which leave similar tracks and sign, are found in some of the westernmost parts of our region.

The Midwest is home to eight species of rabbits, including five species of cottontail (*Sylvilagus* spp.), the Snowshoe Hare (*Lepus americanus*), and Black-Tailed and White-Tailed Jackrabbits (*Lepus californicus* and *Lepus townsendii*). All share a close family resemblance and are instantly recognizable with their long ears, short tails, and powerful hind legs built for jumping.

Widespread and abundant, both rabbits and their tracks are common sights for many Midwesterners. Perhaps because they are so common, and often distinctive, it may be easy to overlook key features of these seemingly familiar tracks. With long, supple toes and heavily furred feet, rabbit tracks can vary enormously and are confused with the prints of other species surprisingly often. Experienced trackers, including me, have at times mistaken rabbit tracks for those of squirrels, skunks, foxes, Domestic Cats, Lynx, deer, and even mice—not just at first glance, but upon close examination.

TRACKS
Rabbit tracks typically have an egg-shaped appearance with a pointed leading edge. When toes splay, the leading edge may appear round or wavy. Thick fur on the soles of the feet usually masks track detail. Toe prints are evident in most tracks, but palm pads are generally indistinct. Stout claws usually register, though they are often obscured by the fur. On firm surfaces, sometimes only the claws register. Rabbits have long, supple toes that can splay widely. When fully spread, tracks can appear almost three times as wide as when the toes are held tightly together. Front tracks appear highly asymmetrical. Though the front foot has five toes, the thumb (toe 1) is reduced in size, sits far back on the foot, and registers lightly if at all. The other four toes (2–5) wrap around the front and outside of the palm in an inverted J-shape. This asymmetric arrangement often makes the front tracks appear duck-footed (turned out), especially when the toes are splayed. Hind tracks are slightly asymmetrical, with four toes (2–5) arranged in front of the palm. As in the front foot, the middle toe (toe 3) is set the farthest forward. The long heel sometimes registers, making hind-track length as variable as width.

TRACK PATTERNS & GAITS
Cottontails and snowshoe hare usually travel in a bound, leaving a distinctive triangular-shaped pattern. Their hind feet register wide apart and point straight ahead. The front feet register close to the center line, either touching or one in front of the other. Jackrabbits typically move in a loose, bounding gallop, with both their hind and front feet offset.

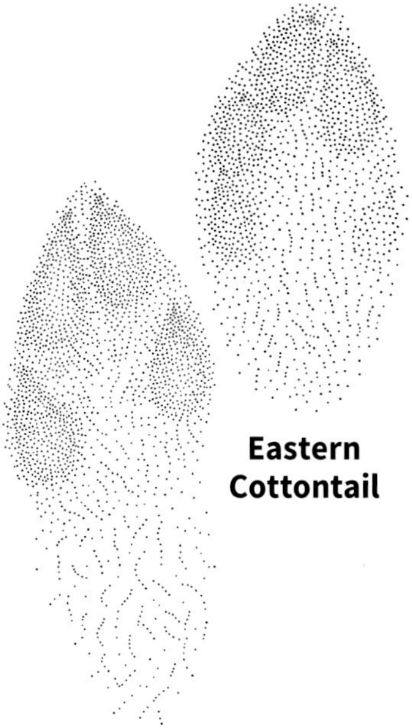

**Eastern
Cottontail**

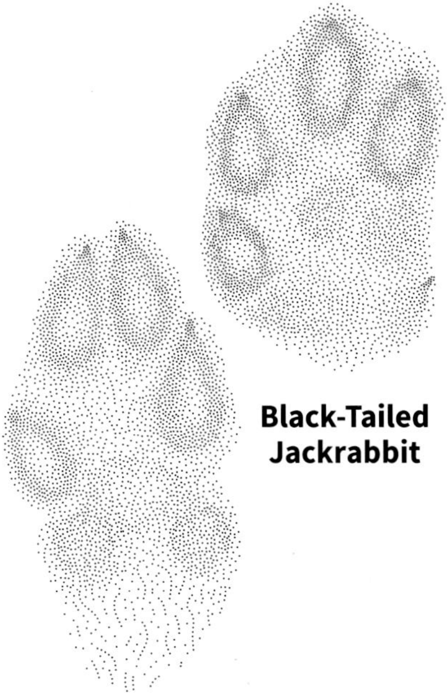

**Black-Tailed
Jackrabbit**

**Snowshoe
Hare**

(See "Track Patterns: Rabbits" on page 316.)

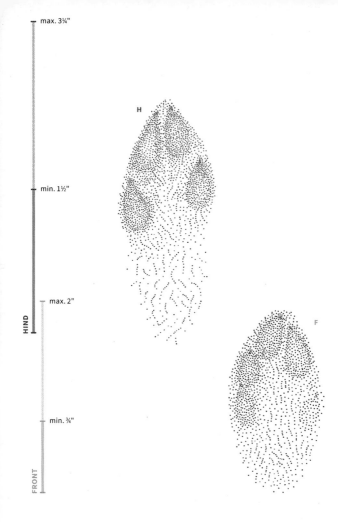

max. 3¼"

min. 1½"

H

max. 2"

HIND

min. ¾"

F

FRONT

(See "Track Patterns: Rabbits" on page 316.)

QUICK ID TIPS

- Egg-shaped tracks form triangular track groups.

- Usually appear pointy, but can be rounded or wavy when splayed.

- Front tracks appear highly asymmetrical. Toes wrap around the palm in an inverted J.

Eastern Cottontail & Relatives

Sylvilagus floridanus and other *Sylvilagus* spp.

TRACKS

Feet are completely covered by fur, often obscuring track detail, but four toes are usually visible on each foot. Palm pads tend to be indistinct but may be visible in good substrate. Stout claws sometimes register clearly as extensions of the toes but may be disguised by the fur. Front tracks are smaller than hinds, but track size can vary widely when toes splay or heels register.

- Front tracks appear highly asymmetrical. Four toes register reliably, wrapping around the palm in an inverted J. The thumb (toe 1) is small, set far back on the foot and registers lightly if at all. The middle toe (toe 3) leads, while the pinkie (toe 5) is set far back. When toes splay, tracks may appear duck-footed (turned out). Front tracks measure ¾"–2" long x ½"–1½" wide.

- Hind tracks have four toes and appear more symmetrical, especially when splayed. The middle toe (toe 3) leads in the track. Toes register in front of the palm, giving some tracks a canine appearance. The long heel may register at low speed or in soft substrates, greatly extending the length of the track. On hard substrates, the hind claws may be the only feature that registers. Hind tracks measure 1½"–3¼" long x ⅝"–2" wide.

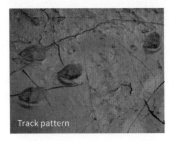
Track pattern

TRACK PATTERNS & GAITS

Bounds almost exclusively, creating one of the most recognizable track patterns. Front feet typically register one in front of the other. When they register side-by-side, they usually touch. The hind feet register wide apart in front of the front feet, pointing straight ahead, giving the group a triangular shape. Occasionally walks for short distances.

HABITAT

Diverse. May be found anywhere with a mix of dense cover and grass or herbaceous growth. Most common in disturbed or altered habitats; along forest borders; and in open, brushy landscapes. Tends to avoid open grasslands and closed forests.

OTHER SIGN

Scat

Scat: Small, round, slightly flattened pellets composed entirely of plant material measuring about ¼"–⅜" across. Dropped individually, unlike deer pellets. A single individual may produce hundreds of pellets a day, which can accumulate in feeding areas. Desert Cottontails and Swamp Rabbits create latrines on elevated stumps, logs, and rocks they use as lookouts.

Forms: Cottontails rest in shallow depressions in the ground, snow, or vegetation. Usually found at the base of shrubs or in heavy vegetation, forms measure about 7" long by 5" wide.

Feeding sign

Feeding Sign: Cuts vegetation off at a 45° angle. Deer tear stems, leaving a ragged tip. Strips bark in the winter, often biting into the heartwood and leaving a rough surface. Rodents, such as Porcupines, usually gnaw bark without gouging the wood, leaving a smoother surface.

ACTIVITY

Active year-round but may hole up when temperatures hover below 10° F. Predominantly crepuscular and nocturnal. Most active close to dawn and in the early evening but may be seen at all times of the day and night.

SIMILAR TRACKS

Snowshoe Hare tracks are larger and show more difference in size between front and hind. **Jackrabbits** leave larger tracks and usually bound with their hind feet offset. Note that splayed cottontail tracks can appear as large as tight hare and jackrabbit tracks. Where ranges overlap, consider substrate, splay, track-pattern measurements, habitat, and behavior. **Gray Fox** tracks can resemble cottontail hinds but are usually more symmetrical, with crisp, distinct toe and palm pads. **Tree squirrel** track patterns usually appear more trapezoidal and less triangular. Their hind feet are usually turned out, while their front feet register side-by-side with a bit of space between them. The leading edge of their hind feet appears blunt, rather than pointed or round.

NOTES

Well adapted to human-altered landscapes and common in many rural, suburban, and even urban areas, cottontail rabbits are among our most familiar wild mammals. There are five species of cottontails in the Midwest, all of which leave nearly identical tracks and sign. The Eastern Cottontail (*Sylvilagus floridanus*) is our most widespread species, found everywhere in the region save some of our most northern forests. The Desert Cottontail (*Sylvilagus audubonii*) inhabits arid lands in our western states, while small populations of Mountain Cottontails (*Sylvilagus nuttallii*), Swamp Rabbits (*Sylvilagus aquaticus*), and Appalachian Cottontails (*Sylvilagus obscurus*) range into the western, southern, and southeastern fringes of the region, respectively.

Cottontails are strict vegetarians, feeding on grasses and herbaceous plants during the growing season and woody vegetation through the winter. They rarely venture far from thick cover, and travel almost exclusively along well-established trails, even when chased. These trails can become obvious in thick ground cover and in snow as they get packed down with repeated use.

Female cottontails produce an average of three to four litters of four to six kits each year. The nest is a shallow excavation lined with fur and covered with grass and leaves. Mothers return to the nest around dawn and dusk to nurse their young but otherwise leave them unattended. Cottontails' prolific breeding make them an important food source for many carnivores and raptors. In many areas, cottontails are the primary prey for Coyotes and Bobcats.

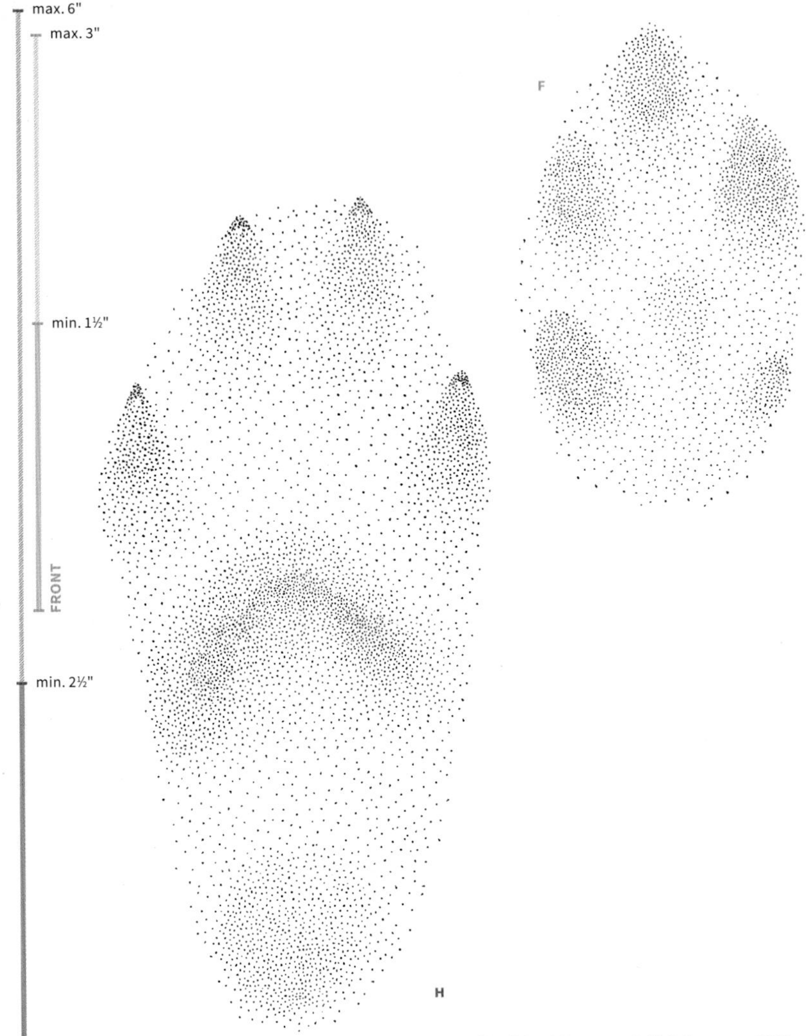

max. 6"
max. 3"
min. 1½"
FRONT
min. 2½"

F

H

HIND

(See "Track Patterns: Rabbits" on page 316.)

QUICK ID TIPS

- Distinctive rabbit-group pattern: egg-shaped tracks with indistinct pads forming triangular groups.

- Front edge of hind track is rounder than for other rabbits.

- Hind track may be much larger than front track when toes are spread.

Snowshoe Hare
Lepus americanus

TRACKS

Similar to cottontail tracks, but larger and with greater size difference between front and hind. Fur on the feet often obscures track details, but four toes are usually visible on each foot. Palm pads tend to be indistinct but may be visible in good substrate. Stout claws often register, but may be disguised by the fur. Hind tracks are much larger than fronts, especially when splayed.

- Front tracks are highly asymmetrical, with the middle toe (toe 3) leading. The four outer toes (2–5) wrap around the palm, forming an inverted J. The small thumb (toe 1) is set far back on the foot and rarely registers. When toes splay, the asymmetry can make the track appear duck-footed (turned out). Front tracks measure 1½"–3" long x 1⅛"–2¼" wide.

- Hind tracks are much more symmetrical than fronts, especially when splayed, and tend to have a round leading edge. The four large toes are arranged in front of the palm, with the middle toe (toe 3) leading slightly, giving many tracks a canine appearance. Splayed tracks are enormous and can resemble those of a Lynx. The furred heel often registers at least part of its length. Hind tracks measure 2½"–6" long x 1½"–5" wide.

TRACK PATTERNS & GAITS

Bounds almost exclusively, leaving track patterns similar to those of cotton-tails. Front feet typically register one in front of the other. Hind feet register ahead of fronts, giving the group a triangle shape. Occasionally walks for short distances.

HABITAT

Snowshoe Hare prefer northern forests with continuous winter snow cover and low, dense vegetation. Ideal habitat has a low understory of conifers for cover and winter browse. When populations swell, hares may expand into marginal habitats and areas with less understory or more variable snow cover.

OTHER SIGN

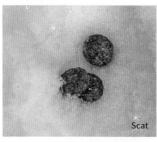
Scat

Feeding sign

Scat: Small, round, slightly flattened pellets composed entirely of vegetation and measuring about ⅜"–½" across. Dropped individually, unlike deer scat. Especially abundant where hares feed.

Forms: Snowshoe Hare rest in shallow depressions in the ground, snow, or vegetation. Usually found under branches or in heavy cover, these forms measure about 9" long x 6" wide.

Feeding Sign: Cuts off vegetation at a 45° angle using sharp incisors. Strips bark from branches and tree trunks, often biting into the heartwood as they do. Hare often stand on hind legs to browse, and feeding sign may appear up to 2' above peak winter snowpack.

ACTIVITY

Active year-round. Predominantly crepuscular and nocturnal. Most active at dusk and before dawn. Seen at all times of the day and night, especially during the summer, when populations swell, long days necessitate daytime feeding, and lush vegetation provides abundant food and cover.

SIMILAR TRACKS

Other rabbit tracks show less difference in size between front and hind, are more likely to have a pointy shape, and are more likely to show the thumb (toe 1) in the front track. **Cottontail** tracks are smaller, but measurements for splayed tracks can overlap. Consider track pattern measurements and habitat along with substrate and track splay. **Jackrabbits** prefer open habitats, usually leave longer track patterns, and typically bound with their hind feet offset. **Lynx** front and hind tracks are more similar in size, and the leading edge of their tracks often has a stepped rather than rounded or wavy profile. **Large dog** tracks will usually have more clearly defined toe and palm pads. They also leave different track patterns and move differently across the landscape.

NOTES

The Snowshoe Hare gets its name from its feet, which are specially adapted for deep snow cover. In soft substrates such as loose snow, a Snowshoe Hare may spread its toes to nearly three times their normal width, leaving tracks the size of a Lynx or a large dog.

Snowshoe Hare are remarkably well adapted to their northern range. Their coats change color with the seasons, from dirty brown in the summer to snow white in the winter. They also subsist remarkably well on meager winter browse. In the spring and summer, Snowshoe Hare feed primarily on herbaceous plants, supplemented with the buds and emerging leaves of trees and shrubs. In the winter, when succulent vegetation has died back or is buried in snow, they browse on conifer needles and tree bark. Snowshoe Hare are solitary but may live in close proximity, particularly in good habitat. Unlike jackrabbits, they rely primarily on stealth and camouflage for safety and generally stay in dense cover, especially during daytime.

Like other rabbits, Snowshoe Hare are prolific breeders. Females typically give birth to two or three litters of three to six kits a year. Kits are born fully furred with their eyes open and leave the birth nest within a few days. Young begin to disperse in mid- to late summer, often moving into more marginal habitats with less cover. Being so abundant and prolific, Snowshoe Hare are an important food source for many carnivores and raptors, and the principal prey for Lynx. Hare populations grow and decline on an 8- to 11-year cycle, leading to a subsequent rise and fall in Lynx and other predator populations.

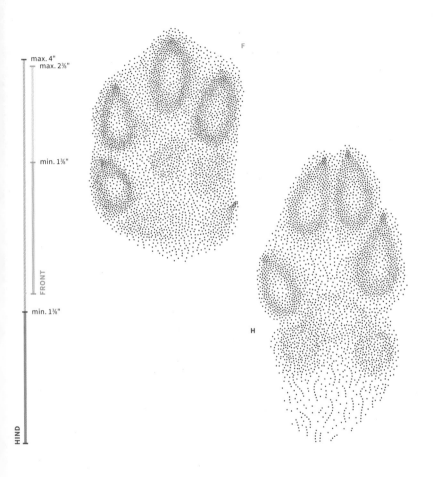

max. 4"
max. 2⅜"

min. 1⅜"

FRONT

min. 1⅜"

HIND

F

H

(See "Track Patterns: Rabbits" on page 316.)

QUICK ID TIPS

- Heavily furred feet make palm pads, and sometimes toe pads, indistinct.
- Usually appear pointy but can be rounded or wavy when splayed.
- Front tracks appear highly asymmetrical. Toes wrap around the palm in an inverted J.

Jackrabbits
Lepus californicus and *Lepus townsendii*

TRACKS

Nearly identical to cottontail tracks but larger. Pads are covered with fur, obscuring track detail, but four toes are usually evident on each foot. Palm pads are usually indistinct but may show in good substrate. Stout claws may register or be hidden by the fur. Front tracks are slightly smaller than hinds, but track size varies widely as toes splay or heels register.

- Front tracks appear highly asymmetrical. Four toes register reliably, wrapping around the palm in an inverted J with the middle toe (toe 3) leading. The small thumb (toe 1) is set the farthest back and may not register, though the claw is often visible. Splayed tracks may appear turned out (duck-footed). Black-Tailed front tracks measure 1⅜"–2⅜" long x 1"–1½" wide; White-Tailed front tracks measure 2⅛"–3½" long x 1½"–2½" wide.

- Hind tracks have four toes and are slightly asymmetrical, with the middle toe (toe 3) leading. Toes register in front of the palm and may appear canine. The long heel occasionally registers. On firm substrates, the hind claws usually register clearly and may be the most visible feature in the track. Black-Tailed hind tracks measure 1⅜"–4" long x 1⅛"–2⅛" wide; White-Tailed hind tracks measure 2¾"–5" long x 1¾"–2¾" wide.

TRACK PATTERNS & GAITS

Jackrabbits typically travel in a bounding gallop, with one hind foot leading the other, creating distinct variations on the typical rabbit-track pattern. Jackrabbits create a remarkable diversity of track patterns and a tremendous variety of trails. They frequently alternate long, fast bounds with shorter, higher "spy jumps" that help them get a better view of the surroundings. They occasionally walk for short distances.

HABITAT

Open grasslands, including cultivated fields, pastureland, and graze lands. Prefer environments with scattered dense shrubs for cover. Black-Tailed Jackrabbits inhabit arid plains; White-Tailed Jackrabbits are adapted for cold winters with persistent snow cover.

OTHER SIGN

Scat

Scat: Small, round, slightly flattened pellets measuring about ⅜"–¾" across. Usually widely scattered but may be abundant in feeding locations.

Forms: Jackrabbits rest in shallow depressions in the ground, usually under low branches or in heavy vegetation. Black-Tailed forms measure about 12" long by 6" wide; White-Tailed forms measure about 14" by 8".

Feeding sign

Feeding Sign: Cuts off vegetation at a 45° angle. Strips bark from branches and tree trunks. Hares often stand on their hind legs to browse, so feeding sign can appear more than 2' above peak winter snowpack.

ACTIVITY

Active year-round. Predominantly crepuscular and nocturnal. Can be seen at any time, especially during the spring and summer, when there is abundant food, populations swell, and long days necessitate daytime feeding. Black-Tailed Jackrabbits typically bed down during the hottest, coldest, and windiest weather. White-Tailed Jackrabbits remain active in all but the most extreme weather and often increase their activity during winter storms.

SIMILAR TRACKS

Other rabbits leave similar tracks and trails, making range, habitat, and behavior important clues. **Cottontails** and **Snowshoe Hare** usually leave more-compact track patterns, with hind feet side-by-side. Snowshoe Hare show greater size difference between front and hind tracks, are less likely to show the thumb (toe 1) in their front tracks, and prefer densely wooded habitat. Cottontails usually stay close to dense cover. Their tracks are smaller, but measurements can overlap, particularly with Black-Tailed Jackrabbits. Compare hind track width, taking splay into account. **Canid** and **felid** tracks usually show a clear palm pad, but under some conditions their tracks can look surprisingly similar. Canid tracks are typically more symmetrical. **Coyotes** and **foxes** have slimmer claws that usually register as dots ahead of the toe pads.

NOTES

Jackrabbits are creatures of the open plains. The larger White-Tailed Jackrabbit *(Lepus townsendii)* is particularly adapted to the cold, growing a thick coat of white fur in the winter. Black-Tailed Jackrabbits *(Lepus californicus)* specialize in arid habitats, gleaning nearly all the water they need from their browse. Obligate vegetarians, jackrabbits feed primarily on grasses and forbs during the growing season and woody vegetation through the winter.

Unlike Snowshoe Hare and cottontails, jackrabbits prefer open habitats and rely on their speed, agility, and acute senses to escape predators. Their long, loose limbs allow them to move at high speeds with remarkable dexterity, and they display some of the most fluid body movements of all Midwestern mammals. Their fluid gaits leave a variety of track patterns, often with indistinct tracks, and some trails are easily confused with those of other animals, particularly canids.

Like other rabbits, jackrabbits are prolific breeders, with most females giving birth to multiple litters of three to six kits each year. Unlike cottontails, jackrabbit kits are born with their eyes open and may leave the nest within a few days. Also like other rabbits, jackrabbits are an important prey animal for many predators, especially hawks, owls, and Coyotes. Local populations of these principal predators often fluctuate with changes in jackrabbit abundance.

Weasels, or mustelids, are inquisitive, energetic carnivores. Mustelids form the largest and most diverse family of carnivores worldwide, with roughly 60 species inhabiting a wide range of habitats. Eight species live in the Midwest, showcasing much of this diversity, from the arboreal Marten (*Martes americana*) to the semi-aquatic River Otter (*Lontra canadensis*) and the diminutive Least Weasel (*Mustela nivalis*) to the fossorial Badger (*Taxidea taxus*). All share a family resemblance, with long, muscular bodies, short legs, and thick fur. They also display exceptional agility and high intelligence, and they have a reputation for punching above their weight. With the exception of River Otters, they are generally solitary animals. Population densities tend to be lower than those of other, similarly sized mammals. Despite this, they are extremely active hunters and can leave abundant tracks and trails.

Most mustelids exhibit pronounced sexual dimorphism, with males much larger than females. This is reflected in track size: in general, tracks at the small end of the range for a given species are female, while those at the large end are male. Ranges also overlap, and the tracks of a male of one species may resemble those of a female of a larger species.

TRACKS

All members of the weasel family have five toes on each foot, though often only four show clearly. Toes are arranged asymmetrically with the thumb (toe 1) set the farthest back. Toes usually register as oval impressions separated from the palm by a tall negative space. Claws usually register. The palm is chevron-shaped, tapering and dropping down toward the inside of the track. Front tracks are more symmetrical than hinds and have a single heel pad that sometimes registers. Hind tracks are highly asymmetrical. The thumb (toe 1) is set far back on the foot and often does not register clearly. When only four toes show, mustelid tracks can resemble canid, felid, or rodent tracks.

TRACK PATTERNS & GAITS

With their long, flexible bodies and short legs, most mustelids have different body mechanics than other mammals and look a bit like Slinkys moving across the landscape. They move in a variety of lopes and bounds and leave diverse but generally distinctive track patterns. In the snow, many mustelids bound leaving an offset 2x2 pattern, with one side consistently leading the other. On firmer surfaces, loping patterns are common. Some mustelids will walk for short distances, large Fisher walk frequently, and Badgers walk almost exclusively.

WEASEL FAMILY

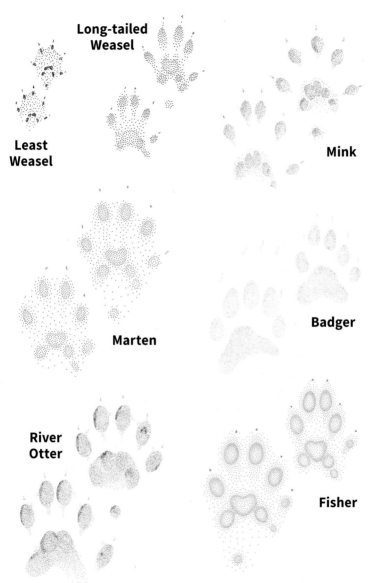

Long-tailed Weasel

Least Weasel

Mink

Marten

Badger

River Otter

Fisher

(See "Track Patterns: Weasels" on pages 318 & 320.)

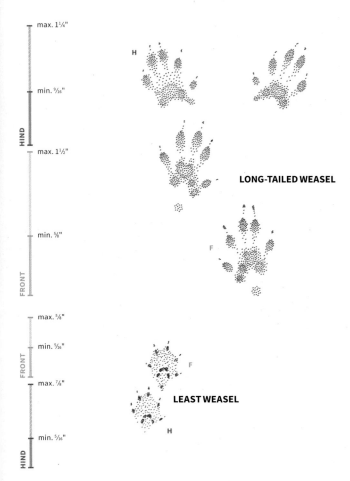

max. 1¼"

min. ⁹⁄₁₆"

HIND

H

max. 1½"

LONG-TAILED WEASEL

min. ⅝"

FRONT

F

max. ⅝"

min. ⁵⁄₁₆"

FRONT

F

max. ⅞"

LEAST WEASEL

min. ⁵⁄₁₆"

HIND

H

(See "Track Patterns: Weasels" on pages 318 & 320.)

QUICK ID TIPS

- Typical mustelid form with five toes, tall negative space, and a crescent-shaped palm.

- Smaller tracks can resemble those of a rodent.

- In snow, 2x2 bounding track patterns show long, variable strides.

Weasels

Mustela nivalis, Mustela richardsonii, and *Neogale frenata*

TRACKS

Weasels display a typical mustelid foot structure, with five toes and a slender, arcing palm on each foot. The thumb (toe 1) is set the farthest back and does not always register, especially on the hind. Toe pads are somewhat bulbous and usually appear separated from the palm by a tall, fur-filled negative space. The fur, which is thickest in winter, may obscure track details. Fine claws tend to show in firm substrate but are often indistinct on looser surfaces. Front and hind tracks are similar in size, and distinguishing them is not always possible. Track widths measure ⁵⁄₁₆"–⁹⁄₁₆" for least, ⅜"–¾" for short-tailed, and ⅝"–1⅛" for long-tailed.

- Front tracks sometimes appear nearly symmetrical, with all five toes radiating evenly from the palm. At other times the middle toes (2–4) register close together, resembling the hind track of a rodent. Occasionally, the thumb (toe 1) appears set nearly as far back as on the hind. A single heel pad may register.

- Hind tracks are less symmetrical than fronts. The thumb (toe 1) often registers lightly or not at all, and the print may resemble the front track of a rodent or look like a miniature canid track. The furred heel sometimes registers. Usually, but not always, hind tracks appear smaller and less splayed than fronts.

Dumbbell track pattern

TRACK PATTERNS & GAITS

Travels in lopes and bounds. Usually bounds in snow, leaving an offset 2x2 track pattern. Stride length is highly variable, with short strides often connected by drag marks, creating a distinctive "dumbbell" pattern. On firmer surfaces the track patterns are more variable but tend to be similar from one stride to the next. Hind tracks may register behind, on top of, to the outside of, or ahead of the fronts. Long-Tailed Weasels often leave a rabbit-like bounding pattern, which may help to differentiate their trails from those of Mink and Short-Tailed Weasels.

HABITAT

Diverse, with each species showing regional variation. Each can be found nearly everywhere small mammals are abundant. Least Weasels are the most tolerant of low, sparse ground cover and are common in meadows, pastures, and marshes. Long-Tailed Weasels seem to prefer brushy areas or woodlands and areas close to water.

OTHER SIGN

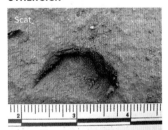
Scat

Scat: Long, slender, rope-like scat is usually heavily twisted with pointy ends. Ranges in size from ⅛" to ⅜" in diameter and ¾" to 3" in length. All three species commonly form latrines near den sites and deposit scat on raised surfaces along trails.

Caches: When prey is abundant, weasels cache excess food. Piles of mice, voles, or shrews are a good sign of weasel activity.

Snow Dives: Weasels occasionally dive into deep snow, emerging some distance away. Tunnel entrances usually measure 1"–2" in diameter.

ACTIVITY

Active year-round. May be active at any time of day or night.

SIMILAR TRACKS

The three weasel species overlap in size, exhibit regional variation, and show strong sexual dimorphism, with males nearly twice the size of females. Trail width, track size, range, and habitat all provide clues, but identifying weasel tracks to species is often not possible. **Mink** tracks are larger, though there is some overlap between a small Mink and a large Long-Tailed Weasel.

Mink loping-track groups usually appear more elongated, less regular, and less "boxy." Their stride length is often more consistent, and they rarely, if ever, leave a rabbit-like bounding pattern. **Rodent** front tracks can closely resemble weasel hind tracks, while rodent hind tracks can appear similar to weasel fronts. The typical **ground squirrel** bound pattern is very similar to the rabbit-like pattern of weasels. **Voles** often leave 2x2 trails in the snow, including "dumbbell" patterns. These rodents tend to take shorter, more consistent strides and show less erratic trails than weasels.

NOTES

The Midwest is home to three small members of the weasel family. Members of these three species have similar behavior, leave similar tracks and sign, and are often referred to simply as weasels. The Least Weasel *(Mustela nivalis)* is found across the Northern Hemisphere and is the smallest member of the family Carnivora. The Short-Tailed Weasel *(Mustela richardsonii)* is a close relative of the European Stoat. The Long-Tailed Weasel *(Neogale frenata)* is the largest of the three and closely related to the Mink. All weasels are energetic, inquisitive, and voracious carnivores. Their diet consists almost entirely of small- and medium-size mammals, supplemented with amphibians, birds, and reptiles. Small but feisty predators, they will prey on animals much larger than themselves. They are such an important control of rodent populations that the genus of the smaller species was named *Mustela,* which means "mouse hunter."

Weasels thoroughly explore their landscapes as they hunt, leaving twisting, winding trails. They move quickly, often stopping and standing on their hind legs to look around them or turning sharply to head off in a new direction. Though they generally forage on the ground, weasels are capable climbers and swimmers, and their trails may begin or end at the edge of a pond or the base of a tree or shrub. In winter, weasels spend much of their time foraging under the snow, where most of their prey is active.

Weasels are active off and on throughout the day and night, alternating periods of hunting with periods of resting in one of their many dens. Dens may be natural cavities or the burrows of small rodents, and usually contain a small nest made of vegetation, fur, or feathers. While formidable, weasels are small and are vulnerable to predation by hawks, owls, snakes, foxes, cats, and other medium-size predators.

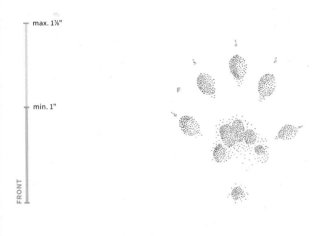

max. 1⅛"

min. 1"

F

max. 1¾"

min. ⅞"

H

(See "Track Patterns: Weasels" on pages 318 & 320.)

QUICK ID TIPS

- Typical mustelid tracks with five toes and a slim, crescent-shaped palm.
- Splays toes more often than other similar-sized mustelids.
- Usually close to open water.

Mink
Neogale vision

TRACKS

Mink leave classic mustelid tracks, with five long toes and slender, crescent-shaped palms. Toes often splay widely and usually appear separated from the palm by a tall negative space. Sharp claws usually register, sometimes as pointy extensions of the toes. The thumb (toe 1) is the smallest, sits the farthest back, and does not always register but is more developed than in Marten and long-tailed weasels. The palm has four pads, which may appear fused, and is wider toward the outside of the track. Front tracks are slightly larger and usually more splayed than hinds. Front and hind tracks often overlap.

- Front tracks often splay widely, with all five toes radiating from the palm. Other times the middle toes (2–4) register close together, like the hind track of a squirrel. A single heel pad sometimes registers. Front tracks measure 1"–1⅞" long x 1"–1¾" wide.

- Hind tracks are less symmetrical than fronts and usually less splayed. The middle and ring toes (toes 3 and 4) are set farther forward and sometimes register fairly close together as the outer toes splay. When the thumb (toe 1) does not register, the resulting 1-2-1 toe pattern can resemble the front track of a squirrel. Hind tracks measure ⅞"–1¾" long x ¾"–1¾" wide.

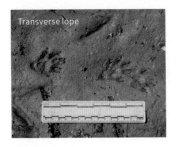
Transverse lope

TRACK PATTERNS & GAITS

Usually lopes while traveling on firm surfaces. Displays both transverse and rotary lopes, leaving elongated patterns with tracks registering individually or partially overlapping. Stride length tends to be consistent, while track patterns sometimes vary one stride to the next. Generally bounds in deeper snow leaving an offset 2x2 pattern. Occasionally walks.

HABITAT

Almost always found close to open water and most common in Muskrat habitat. Prefers areas where trees or rocks provide shelter along shorelines. May travel long distances between bodies of water.

OTHER SIGN

Scat

Scat: Ranges from ¼" to nearly ½" in diameter and 1"–4" in length. Most common form is a long, twisted, rope-like scat made up mostly of rodent remains. Less commonly contain large amounts of fruit and berry seeds, scales, feathers, or crayfish shells. These scat tend to be more tubular, with smoother surfaces and less twisting. Often deposited on rocks, logs, or vegetation next to water, near Muskrat burrows, or on Beaver lodges.

Slides: Sometimes slides short distances on the snow like a River Otter. Slides are typically 3"–5" wide.

Dens: Mink commonly den in streambanks. Entrances are typically 4" across. May also den in hollow logs or abandoned Muskrat burrows. All dens are temporary, as Mink change dens frequently.

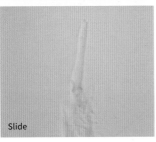
Slide

Snow Dives: As with the smaller weasels, Mink occasionally dive into deep snow and explore under the surface, emerging some distance away. Tunnel entrances measure about 2" in diameter.

ACTIVITY

Active year-round. Predominantly crepuscular and nocturnal but may be active at any time of day or night.

SIMILAR TRACKS

Marten tracks are usually larger and less likely to splay. They have proportionally larger feet, and their tracks tend to fill more of the area of their track patterns. Most **Long-Tailed Weasel** tracks are smaller and less splayed. Their loping track groups are usually more regular, compact, and "boxy." They often show more variation in stride length and sometimes leave a rabbit-like bounding track pattern. **Squirrel** front tracks can closely resemble Mink hinds, while squirrel hind tracks can resemble Mink fronts. Study the track pattern to distinguish fronts from hinds. Squirrel hind tracks will have parallel rather than splayed toes and a flat, rather than curved, leading edge. Squirrel palm pads are more substantial, and their heels are quite different. Mink often travel along shorelines, while squirrel trails are usually perpendicular to the shore.

NOTES

An amphibious member of the weasel family, Mink are equally at home in water and on land. They generally live close to water, and trails are common along shorelines. Most Mink spend the majority of their time foraging in water, but they are also adept climbers and hunt on land and occasionally in trees. Their preferred prey is Muskrat, but Mink are opportunistic carnivores, feeding on fish, frogs, crayfish, turtles, small rodents, cottontails, waterfowl, eggs, worms and insects.

Like all mustelids, Mink are energetic and inquisitive. Their trails seem to connect every nook and cranny across a wide variety of terrain. A trail may weave through underbrush, cross swamps, follow streams, disappear into lakes or ponds, or even lead up a tree.

Mink are solitary and intolerant of intruders. As they move about their home ranges, Mink mark their territories with a discharge from their anal glands. This discharge is nearly as pungent as a skunk's, though it does not carry as far and is not quite as objectionable. Mink tolerate human habitation fairly well and are fairly common in suburban areas with adequate open space. Highly prized for their fur, Mink were once heavily trapped. Today, most Mink fur comes from farms. Though no longer trapped in significant numbers, Mink are preyed upon by foxes, Coyotes, Wolves, Fisher, Bobcats, Lynx, and Great Horned Owls.

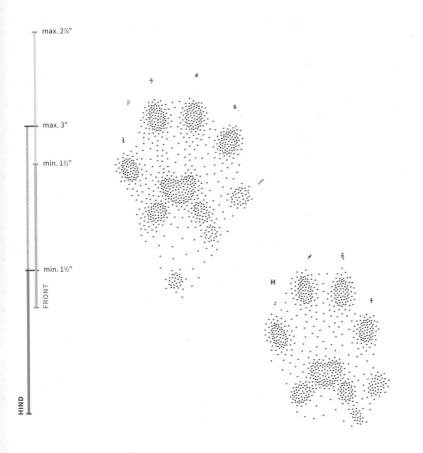

max. 2⅞"

max. 3"

min. 1½"

min. 1½"

F

H

FRONT

HIND

(See "Fisher," page 154, for additional details.)

QUICK ID TIPS

- Typical weasel tracks and trails.

- Very large feet relative to body size.

- Front tracks splay less often than those of Mink or Fisher.

American Marten
Martes americana

TRACKS

Typical weasel track form with five toes on each foot; a tall negative space; and a slender, chevron-shaped palm. The thumb (toe 1) is set the farthest back and often does not register clearly, especially on the hind. Toe pads appear oval or teardrop-shaped and register separately from the palm. The asymmetrical palm tapers toward the inside of the track and may appear lobed or made up of several distinct pads. Fur between the pads may blur track detail or make pads appear smaller, especially in winter when it is thickest. The fur-covered heels often register, and sharp claws often show. Tracks of females are smaller than those of males.

- Front tracks are more symmetrical and slightly larger than hind. Toes splay less often than in Mink or Fisher. A single heel pad often registers. Front tracks measure 1½"–2⅞" long x 1½"–2¼" wide.

- Hind tracks are highly asymmetrical and can appear canine when the thumb (toe 1) does not register clearly. Hind tracks measure 1½"–3" long x 1⅛"–2¼" wide.

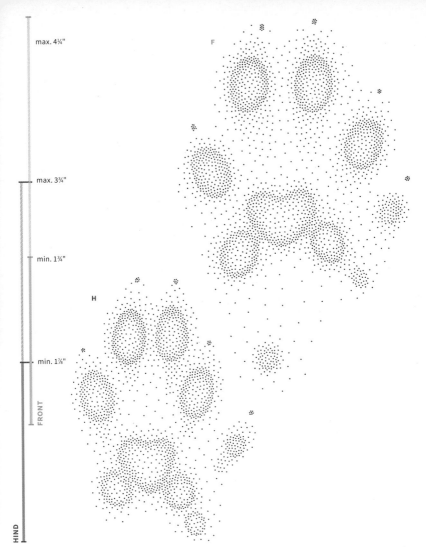

max. 4¼"

F

max. 3¾"

min. 1¾"

min. 1⅞"

FRONT

H

HIND

(See "Track Patterns: Weasels" on pages 318 & 320, and "Track Patterns: Cats & Dogs" on page 328.)

QUICK ID TIPS

- Typical mustelid tracks with five toes and a slender palm.

- Large feet relative to body size.

- Front tracks larger and usually more splayed than hind.

Fisher

Pekania pennanti

TRACKS

Fisher display typical weasel-family track form, with five toes, a tall negative space, and a crescent-shaped palm. The middle and ring toes (3 and 4) lead in the track, while the thumb (toe 1) is set the farthest back and often does not register clearly, especially on the hind. Fur between the toes may blur some track detail and exaggerate the negative space. The palm may appear as several discrete pads or continuous with distinct lobes. The pads on the inside of the track are smaller and set farther back than those on the outside. Sharp claws usually register. Males are nearly twice the size of females and leave much larger tracks.

- Front tracks are larger, more symmetrical, and typically more splayed than hind. Fully splayed, they can approach the size of Lynx tracks. There is a single pad on the heel which sometimes registers. Front tracks measure 1¾"–4¼" long x 1¾"–3¼" wide.

- Hind tracks are highly asymmetrical, smaller, and less likely to splay. When toe 1 does not register, tracks appear symmetrical, similar to a canid track. The fur-covered heel occasionally registers. Hind tracks measure 1⅞"–3¾" long x 1⅜"–3⅛" wide.

TRACK PATTERNS & GAITS

Marten and Fisher regularly lope and bound. Marten most often use a rotary lope, leaving 3x4 track patterns. Fisher use both rotary and transverse lopes, leaving a wider variety of patterns. Both species bound in deeper snow, leaving an offset 2x2. Fisher sometimes leave a highly offset 2x2 pattern, with one pair of tracks far in front of the other. Fisher also walk frequently, leaving trails similar to those of Lynx, Bobcats, or Coyotes.

HABITAT

Forests, especially mature coniferous or coniferous–deciduous forests with a closed canopy, large cavity trees, and extensive debris on the ground. Marten prefer areas with deep winter snow cover. Fisher extend into fragmented forests and even some suburban areas.

OTHER SIGN

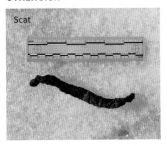

Scat

Scat: The typical form is heavily twisted and tapered rope-like scat with pointy ends. In summer, Marten and Fisher may eat large amounts of fruits and berries and produce scat that is more cylindrical with little or no twisting. Fisher scat occasionally contains Porcupine quills. Scat ranges in size from ¼" to ¾" in diameter and 2"–7" in length. Marten commonly leave scat on elevated surfaces along well-used trails. Fisher commonly leave scat near den sites and in Raccoon latrines.

Snow Dives: Like smaller members of the weasel family, Martens occasionally dive into deep snow and explore under the surface, emerging some distance away. Tunnel entrances measure about 3" in diameter.

ACTIVITY

Active year-round but may reduce activity in winter. Daily schedule varies geographically and seasonally based on prey and may be diurnal, crepuscular, nocturnal, or arrhythmic.

SIMILAR TRACKS

Marten tracks and trails are generally smaller than Fisher tracks, but there is overlap. In snow, Marten use a 2x2 bound more consistently, take longer bounding strides, and do not sink as deeply into the snow. They also investigate smaller nooks and crannies. Fisher walk much more often. **Mink** tracks are smaller but overlap slightly with Marten tracks. Marten have proportionally larger feet, and tracks fill more of the area of the track pattern. Mink are more likely to splay their toes. **River Otter** hind tracks are larger than front. Their palm pads are proportionally larger, and webbing may be visible between their toes. In deeper snow, the heavier River Otter sinks more deeply, may show a tail drag, and frequently slides while traveling. River Otters often travel in groups and tend to follow direct routes, while Fisher are generally solitary and usually meander across the landscape. **Raccoons** have longer toes that usually connect to the palm pad. Their palm pad is larger, has a smooth leading edge, and makes up more of the total area of the track. The lead track in the Raccoon walk switches from right to left with each step. The lead track in the Fisher 2x2 bound is consistently on one side of the trail. **Bobcats, Lynx, foxes,** and **Coyotes** usually show larger palm pads and less negative space between the toes and the palm. Their walking trails tend to be narrower and more regular.

NOTES

Marten and Fisher are semi-arboreal mustelids, adapted to life in the northern forests. Once targeted for their pelts, they were nearly wiped out of the Midwest by trapping and habitat loss. Today their populations are recovering, and Fisher range is expanding toward its historical limits.

Adept climbers, Marten and Fisher can rotate their hind feet 180°, enabling them to move down trees headfirst like squirrels. Though they hunt primarily on the ground, they often den in trees and sometimes travel through the canopy. Larger male Fisher take to the trees less often than females or Marten. Generally solitary, except for mating and raising young, they travel widely across large home ranges. They tend to follow their own travel routes, ignoring trails made by other animals, and their tracks can be difficult to find in the summer. In snow, however, the trails of these active hunters are often more common than their low population densities would suggest.

Marten and Fisher are energetic, efficient predators that hunt where prey is both abundant and easy. They rarely run down prey, preferring to surprise animals resting in shelter. Their trails zigzag across the landscape, investigating snags, logs, crevices, cavities, and other hiding places. They primarily hunt small to medium-size mammals but are more omnivorous than other mustelids. Marten hunt mainly voles but also actively hunt squirrels and Snowshoe Hare. In winter, they sometimes forage under the snow, where smaller prey is active. Fisher prefer either Porcupine or Snowshoe Hare. Where these species are rare, they often focus on squirrels.

Both of these boreal weasels have large feet relative to their body size. This trait is most developed in the Marten and gives the smaller animal an advantage in deep snowpack. In areas where the two species overlap, Marten usually do best in habitats with the deepest snow cover, while Fisher dominate in areas where snow is shallower or firmer.

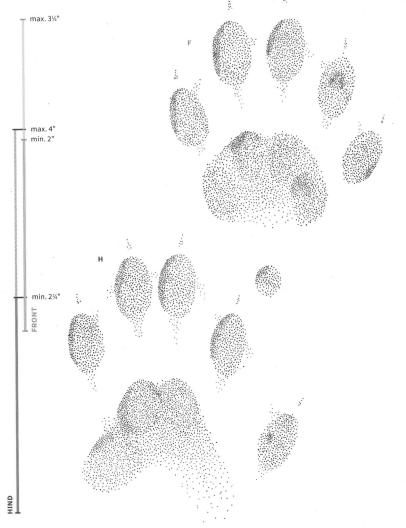

max. 3¼"

F

max. 4"
min. 2"

min. 2¼"

FRONT

H

HIND

(See "Track Patterns: Weasels" on pages 318 & 320.)

QUICK ID TIPS

- Typical mustelid tracks form with five toes and a crescent-shaped palm.
- Highly aquatic, tracks are usually found close to waterways.
- Typically lopes, leaving diagonal lines of tracks. Slides on snow.

Northern River Otter
Lontra canadensis

TRACKS

River Otters' feet are highly adapted for swimming but retain the basic mustelid form, with five toes and an arching palm pad on each foot. Toes have bulbous tips that appear oval or teardrop shaped and are connected by webbing, which is sometimes visible, though generally subtle. The shafts of the toes are often visible. Palm pads are fused but remain distinctly lobed. The thumb (toe 1) and the innermost lobe of the palm often fail to register clearly. Short, sharp claws often register. Hind tracks are slightly larger than fronts.

- Front tracks are slightly asymmetrical, with the toes arranged in an arc around the palm. The palm pad sometimes appears large and smooth, but two leading lobes are usually evident. A single heel pad often registers. Front tracks measure 2"–3¼" long x 1⅞"–3" wide.

- Hind tracks are asymmetrical. The thumb (toe 1) is set farthest back but is longer and more developed than in most mustelids. The arching palm extends much farther back on the inside of the track. When toe 1 doesn't register, the tracks can resemble those of a canid or felid. Hind tracks measure 2¼"–4" long x 2⅛"–3¾" wide.

TRACK PATTERNS & GAITS

Usually travels on land in a transverse lope, with the body angled slightly to the line of travel. Track patterns include diagonal lines, 1-2-1 arrangements, and boxy groupings, and are generally consistent one stride to the next. Prints sometimes overlap, but usually all four tracks are visible in each group. Sometimes walks, leaving an indirect-register pattern. Bounds in deeper snow, leaving an offset 2x2 pattern. Frequently slides while traveling across snow or ice. Tail marks are sometimes visible in deep or loose substrates.

HABITAT

Lakes, ponds, streams, rivers, marshes, and reservoirs with adequate shore-line cover and abundant fish. Much more common in less developed areas.

OTHER SIGN

Scat

Scat: Typically found as a loose, crumbly pile of fish scales. Consistency depends on diet. May range from a loose, liquid patty to a tubular scat measuring ⅜"–1" in diameter and 3"–6" long. Scat consisting of amphibian remains is the most liquid, while scat made of crustacean remains is cylindrical and most likely to hold together.

White Secretion: River Otters deposit a white, sticky secretion with a strong musky odor. These secretions are usually less than 1" wide and often found near scat.

Scent Rolls and Twists: River Otters create scent posts near the water's edge in their territories. Here the Otter rolls, matting down the vegetation and often forming a shallow depression. Scat is often deposited on the edges of these rolls. Frequently, River Otters mound or twist together vegetation that is then scented or used as a post to deposit scat.

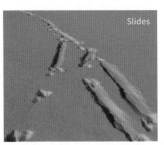

Slides

Slides: River Otters are well known for sliding down hills, and even across level ground when surfaces permit. Slides are typically 6"–10" wide and limited in length only by the terrain. On longer slides, an Otter may give itself an extra push, as if swimming across the ground.

Active year-round. Predominantly crepuscular and nocturnal. Least active around midday.

SIMILAR TRACKS

Fisher front tracks are larger than hind, and their palm pads appear more slender. In deeper snow, the lighter Fisher does not sink as deeply and rarely shows tail drag. Fisher do not slide but sometimes make short, slide-like drag marks along their trails. Fisher are generally solitary and tend to meander across the landscape, while River Otters often travel in groups and generally follow more direct travel routes. **Raccoons** have longer, more slender toes that register at the same depth from tip to base and usually connect to the palm in the track. Their palm pads usually make up more of the total area of the track and almost always have a smooth, rather than lobed, leading edge. Raccoons usually walk leaving a distinctive paired track pattern, with the lead track alternating sides with each step. **Bobcats** show four toes in both front and hind tracks and leave different track patterns. Their tracks usually show less negative space between the toes and the palm.

NOTES

A famously playful and adventurous member of the weasel family, River Otters are completely at home in the water. They hunt in water exclusively but come to land to den, mate, and move from one water body to another. While their lives revolve around water, River Otters may travel dozens of miles across land between bodies of water. While widespread and fairly common, they are sometimes quite secretive.

River Otters eat mostly fish, usually preferring the most abundant slow-moving fish in the area. Their diet also includes aquatic crustaceans such as crayfish, large aquatic insects, amphibians, turtles, and occasionally Muskrat, Beavers, and waterfowl.

Efficient hunters, River Otters have a great deal of energy, and their inquisitive behavior can look quite playful. Naturally curious and completely at home in the water, they will sometimes come investigate small boats they encounter. On land they move fluidly, if somewhat comically, and look a bit like giant Slinkys as they lope or bound. They often slide on their bellies across snow or ice and are sometimes seen sliding down hills repeatedly—apparently out of sheer enjoyment. River Otters are highly mobile and may move miles across their ranges each day—usually by water—to find optimal foraging, seek a mate, or perhaps simply to swim and explore.

Tracks and sign are usually concentrated at scent-roll sites and along runs between water systems. Runs are most apparent at the narrowest point between two bodies of water.

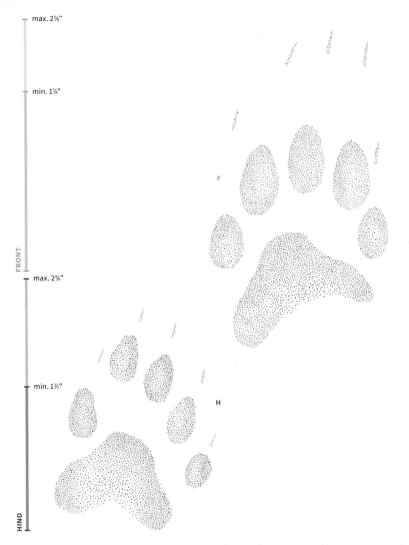

max. 2⅝"

min. 1⅞"

FRONT

F

max. 2⅝"

min. 1½"

H

HIND

(See "Track Patterns: Weasels" on pages 318 & 320.)

QUICK ID TIPS

- Robust-looking tracks with large toes, broad palms, and long front claws.
- Front tracks are significantly larger and wider than hind.
- Walks pigeon-toed, with feet turned in sharply.

American Badger
Taxidea taxus

TRACKS

Highly specialized for digging, Badgers' robust feet still have recognizable mustelid features, with five toes in front of an arching palm that is widest toward the outside. The thumb (toe 1) is the smallest, set farthest back, and may not register. Toe pads are large and may appear curved or warped. Toes often angle inward and rarely splay. The fully fused palm pads are larger than in most mustelids. The leading edge of the palm often points in a slightly different direction than the toes. The trailing edge of the palm is distinctly concave or notched. Front tracks are significantly larger than hind.

- Front tracks have long, stout claws that register reliably, though sometimes faintly. Claws often extend more than 1" from the toes and may be overlooked. The middle toes (2–4) register farthest forward, with toe 3 leading slightly. Toe pads are teardrop-shaped. The palm is wider than tall. A small heel pad may register. Front tracks measure 1⅞"–2⅝" long x 1⁹⁄₁₆"–2½" wide.

- Hind tracks are smaller and narrower than fronts. Toe pads are oval or teardrop-shaped. When all five toes register, the inner four toes (1-4) form a nearly straight, diagonal line. Claws are much smaller than on the front foot. Hind tracks measure 1½"–2⅝" long x 1¼"–2⅛" wide.

TRACK PATTERNS & GAITS

Walks when foraging. Often travels in a trot. Lopes or gallops when alarmed. Walks and trots with feet pointed sharply inward (pigeon-toed)—a defining characteristic of the species—leaving direct-register and indirect-register track patterns. Plows through deep snow, leaving a prominent trough.

HABITAT

Open plains and prairies, and occasionally the edge of open woodlands.

OTHER SIGN

Scat

Scat: Similar to that of other medium-size carnivores. May be twisted and pointy, or tubular and partially segmented. Typically measures ⅜"–¾" in diameter and 3"–6" long. Usually deposited underground or buried in the throw mound near den entrances, it is rarely encountered. Sometimes deposited along travel routes or near the entrance to a ground squirrel or prairie dog burrow.

Burrow

Burrows: The quintessential Badger sign, burrows have an elliptical entrance, about 8"–12" across, to accommodate the animal's squat profile. Entrances are surrounded by a large mound of excavated earth, sometimes littered with bones, fur, or droppings. There are frequently other elliptical holes nearby where the Badger dug in search of food.

ACTIVITY

Active year-round but may become torpid during the coldest parts of the winter, remaining in its burrow for days or even weeks at a time. Predominantly nocturnal but sometimes active during the day.

SIMILAR TRACKS

Bobcats and **Coyotes** show four toes and have sharper claws that are much shorter on the front foot. Their palm pads lack the clear notch along the trailing edge that is seen in Badgers and generally appear more symmetrical and aligned with the toes. They walk with their feet pointing straight ahead rather than pigeon-toed. **Porcupines** can leave similar-looking troughs in the snow and also walk pigeon-toed, but their feet are long and narrow.

NOTES

Badgers are consummate burrowers, and their lives revolve around burrows and burrowing. The Badger's squat, stocky body, powerful forelimbs, and long claws make it supremely adapted for a life of digging. They dig to hunt and to escape danger, using burrows for shelter from the heat and cold, for denning, and to store food. Badgers keep many active burrows and dig new ones frequently. In summer, Badgers sometimes dig a new burrow every day. In cold weather, Badgers may retreat to dens for extended periods, plugging the entrance to keep the cold out. Not surprisingly, burrows are the most conspicuous and reliable sign of Badger activity. Though primarily burrowers, Badgers swim well and may rest in shallow water on hot days.

Badgers prey primarily on burrowing rodents, including ground squirrels, pocket gophers, rats, and mice. They forage by digging out burrows and can quickly destroy an entire colony of ground squirrels. In the winter, they also dig up animals hibernating underground. Badgers also eat insects, birds, carrion, and reptiles, and they seem to have a particular fondness for rattlesnakes. Badgers are well protected by thick fur and a tough hide, and they appear to be highly tolerant of rattlesnake venom. As with many other members of the weasel family, Badgers cache excess food for later consumption. Caches, of course, are located in underground burrows.

Badgers have few natural enemies. They are formidable fighters, with strong claws, a tough hide, and a powerful neck. Nonetheless, they rarely pick a fight and generally retreat to a burrow if threatened. If a burrow isn't close enough at hand, a Badger may dig one on the spot, throwing dirt into its attacker's face and disappearing underground with remarkable speed.

This section covers a diverse group of species from seven families and three orders of mammals. Among the seven families, only the skunks have two representatives in the Midwest, and one of those is quite rare.

The Virginia Opossum (*Didelphis virginiana*), the Midwest's only marsupial, is in the family Didelphidae and the order Didelphimorphia. The large rodents represent three families in the order Rodentia. Muskrat (*Ondatra zibethicus*) are large voles in the family Cricetidae, American Beavers (*Castor canadensis*) belong to the family Castoridae, and North American Porcupines (*Erethizon dorsatum*) are in the family Erethizontidae. The other species are in the order Carnivora. The Striped Skunk (*Mephitis mephitis*) and Eastern Spotted Skunk (*Spilogale putorius*) are members of the family Mephitidae, Northern Raccoons (*Procyon lotor*) are part of the family Procyonidae, and American Black Bears (*Ursus americanus*) are in the family Ursidae.

Though most of these animals are not closely related, they share some characteristics of interest to us as trackers. Each has a plantigrade posture. Like humans, they can easily walk on the soles of their feet, with the bones of the palm flat to the ground and their heels bearing weight. This contrasts with digitigrade animals like cats and dogs, which walk on their toes with their heel bones high off the ground. All show five toes in their hind tracks, and all but the rodents show five in their front tracks as well. Except for the Spotted Skunk, which is rare in the Midwest, all commonly or exclusively walk when traveling.

TRACKS

The tracks of these animals are as diverse as their relationships. Skunk tracks are compact and blocky, with long claws and small toes that do not splay. The large rodents have feet highly specialized for an arboreal or aquatic lifestyle, and each leaves distinctive tracks. Opossum, Raccoon, and Black Bear tracks are unique but all resemble human hand- or footprints in some way.

TRACK PATTERNS & GAITS

All of these species except for the Spotted Skunk walk much of or most of the time. Striped Skunks, Porcupines, and Black Bears usually leave direct-register or overstep track patterns, with the tracks sometimes registering pigeon-toed. Opossums, Muskrat, and Beavers usually leave indirect-register patterns, with the hind foot partially or fully overlapping the front. Raccoons leave a distinctive overstep track pattern that is unique to this species.

SKUNKS, LARGE RODENTS, OPOSSUMS, RACCOONS & BEARS

Spotted Skunk

Striped Skunk

Muskrat

Beaver

Porcupine

Raccoon

Opossum

Bear

(See "Track Patterns: Flat-Footed Walkers & Armadillos" on pages 322, 324 & 326.)

max. 1⅜"

min. ⅞"

FRONT

F

max. 1¼"

min. ⅞"

HIND

H

(For more details, see "Striped Skunk," page 169.)

QUICK ID TIPS

- Small toes register close together in front of the broad palm.

- Two heel pads usually register on each foot.

- Walking trails are often irregular, while bounding trails can resemble those of weasels or small squirrels.

Eastern Spotted Skunk
Spilogale putorius

Historical range ⬛ Current known range ⬛

TRACKS

Similar to Striped Skunk tracks but generally smaller and more delicate-looking, sometimes resembling the tracks of a Mink, Long-Tailed Weasel, or small squirrel. There are five toes on each foot, with the thumb (toe 1) set the farthest back. The other toes are partially fused, tend not to splay, and register in front of the broad palms. There are four distinct palm pads on each foot, along with two heel pads that usually register. The pads are bare of fur and register crisply. Front and hind tracks are similar in size.

- Front tracks have long claws which, though significantly smaller than those of Striped Skunks, are usually prominent. The three middle toes (2–4) form a curved line. Front tracks measure ⅞"–1⅜" long x ½"–1" wide.

- The three middle toes on the hind track register close together in a nearly straight line. Hind claws are smaller than those on fronts and may not register clearly. Hind tracks measure ⅞"–1¼" long x ⅝"–1" wide.

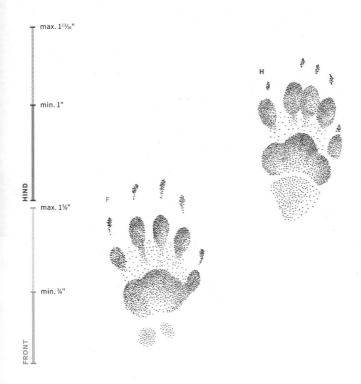

max. 1¹³⁄₁₆"

min. 1"

HIND

max. 1⅝"

min. ¾"

FRONT

H

F

(See "Track Patterns: Flat-Footed Walkers & Armadillos" on pages 324 & 326.)

QUICK ID TIPS

- Small, compact tracks with toes that never splay.
- Long, prominent claws on the front foot.
- Tracks and trail patterns often resemble those of a bear in miniature.

Striped Skunk
Mephitis mephitis

TRACKS

Skunks leave small, blocky tracks. They have five stout, partially fused toes on each foot. Unable to splay, the toes register parallel to each other. The thumb (toe 1) is the smallest, sits the farthest back, and does not always register clearly. Toes sometimes connect to the palm in the track, but are usually separated by a narrow negative. Palm pads are broad, smooth, trapezoidal, or kidney bean–shaped, and prominent in the tracks. Front and hind tracks are similar in size.

• The front track has long, stout claws that are prominent in most tracks. Claws on the middle three toes (2–4) are usually most evident and often register nearly ½" in front of the toes. Two heel pads sometimes register. Front tracks measure ¾"–1⅝" long (plus claws) x ¾"–1¼" wide.

• The hind claws are stout but much shorter than the front claws and do not always register clearly. A single, large heel pad sometimes registers, clearly separated from the palm by a thin crease. Hind tracks measure 1"–1¹³⁄₁₆" long x ⅞"–1¼" wide.

TRACK PATTERNS & GAITS

Leaves distinctive but sometimes confusing track patterns. Walks when foraging and travels in an overstep walk or lope. Walking gaits are often irregular and leave a variety of indirect register and overstep patterns, including some that look surprisingly similar to a lope. Uses a direct-register walk in deep snow, leaving a track pattern similar to that of a House Cat. Spotted Skunks often bound, leaving track patterns—and tracks—similar to those of a Long-Tailed Weasel or small squirrel.

HABITAT

Diverse habitats including open woodlands, brushlands, grasslands, and suburbs. Usually close to water in more arid landscapes.

OTHER SIGN

Scat: Varies with the diet of this opportunistic omnivore. Commonly, scat consists mostly of insect parts and breaks apart easily. The typical form is a smooth cylinder with blunt ends measuring ⅜"–⅞" in diameter and 2"–5" long. Skunks drop scat randomly but may also form latrines near den sites or in a prominent location on a regular travel route.

Odor: The skunk's odor is its most distinctive sign and may carry for up to a mile. Catching a whiff may mean a skunk is near or one has sprayed recently. Foxes and weasels have a similar odor that doesn't carry as far.

Digs: Striped skunks frequently dig for insects, making small, shallow holes about 1½"–3" in diameter. Digs can look similar to those made by other animals.

ACTIVITY

Active year-round in warm climates. In cold climates, spends much of winter holed up in its den. Does not hibernate and may emerge on warm winter days to forage. Primarily nocturnal.

SIMILAR TRACKS

Spotted Skunk tracks are smaller and more delicate, with shorter, finer claws. They show four discrete palm pads and have two heel pads on each foot. Their tracks and trails may resemble those of a Mink, weasel, or small squirrel. **Mink** and other **weasels** have smaller claws, smaller palm pads, and distinct heels that don't typically register. When loping, they tend to show longer strides and more-compact track groups. **Cat** tracks tend to look more circular, even when details are obscured in loose substrate. When cat claws register, they appear shorter and much sharper.

NOTES

Common, widespread, and abundant, skunks are perhaps best known for their chemical defense. When threatened, they may spray a noxious musk up to 15' with remarkable accuracy. Mist can drift three times that far, and the smell can carry for a mile. A direct hit to the eyes can temporarily blind an attacker, and consuming musk glands can be fatal. Unlike most mammals, which have coloration that allows them to blend in with the surroundings, the skunk's bold white-on-black pattern advertises its presence and its formidable chemical weaponry. Many predators quickly learn to avoid encounters with skunks. Some, particularly Great Horned Owls, seem undeterred by skunks' defenses and readily prey on them.

Like Black Bears, Striped Skunks are generally docile foragers. They don't chase their food, rarely flee from predators, and tend to move about with a relaxed disposition. Indeed their tracks, trails, and feeding sign often resemble those of Black Bears in miniature. They feed primarily on insects and other invertebrates, which they dig for with their long front claws. Their diet also includes eggs, fruits, berries, carrion, some vegetable matter, and occasional birds or small mammals.

Generally solitary but not territorial, they range freely and den in nearly any available shelter, including abandoned burrows, natural cavities, and under buildings. They often line their dens with grasses to make a nest. In the winter, Striped Skunks sometimes den communally and may congregate in areas with abundant food, such as a dump. They tend to move along established travel routes, including roadways. They can often be seen foraging on roadsides in late evening where, to the detriment of all involved, many are struck by cars. Sadly, Striped Skunks are also one of the primary rabies vectors in the U.S. Although few people need an extra incentive to avoid skunks, this is another reason to give them a wide berth.

The smaller, more agile, and weasel-like Spotted Skunk was once common on farms across much of the Midwest, but their populations have declined dramatically since the 1940s. Outside of South Dakota, where some small populations persist, there have been only a handful of sightings across the Midwest in the past decade.

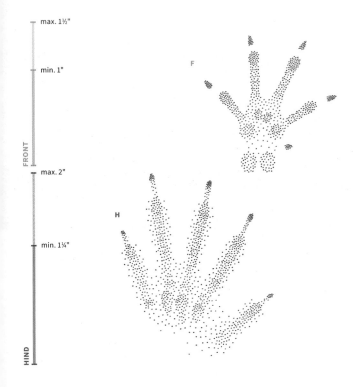

max. 1½"

min. 1"

FRONT

F

max. 2"

min. 1¼"

HIND

H

(See "Track Patterns: Flat-Footed Walkers & Armadillos" on pages 322 & 326.)

QUICK ID TIPS

- Front tracks show typical rodent structure. Hind tracks are significantly larger.

- Long, "fingery" toes and prominent claws.

- Walking trails often show tail drag.

Muskrat
Ondatra zibethicus

TRACKS

Muskrat tracks have four long, slender toes on the front and five on the hind. Toes may appear ribbed and usually connect to the palm in the track. Long, stout claws usually register prominently.

- Front tracks show typical rodent form. The outer toes (2 and 5) splay widely, while the middle toes (3 and 4) point straighter ahead. The tiny thumb (toe 1) has a stout claw that often registers as a dot. The palm shows three pads, arranged in a triangle. Two large heel pads usually register. Front tracks measure 1"–1½" long x ⅞"–1⅜" wide.

- Hind tracks are much larger and more variable. Each toe is surrounded by a shelf of stiff hairs. When these hairs register, toes appear wide and stout. When they do not, toes appear long and spindly. All five toes radiate out from the wide palm. The middle toes (2–4) are grouped together, but less distinctly than in many rodents. The outer toes (1 and 5) often register more lightly or not at all. The palm often registers weakly, and the heel rarely shows. Palm pads are rarely visible, but knuckle imprints often show. The larger hind tracks often register more faintly than the smaller fronts. Hind tracks measure 1¼"–2" long x 1⅜"–2¼" wide.

TRACK PATTERNS & GAITS

Usually walks leaving indirect-register patterns. Hind tracks may appear ahead, behind, beside, or on top of the front. A drag mark from the long, narrow tail is often visible snaking between the tracks. Lopes or bounds when threatened. Walks in snow, often showing foot drags. Plows a trough in deep snow.

HABITAT

Marshes, ponds, streams, lakes, rivers, and canals. Generally avoids strong currents. Especially common in shallow cattail marshes and Beaver ponds.

OTHER SIGN

Scat

Scat: Generally an oblong pellet with rounded ends about ¼" in diameter up to 1" long. Dry, hard pellets are smaller and more distinct. Wet, soft pellets are larger and clump together more often. Often accumulates on elevated surfaces near the water's edge such as rocks, logs, and Beaver lodges.

Burrows: Muskrat frequently create burrows in streambanks and pond banks. Entrances to burrows may be above or below the water line and typically measure 3½"–6" across.

Lodge

Lodges: Similar to Beaver lodges but smaller. Instead of wood, they are constructed of reeds, cattails, and similar plants mixed with mud. Mounded material extends 1½'–4' above the water line. Underwater entrances and denning cavities are excavated from below.

Feeding Stations: In winter, Muskrat push mud and plant matter up though holes in the ice. This debris helps keep the hole open and provides some protection from predators. In summer, Muskrat create feeding platforms of cut vegetation, creating a somewhat-solid surface in a marsh. Platforms vary widely in size and may even resemble a lodge.

ACTIVITY

Active year-round. Predominantly nocturnal and crepuscular but may be active at any time. Most active by day in the late spring and early summer.

SIMILAR TRACKS

Clear tracks are unmistakable. **Squirrel** front tracks can appear similar, but hind tracks are distinct. **Raccoon** tracks and **Beaver** front tracks occasionally resemble Muskrat hind tracks and may be found in the same locations.

NOTES

Muskrat are highly aquatic rodents with habitat and behavior similar to those of Beavers. Like Beavers, Muskrat frequent ponds and wetlands, build lodges, and spend most of their time in the water. They often make their homes in Beaver ponds and may even move into an occupied Beaver lodge. They do not fell trees or gnaw sticks, instead building lodges and feeding platforms out of cattails, reeds, and aquatic plants.

While Muskrat do not build dams, they create open water in marshy wetlands by digging channels and by consuming large quantities of cattails and other plants. This supports wetland diversity, providing habitat for waterfowl. Muskrat are primarily herbivores but also eat fish, crayfish, and clams; clamshells sometimes accumulate at feeding platforms or near burrows.

Muskrat are essentially a wetland species yet have flourished even as wetlands have declined—they are highly adaptable and have adjusted well to human land uses. They have become quite abundant in rural, suburban, and even urban streams, ponds, and canals. Males are generally territorial, especially during breeding. A lodge or burrow is usually shared by a breeding pair and offspring. Young disperse in spring and may travel some distance to find homes. In winter, males are less territorial, and several may share a lodge or burrow.

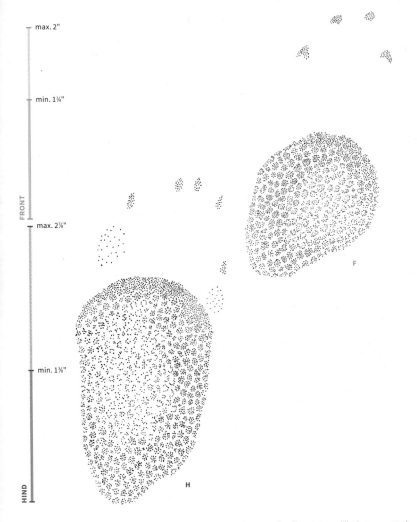

max. 2"

min. 1¼"

FRONT

max. 2⅞"

min. 1⅜"

HIND

F

H

(See "Track Patterns: Flat-Footed Walkers & Armadillos" on page 324.)

QUICK ID TIPS

- Round or oval tracks often show a unique pebbly texture.
- Toes rarely register.
- Long, prominent claws register far in front of soles.

North American Porcupine
Erethizon dorsatum

TRACKS

Porcupine feet are highly adapted for climbing and leave distinctive tracks. As with most rodents, there are four toes on the front foot and five on the hind, but that is where the family resemblance ends. Stout claws register in a prominent arc well in front of the palm. The toes themselves are held off the ground by the long nails and rarely register. The toes, and thus the claws, never splay. The palm and heel form a broad, continuous sole. The bottom of the foot is textured like a basketball, giving tracks a pebbly appearance.

- Front tracks have a lopsided sole that is taller along the outside and narrows toward the heel. If the heel does not register, tracks appear round. When the heel registers fully, tracks appear more triangular. The sole of the front track measures 1¼"–2" long by 1"–1⅝" wide. Claws add about 1½".

- Hind tracks are larger, longer, and more symmetrical than fronts, with slightly shorter claws. The sole may register as a long oval or taper slightly toward the heel. Sometimes a raised mound is evident along the centerline. Occasionally this mound is so prominent that the two sides of the track resemble the two cleaves of a deer hoof. The sole of the hind track measures 1⅜"–2⅞" long x 1"–2" wide. Claws add about 1¼".

TRACK PATTERNS & GAITS

Walks almost exclusively, usually leaving a direct-register or slight overstep pattern. Tracks often register pigeon-toed (pointed in). A brush-like tail drag is sometimes visible. May lope or bound briefly if startled. Walks in deep snow, plowing a trough. Often follows well-established runs, particularly in winter.

HABITAT

Predominantly arboreal. Common in deciduous, coniferous, and mixed forests. Lives in brushland in some arid regions.

OTHER SIGN

Scat

Debarked tree

Scat: Irregular fibrous pellets measuring ¼"–½" in diameter and ½"–1¼" in length. Pellets have round or pointy ends and most are slightly curved. Scat often accumulates in large quantities wherever Porcupines feed, travel, or rest.

Debarked Trees: During the winter, Porcupines feed heavily on the inner bark of trees. They strip large, irregular patches of bark from a wide variety of hardwoods and conifers. Freshly bared wood is usually bright yellow and fades over time. While bark may be stripped from any part of the tree, it is most commonly done high off the ground, where the bark is more succulent and the Porcupine is safer from predators.

Nip Twigs: When feeding, Porcupines bite off branches too thin to support them to reach nuts or succulent growth; these branches fall to the ground or lodge in the canopy.

ACTIVITY

Active year-round but may hole up for days during inclement winter weather. Primarily nocturnal. Occasionally active during the day.

SIMILAR TRACKS

Clear prints are unmistakable. **Badger** trails in the snow can appear similar, but Badger tracks are much wider and show clear toe impressions. **Turtle** tracks can also show long, stout claws and oval soles with a pebbly texture, but turtles leave wider trails with shorter strides.

Porcupines are large rodents best known for the sharply barbed quills on their body and tail. When threatened, a Porcupine contracts muscles under its skin, causing its quills to stand firmly on end. Porcupines are not aggressive and cannot throw their quills, but if provoked they can strike with their barbed tail with surprising speed and force. The quills easily come loose and work their way into skin, where they can cause infections. With their strong defense, Porcupines have developed a relaxed manner. They move about slowly and have very small home ranges that they rarely stray from. Yet despite their quills, Porcupines are actively hunted by Fishers and some Cougars, and they occasionally fall prey to Bobcats and Coyotes.

Porcupines are herbivores, feeding on the buds of trees in spring, tree leaves and herbaceous plants in summer, nuts and fruits in fall, and the inner bark of trees in winter. They are excellent climbers and spend a great deal of time in the trees. Their long claws and textured foot pads aid in climbing, as does their stout tail, which they use as a brace. They tend to stay close to the trunk, as thinner branches cannot support their weight and they are heavy enough to injure themselves if they fall.

When walking, Porcupines sometimes hold their tail straight out behind them and sweep it side-to-side along the ground, brushing away their tracks. Porcupines create well-worn runs between denning sites and preferred feeding areas. In warm weather, they sleep on branches high in trees. In cold weather, they rest in a variety of cavities and shelters, including rock ledges, hollow logs, root tangles, and underground burrows. Porcupines are generally solitary but may gather in large numbers at good feeding or denning sites.

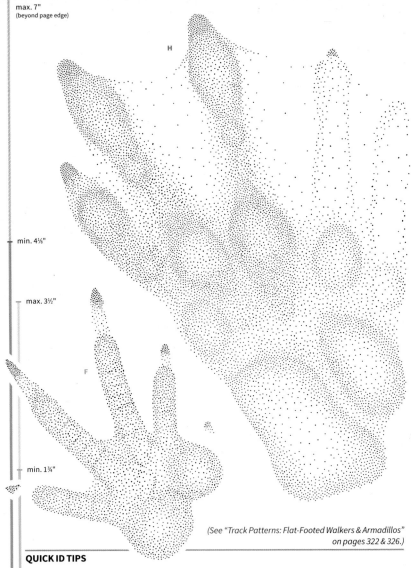

max. 7"
(beyond page edge)

H

min. 4⅛"

max. 3½"

F

min. 1¾"

(See "Track Patterns: Flat-Footed Walkers & Armadillos" on pages 322 & 326.)

HIND FRONT

QUICK ID TIPS

- Extremely large, fingery hind tracks; clear prints are unmistakable
- Partial tracks and overlapping prints are common
- Trails usually lead directly to or from a body of water

American Beaver
Castor canadensis

TRACKS

Beaver feet are highly specialized for their unique lifestyle. Tracks are unusual but display some rodent characteristics. Long toes connect to the palms. Stout nails register reliably but are often indistinguishable from toes. Large palms and heels register prominently. Hind tracks are more than twice the size of fronts and often cover them in the track pattern.

- Front tracks show typical rodent features. Four toes usually register, though often only two or three are distinct. Toes usually angle or curve inward. The thumb (toe 1) is well developed and has a claw that often registers. The palm is featureless and difficult to distinguish. Two large, round heel pads usually register, giving the trailing edge of the track a square profile. Front tracks measure 1¾"–3½" long x 2"–2¾" wide.

- Hind tracks are large and unlike those of any other Midwestern animal. Five long, slender toes are connected by webbing, which is often visible. The three outer toes (3–5) carry most of the weight and register reliably. The two inner toes (1 and 2) often register lightly or not at all. The knuckles often leave conspicuous impressions. The broad palm and large heel register reliably. Hind tracks measure 4⅛"–7" long x 2⅜"–5⅛" wide.

TRACK PATTERNS & GAITS

Walks typically leaving a direct-register or indirect-register pattern. Hind tracks usually partially or fully cover the front tracks. May bound when alarmed, leaving a large squirrel-like track pattern. Plows though deeper snow, creating a wide trough.

HABITAT

Swamps, rivers, streams, marshes, lakes, and ponds in wooded areas.

OTHER SIGN

Scat

Lodge

Gnawed trees

Scat: Beavers defecate in water, so scat is rarely seen. If found, the typical form is an oval pellet ¾"–1½" around made of wood and plant fibers.

Lodges: Easily recognizable, Beaver lodges are large domes of sticks and mud with underwater entrances. Carefully built and maintained, lodges are quite sturdy and may be used for many generations. If abandoned, they may be reclaimed by other Beavers or persist for years. Look for other Beaver sign to identify active lodges.

Dams: Impressive structures constructed of wood and mud. Far from being haphazard piles of debris, dams are engineered with large anchor poles and a lattice of sticks to hold mud in place. Dams are nearly waterproof and may be as large as 10' high or hundreds of yards long. Beavers often build a series of dams along a waterway.

Chews: When Beavers feed, they leave behind sticks and small logs stripped of bark with ends gnawed to a point. Tooth marks on chews range from ⅛" to ¼" wide. Beavers also chew on the bark of standing trees.

Canals: Beavers sometimes dig canals from ponds to provide safer travel and to float logs to the lodge or dam. Canals can measure 2' wide x 2' deep and may be several hundred yards long.

Scent Posts: Beavers mark piles of vegetation and mud with a substance called castoreum, secreted from a specialized scent gland. The odor, reminiscent of a barn, is evidence of current Beaver activity.

ACTIVITY

Active year-round. In northern climates, spends most of winter in its lodge or under the ice. Predominantly nocturnal and crepuscular.

SIMILAR TRACKS

Clear prints are unmistakable, but partial tracks are common. Front tracks occasionally resemble **Muskrat** hind tracks but have a more robust palm and heel. When only three toes register clearly, hind tracks are easily mistaken for **large bird** tracks at a glance. When only the tips and nails of toes 3 and 4 register clearly, hind tracks can bear a striking resemblance to splayed, weathered **deer** tracks. Rarely, when the knuckles in the palm are the most prominent feature, hind tracks can resemble those of a **River Otter.**

NOTES

Common and widespread, Beavers are best known for dramatically altering their landscape. These large, highly aquatic rodents are a keystone species and among the most ecologically significant animals in North America. While it can be uncommon to find clear Beaver tracks, other signs of their presence are easy to spot. The distinctive lodges, dams, felled trees, and chewed sticks all point unmistakably to this animal. Beavers also make trails between feeding areas or bodies of water and clip them clear of protruding branches. The Beaver's reputation as highly industrious is well earned. Dams can reach enormous proportions and dramatically transform the surrounding landscape.

While Beavers primarily eat green plants and roots during summer, in the winter they rely on the inner bark of trees such as aspen, cottonwood, birch, maple, and willow. They cut down trees with remarkable speed by gnawing through the trunk with their sharp incisors. They regularly drop trees over 6" in diameter and have been known to fell trees over 2' across. Trees are cut into small sections to transport. Larger pieces are used in construction, while smaller branches may be stored underwater for food in winter. Where natural water levels are high, such as large streams and rivers, Beavers forgo building and simply burrow into the bank. Such "bank beavers" still fell trees to feed on in winter.

max. 2"

min. 1"

FRONT

F

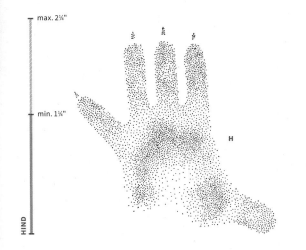

max. 2¼"

min. 1¼"

HIND

H

(See "Track Patterns: Flat-Footed Walkers & Armadillos" on pages 322 & 324.)

QUICK ID TIPS

- Widely splayed front tracks have a star-like shape.
- Hand-like hind tracks show a prominent opposable thumb.
- Front and hind tracks often overlap, creating a confusing but distinctive jumble of pads.

Virginia Opossum
Didelphis virginiana

TRACKS

Opossum front and hind tracks look quite different from each other, and from the tracks of any other animal. Both show five long toes connected to a large palm. Toes usually have an even width and register their full length. Palms register prominently, show four discrete pads, and are sometimes the clearest feature in the tracks. Small, sharp claws often register. Hind tracks often over-lap fronts, creating a confusing but distinctive jumble of pads.

- Front tracks splay widely, with toes radiating out from a round palm in a "rising sun" shape. The front track is nearly symmetrical, and there is no reliable way to distinguish right from left. Palm pads are arranged in a partial circle that may resemble the dimples on the bottom of an apple. Two heel pads rarely register. Front tracks measure 1"–2" long x 1¼"–2⅜" wide.

- Hind tracks show a distinctive opposable thumb that is often the most prominent feature in the track. The large thumb (toe 1) lacks a claw and usually splays 90° or more from the rest of the foot. The other toes are much thinner, register close together, and point to the outside of the trail. The middle toes (2–4) register parallel, while the pinkie (toe 5) usually splays slightly. Hind tracks measure 1¼"–2¼" long x 1¼"–2½" wide.

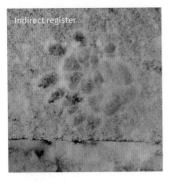
Indirect register

TRACK PATTERNS & GAITS

Usually walks or trots, leaving a slight understep or indirect-register pattern. Hind tracks usually fall slightly behind and outside of fronts, leaving the front track cradled in the crook of the hind thumb. Sometimes hind tracks register farther outside, and fronts and hinds appear side-by-side. This pattern can resemble the paired track pattern of a Raccoon but is made by feet on the same side of the body. Tail drag is sometimes visible.

HABITAT

Prefers fragmented wooded or brushy areas near water. Also common in cultivated lands, suburbs, and some urban areas. Rare in northern coniferous forests.

OTHER SIGN

Scat

Scat: Because Opossums' diets are so diverse, their scat varies widely and is not easily distinguished. Scat also tends to break down quickly and is rarely found. Scat may range from ⅜"–1⅛" in diameter and 1"–4½" in length and may be composed of nearly anything.

ACTIVITY

Doesn't hibernate but is generally inactive when temperatures are below 20°F. May hole up for days or weeks at a time during winter. Most active in the spring. Primarily nocturnal.

SIMILAR TRACKS

Raccoon toes point more forward than those of Opossums. They don't splay as wide as Opossum fronts and don't angle sharply outward like Opossum hinds. Raccoons have large, smooth palms rather than multiple distinct pads and lack the pronounced opposable thumb of the Opossum hind track.

NOTES

One of the most common arboreal animals in the southern part of the Midwest, the Virginia Opossum is North America's only marsupial. Like other marsupials, Opossums climb to their mother's pouch shortly after birth, where they nurse for two months before venturing outside. The Virginia Opossum migrated to the United States at about the same time European settlers first arrived and has been expanding its range northward ever since.

Remarkably hardy, Opossums tolerate a wide range of climate conditions. While they are poorly adapted to deal with extreme cold and prone to frostbite on their naked feet and tails, they continue to expand their range northward and increase their population throughout most of the Midwest. In cold climates, Opossums greatly reduce their activity in winter, but they do not hibernate and need to leave their dens to forage. In the northern states, it's not uncommon to see an Opossum that has lost toes or part of its tail to frostbite or to find blood on their trails in winter.

Opossums adjust well to human habitation and can eat nearly anything. Their highly varied diet is made up primarily of insects but also includes carrion, frogs, birds, eggs, snakes, small mammals, worms, fruits and berries, corn, and garbage. They often forage along streams and are known to raid henhouses. As slow-moving, nocturnal carrion eaters, many are struck by cars while feeding on the remains of other roadkill.

Opossums are solitary, non-territorial, and semi-nomadic. They den up during the day and forage at night across a constantly shifting home range. They commonly travel along roads and established trails and den up in almost any convenient shelter, including abandoned burrows, hollow logs, rock crevices, and buildings. They may line their dens with leaves, which they carry with their prehensile tail.

Excellent climbers, Opossums spend much of their time in trees. When threatened, an Opossum may hiss and bare its teeth, or it may "play 'possum," falling limp, drooling, and excreting a foul-smelling substance from its anus. This unique display is apparently unusual enough—or revolting enough—to dissuade most predators.

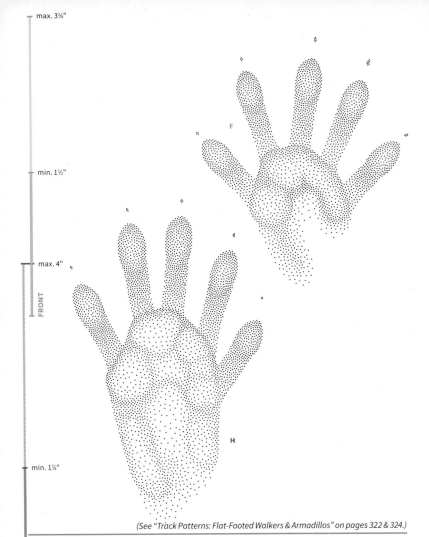

max. 3⅛"

min. 1½"

F

max. 4"

FRONT

min. 1⅞"

H

HIND

(See "Track Patterns: Flat-Footed Walkers & Armadillos" on pages 322 & 324.)

QUICK ID TIPS

- Tracks may resemble human handprints, with five long fingers and a large palm.

- Distinctive paired track pattern is unique to this animal.

- One of the most common—and most commonly misidentified—tracks in the Midwest.

Northern Raccoon
Procyon lotor

TRACKS

Raccoon tracks have five finger-like or cigar-shaped toes that typically connect to a large, curving palm. Tracks are slightly asymmetrical with the thumb (toe 1) set lowest on the foot. The fully fused palm pad is roughly C-shaped and slightly larger on the outside of the track. The bottoms of the feet are hairless and leave clear impressions. Short, sharp claws often register. Though generally distinctive, Raccoon tracks can be highly variable and occasionally resemble the tracks of other animals.

- Front tracks tend to splay more than hinds and often resemble tiny human handprints. The indent along the trailing edge of the palm is often sharply defined, and the C-shaped pad sometimes cups a small mound at the rear of the track. Rarely, a single heel pad registers on the outside edge of the foot. Front tracks measure 1½"–3⅛" long x 1¼"–2⅞" wide.

- Hind tracks are slightly less symmetrical than fronts, tend to splay less, and have larger, blockier palm pads. The trailing edge of the palm is less sharply defined and may appear straight rather than indented. A large, rounded heel pad sometimes registers. Slightly larger than front tracks overall but sometimes narrower, hind tracks measure 1⅞"–4" long x 1⅜"–3" wide.

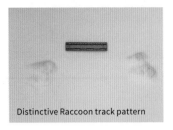
Distinctive Raccoon track pattern

TRACK PATTERNS & GAITS

Raccoons leave one of the most distinctive track patterns in nature. When they walk, they place their hind foot next to the opposite front, leaving an alternating paired track pattern. Hind tracks may register slightly ahead of, behind, or exactly beside the fronts. Unlike the canine side-trot, front and hind tracks appear on alternate sides of the trail with each step. When tracks are obscure, the size difference between fronts and hinds gives many trails a "boot-mitten, mitten-boot" appearance. In deeper snow, Raccoons may leave a direct-register pattern, similar to a Fisher or Bobcat. They occasionally lope, bound, or gallop.

HABITAT

Preferred habitat is waterways or wetlands near stands of hardwood trees for denning. Common in suburban areas, where they reach their highest population densities, and many cities. In rural areas, they most often live in lowland woodlots, shelterbelts, or fencerows but occasionally den underground in upland pastures, grasslands, or croplands.

OTHER SIGN

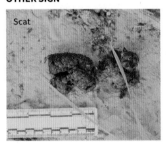
Scat

Scat: Usually tubular with blunt ends, measuring about ½"–1" in diameter and 3½"–7" long. Often granular and crumbly, with contents varying widely with diet. ***Warning:*** Raccoons can carry a parasitic roundworm called *Baylisascaris procyonis*, which can be fatal in humans. Use caution when handling Raccoon scat.

Latrines: Scat often accumulates in latrines at the base of prominent trees, under overhangs, and along natural bridges such as fallen trees. Large latrines may be used communally and maintained for many years.

ACTIVITY

Inactive during the coldest winter weather but not a true hibernator. In southern parts of the Midwest, they may hole up for a few days during snowstorms. In northern states, they may go dormant for months, leaving the den only occasionally from November through February.

SIMILAR TRACKS

The Raccoon's supple toes lead to a wide variety of track shapes, and Raccoon prints are frequently misidentified. But no other animal leaves the Raccoon's distinctive alternating track pattern. **Canids** and **mustelids** can leave similiar looking patterns, but the leading track in these patterns is consistently on one side of the trail. **Fishers** and **River Otters** have bulbous, arching toes that register deeper and wider at the tip than along their length. Their palm pads tend to be proportionally smaller and have distinct lobes on the leading edge. **Bobcats** have four toes front and hind, though Raccoon tracks sometimes show only four toes. Bobcat toes appear wider and usually somewhat teardrop-shaped, and they register separate from the palm. Bobcat palm pads generally show two leading lobes and three trailing lobes. **Opossum** tracks also look "fingery" and sometimes appear side-by-side in the track pattern. However, their palms show several distinct pads, their front tracks splay more widely, and their hind tracks show a large, distinctive opposable thumb.

NOTES

Raccoons are one of the most common medium-size mammals in North America. They adapt well to human habitation and thrive in suburban and urban areas, reaching their highest population densities in some of the Midwest's largest cities. Raccoons also frequent muddy shorelines, making them one of our most prolific track-makers. Because their tracks are so common, and so variable, they are frequently misidentified. Members of the Minnesota Wildlife Tracking Project jokingly describe all medium-size tracks as being "Raccoon until proven otherwise."

Omnivorous opportunists, Raccoons have diverse diets that vary seasonally and geographically. Plant foods, including fruits, berries, nuts, seeds, grasses, and sweet corn, usually make up most of their diet. They also eat carrion, eggs, invertebrates, and small vertebrates, especially aquatic creatures. Their habit of foraging for crayfish, frogs, fish, clams, and aquatic insects along muddy shorelines makes their tracks and trails particularly common. The Raccoon's dexterous fingers are capable of untying knots, unscrewing jar lids, and turning doorknobs. In developed areas, they commonly climb into garbage cans and compost bins and may raid food stores.

Adults are generally solitary, though they sometimes den communally when populations are high or temperatures are low. Young stay with their mothers for most of their first year, and families are often seen together in late summer. Raccoons are excellent climbers and often take refuge in trees. They may sleep on branches in mild weather, and they commonly den in tree cavities. They also den in rock crevices, abandoned buildings, culverts, brush piles, and the abandoned dens of other animals. Outside of natal dens and winter dormancy, they commonly change den sites every night. Raccoons usually make their own trail systems, connecting dens and foraging sites. They sometimes follow roads but more often cross them; many are killed while doing so.

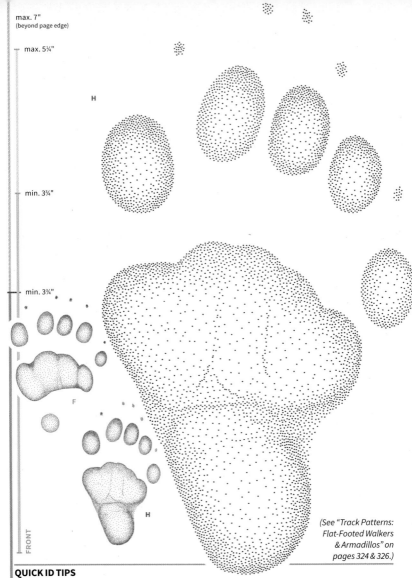

max. 7"
(beyond page edge)

max. 5¼"

min. 3¾"

min. 3¾"

H

F

H

FRONT

HIND

(See "Track Patterns:
Flat-Footed Walkers
& Armadillos" on
pages 324 & 326.)

QUICK ID TIPS

- Among the largest tracks in our region; clear prints are unmistakable.

- Each foot has five toes and a wide, robust palm pad.

- When heel pads register, hind tracks may resemble a large, bare human foot.

Black Bear

Ursus americanus

TRACKS

Black Bear tracks are dominated by broad, robust palm pads, which cover a larger area than all of the toe pads combined. The palm pads are largest on the outside of the track and narrower toward the inside. Five toes are arranged in an arc in front of the palm, separated by a wide, slightly curved negative space. Opposite that of a human footprint, the pinkie (toe 5) on the outside of the track is the largest, while the thumb (toe 1) on the inside is the smallest and sometimes does not register clearly. Stout claws are sometimes prominent but may not register on firm substrates.

Front tracks are wider than hinds. A single heel pad, similar in size to the largest toe, sometimes registers behind the palm. Front tracks measure 3¾"–5¼" long x 3¼"–5½" wide.

Hind tracks are longer than fronts when the heel registers, which it usually does. A single, large pad covers the entire heel. There is a wedge of fur between the palm and the heel on the inside of the track, analogous to the arch in our own feet. Hind tracks measure 3¾"–7" long x 3½"–5" wide.

TRACK PATTERNS & GAITS

Black Bears typically walk leaving an overstep track pattern. The front feet often toe in, especially in larger males. Bears sometimes trot and lope and are capable of galloping for short distances.

HABITAT

Primarily wooded areas, including wooded swamps. Most common in large forests.

OTHER SIGN

Scat

Scat: Bear scat varies greatly with diet, from firm logs to amorphous plops. One common form is a wide, segmented cylinder with blunt ends measuring 1"–2½" in diameter and 5"–12" in length. Segments may be linked together or completely separate. Most scat breaks apart easily and often includes easily recognizable insect remains, nut shells, fruit or berry seeds, or grasses. Bears deposit scat six to eight times per day, apparently at random. Scat may accumulate along travel routes, near bedding sites, or in areas with abundant food.

Bear Trails: On specific sections of trail, Black Bears will step in exactly the same spots each time they pass, stomping to deposit scent from glands on their feet. Over time, this wears a series of distinct oval impressions into the trail. These "stomp trails" are commonly associated with marking trees. Black Bears also create smooth trails along regular travel routes and use human trails when convenient.

Marked cedar post

Marking Trees: Black Bears rub, bite, and claw trees as a way of communicating with other bears. Red Pines are common targets, as are utility poles and other creosote-treated wood, trail signs, and cedar posts. Rubbing often leaves hairs lodged in the grain or bark. Bites can resemble damage from a .22 rifle or appear as diagonal "dot and dash" gouge marks. Claw marks may be visible, though most claw marks on trees are from climbing. Black Bears also straddle and walk over saplings, and they break or bite the tops off of conifers. Marking trees is common along regular travel routes.

ACTIVITY

Hibernates through the winter in northern climates. When not hibernating, bears may be active at any time. Often diurnal in wilderness areas but usually nocturnal near human habitation.

SIMILAR TRACKS

In the Midwest, clear prints are unmistakable. **Cougars** have proportionally smaller, trapezoid-shaped palm pads. Toes are arranged in a stronger arc around the palm, leaving a C-shaped negative space.

NOTES

The Black Bear is both the largest carnivore in the Midwest and our most common large carnivore. The Midwest is home to about 65,000 Black Bears, primarily in the northern forests, compared with just 4,500 Wolves and 250 Cougars. Though members of the Carnivora order, Black Bears eat a diverse diet that is mostly plant-based and includes grasses, herbaceous plants, fruits, berries, nuts, insects, and only occasional meat, including carrion. In populated areas, they may forage through garbage and at bird feeders.

The Black Bear's fluid, rolling walk may appear lumbering or even clumsy, but they are both incredibly strong and remarkably agile. They can sprint as fast as a deer and are good swimmers and excellent climbers, often foraging in trees and climbing to escape perceived threats. They are strong diggers and capable of excavating hibernation dens in hard, rocky soils. They can turn over large rocks and tear apart logs in search of insects and move easily across the landscape, walking directly through dense vegetation, in a near-constant search for food.

Black Bears are generally solitary, except when raising cubs. Litters of one to three cubs are born in the hibernation den and often stay with their mother until the following spring. Black Bears may also congregate in areas with abundant food, including garbage dumps. Mature Black Bears have no natural enemies, but they evolved in a time of much larger predators and can be surprisingly skittish—more like their smaller cousin the Raccoon than the region's largest carnivore. Though generally relaxed, they are shy and easily startled. When surprised, they typically run away and may climb a tree. Though generally timid, they are still powerful carnivores and can cause significant damage even if they are not being intentionally aggressive.

ORDER CARNIVORA; FAMILIES FELIDAE & CANIDAE

The Midwest is home to four species of felids and six species of canids. Colloquially known as cats and dogs, these two families of carnivores include some of the most charismatic species in nature, such as the Gray Wolf (*Canis lupus*) and Cougar (*Puma concolor*), as well as our most familiar companion animals, the Domestic Dog (*Canis familiaris*) and Domestic Cat (*Felis catus*). Each family has a recognizable body form: canids look like dogs, and felids look like cats.

Canids and felids are cursorial mammals: animals adapted for running fast or for long periods of time. Most canids do both, galloping in short bursts and traveling in a brisk trot. Felids typically run only when pursuing prey or fleeing. Cats are natural sprinters, very dangerous over short distances. To aid in running, cats and dogs have evolved flexible shoulders, long legs, and what is known as a digitigrade posture—walking on their toes with their heels high off the ground.

TRACKS

Cats and dogs have similar foot structures and leave similar-looking tracks that show four toes (numbered 2–5) and a fully fused palm pad. Front feet have a small, clawed thumb (toe 1) and a single heel pad that rarely register. Hind feet lack a thumb (toe 1). Front tracks are generally wider and rounder and have larger palm pads than hinds. Hind tracks tend to show greater symmetry and a taller negative space. Distinguishing felid and canid tracks is occasionally difficult, and many popular diagnostics are not reliable. Cat tracks are not all round, while some dog tracks are; dog tracks don't always show claws, while some cat tracks do.

Felids have large palms that usually make up most of the area of the track. Palm pads are trapezoidal, with two leading lobes and three trailing lobes. Tracks are asymmetrical, with the middle toe (toe 3) leading. The negative space between the toes and palms is usually narrow and C-shaped (think *C* for "cat"). Toes and palms tend to register at the same depth. Sharp, retractable claws register only occasionally.

Canids have large toes that usually make up most of the area of the track. Palm pads tend to be smaller and roughly triangular, showing a single leading lobe. Tracks usually appear symmetrical and have a taller X- or H-shaped negative space. Toes often register deeper than palms, particularly in hind tracks. Claws register reliably in some species but inconsistently in others, including Domestic Dogs.

CATS & DOGS

Cat

Bobcat

Lynx

Cougar

Swift
Fox

Gray
Fox

Red
Fox

Dog

Coyote

Gray
Wolf

FRONT

max. 1⁹⁄₁₆"

min. 1"

F

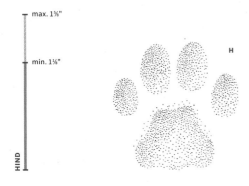

HIND

max. 1⅝"

min. 1⅛"

H

(See "Track Patterns: Cats & Dogs" on pages 328 & 330.)

QUICK ID TIPS

- Round tracks between the size of a quarter and a ping-pong ball.
- Oval toes asymmetrically arranged in a shallow arc in front of the palm.
- Retractable claws rarely show.

Domestic Cat
Felis Catus

TRACKS

Domestic Cats leave round, blocky-looking feline tracks, with four toes and a trapezoidal palm pad. The toes appear oval and are proportionally larger and arranged in a straighter line than in other felids. The toes are arranged asymmetrically, with the middle toe (toe 3) registering the farthest forward. The palm pad, though less prominent than in Bobcat tracks, is still large and has two leading and three trailing lobes, though these are not always distinct. The negative space between the toes and the palm is typically C-shaped. Toes and palm register at the same depth. Sharp, retractable claws do not register often.

- Front tracks have a larger palm pad and thinner negative space than hinds. They are usually less symmetrical and often larger and rounder, but not always. A clawed thumb (toe 1) and small heel pad high on the foot rarely register. Front tracks measure 1"–1⁹⁄₁₆" long x 1"–1¾" wide.

- Hind tracks are usually more symmetrical, longer, and narrower than fronts. They have a smaller palm and a larger negative space that sometimes appears H-shaped. Hind tracks measure 1⅛"–1⅝" long x 1"–1⅝" wide.

TRACK PATTERNS & GAITS

Usually walks leaving a direct-register, indirect-register, or overstep track pattern and slightly meandering trails. Speeds up into lopes, bounds, and rotary sequence gallops. Cats walk with a direct register in snow, often sweeping their feet to the outside of the trail in a way that leaves a pattern of closely spaced triangles.

HABITAT

Most common in urban, suburban, and rural areas but may be found almost anywhere with sufficient cover and available small prey. Prefers transitional areas with a mix of cover and open ground.

OTHER SIGN

Scat

Scat: Long, cylindrical scat, typically segmented with blunt ends and little or no twisting. Measures about ⅜"–⅞" in diameter and 2"–5" long. Frequently deposited in a scrape and often covered. Most commonly left on soft substrates, which make the scat easier to cover.

Spray/Scent Posts: Cats spray urine onto marking posts to communicate with each other. Usually visible only in the winter, but the distinctive "litter box" smell of cat urine is detectable any time of year.

ACTIVITY

Active year-round. Activity patterns depend on how accustomed the individual is to humans. An outdoor house cat or neighborhood stray may be quite active during the day, while a completely feral cat is likely to be fully nocturnal and highly elusive.

SIMILAR TRACKS

Gray Foxes have larger toes arranged in a steeper arc around the palm. They have proportionally smaller, triangular palm pads and a larger, X-shaped negative space. **Bobcat** tracks are usually larger and have proportionally larger palm pads. Their toes are more teardrop-shaped and are arranged in a steeper arc. Front tracks typically appear more asymmetrical, while hind tracks are longer and have a taller negative space.

NOTES

Thanks to their exceptional hunting skills and their long, close association with people, Domestic Cats have become the most abundant and widespread carnivore in the world. There are about 40 million cats in the Midwest alone: 25 million share our homes, and another 15 million or so live fully outdoors. Agile, graceful, and loaded with personality, Domestic Cats make wonderful companions. I have always lived with cats and usually have one sitting on my lap when I am writing. Since learning about the toll they take on wildlife, however, I no longer allow any cat in my care to venture outdoors.

Cats are common in urban, suburban, and rural areas and occasionally show up in remote wilderness far from human habitation. Skilled and efficient hunters, they prey primarily on small rodents—the reason they were domesticated— and birds. Tragically, Domestic Cats kill between 1.3 and 4 billion (with a *b*) wild birds every year in the United States alone. Most are killed by cats that live outdoors full-time, but 30% are taken by cats that share our homes. Cats are naturally surplus killers, hunting when prey is available, not just when they are hungry. Even well-fed house cats will hunt songbirds as readily as they play with a feather or laser toy. One of the largest single threats to wild bird populations, Domestic Cats have been implicated in the extinction of 40 bird species worldwide—one quarter of all those in modern times.

When living with people, Domestic Cats show a number of kitten-like behaviors: tolerating other cats, looking to people for food, and sleeping close to people and other cats. Away from people, they easily revert to the wild and may avoid human contact. As with other felids, cats are quite secretive and may go unnoticed even where populations are large. Outdoor cats are generally solitary animals, like our native wildcats. However, in areas where food is concentrated—including where they are fed by people—they may form colonies. These colonies are groups of females and juveniles, with roving males moving in and out.

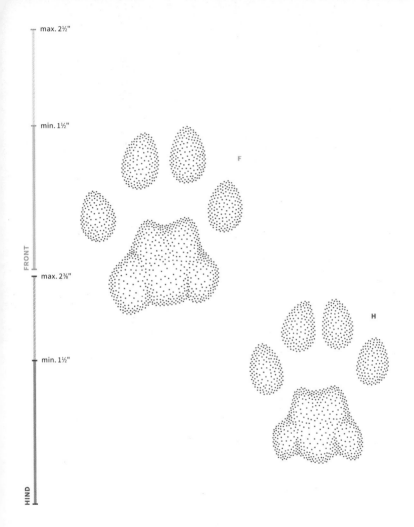

max. 2½"

min. 1½"

F

max. 2⅜"

min. 1½"

FRONT

HIND

H

(See "Track Patterns: Cats & Dogs" on pages 328 & 330.)

QUICK ID TIPS

- Round tracks between the size of a golf ball and a tennis ball.

- Front tracks are asymmetrical, with a large palm.

- Hind tracks are more symmetrical, with a smaller palm and taller negative space.

Bobcat
Lynx rufus

TRACKS

Bobcat tracks have a typical felid form, showing four toes and a large trapezoidal palm pad. The toes appear oval or egg-shaped and wrap around the front of the palm in a steep arc. The leading edge of the palm is indented, and the trailing edge may appear concave or tri-lobed. The pads are hairless and leave clear impressions in good substrate. Tracks are flat, with toes and palm registering at the same depth. Sharp, retractable claws rarely register.

- Front tracks are larger, rounder, and more asymmetrical than hinds. The middle toe (toe 3) is farthest forward, and the palm pad often appears tilted. The large palm is about the size of all four toe impressions combined. The negative space is slender and distinctly C-shaped. A small, clawed thumb (toe 1) high on the foot and a single heel pad rarely register. Front tracks measure 1½"–2½" long x 1⅝"–2½" wide.

- Hind tracks are more symmetrical than fronts and have a smaller palm pad. The negative space between the palm and toes is taller than in the front and may appear C- or H-shaped. Hinds are typically narrower than fronts and may appear oval rather than circular overall. Hind tracks measure 1½"–2⅜" long x 1½"–2½" wide.

TRACK PATTERNS & GAITS

Trail in the snow

Usually walks leaving a direct register or, more often, an overstep pattern. May trot across open spaces leaving a direct register. Speeds up into lopes, bounds, and rotary-sequence gallops when chasing or fleeing. Walks in deep snow, leaving a direct-register pattern. The feet tend to drag along the outside of the trail, sometimes creating a string of closely spaced triangles.

HABITAT

Bobcats are habitat generalists that can live nearly anywhere with sufficient cover and adequate prey. They do well in second-growth forests with heavy underbrush, swamps, and old fields, and along bluffs and rock outcroppings. They tend to avoid large, open areas and may do poorly in areas that are heavily impacted by agriculture.

OTHER SIGN

Scat

Scat: Long, cylindrical scat, often segmented with blunt ends measuring ½"–1" in diameter and 3"–9" long. Scat contains only animal matter and occasionally a bit of grass. Scat is dense, does not flatten as easily as that of Coyotes, and can be difficult to break apart. The interior is often a twisted, compacted mat of fur and bones, but the exterior is usually smooth, and bones rarely protrude. Bobcats do not usually cover their scat but may deposit it in scrapes.

Scratching Posts: Bobcats sharpen their claws by scratching on trees, logs, and stumps. Claw marks are generally about 3'–4' off the ground.

Spray/Scent Posts: Bobcats spray urine onto marking posts as communication. Stumps, rocks, and low-hanging branches along trails are common targets. Posts can usually only be seen in winter, when urine colors the snow, but can be smelled any time of year and have a distinctive odor similar to that of a litter box.

Cached Kills: Like other cats, Bobcats may rake dirt and debris over kills with their front paws. Rake marks usually range from 1'–1½' long, compared with 1' or less for a Domestic Cat and 1½'–3' for a Cougar. Larger carcasses may be only partially covered.

ACTIVITY

Active year-round. Mainly crepuscular and nocturnal, Bobcats are most active from late afternoon to midnight and in the hours before sunrise.

SIMILAR TRACKS

Domestic Cat tracks are smaller, with proportionally larger toes arranged in a straighter line and a slimmer negative space in the hind track. **Cougar** and **Lynx** tracks are larger. **Canid** tracks are more symmetrical, with proportionally larger toes and smaller palms. The negative space is usually taller and often X-shaped. **Coyote** tracks are typically larger and usually show claw marks. **Gray Fox** tracks, which often do not show claws, are usually smaller, and their hind tracks are typically narrower. **Raccoon** tracks can look similar when only four toes show. Raccoon toes are longer and narrower. Their palms are smoother and often show a more deeply indented trailing edge.

NOTES

Bobcats are roughly twice the size of a typical house cat, with males roughly a third larger than females. The most common wildcat in North America, they range from southern Canada to central Mexico and were once found everywhere in what is now the Lower 48. A combination of hunting, lethal predator control, and conversion of land for agriculture from the early 1800s to the mid-1900s extirpated Bobcats from most of the Midwest. In recent decades, they have begun to return to much of their historical range. Though widespread and common in some areas, they are usually secretive, making sightings rare.

Like most cats, Bobcats are obligate carnivores subsisting exclusively on meat. They occasionally eat small quantities of grass but do not consume fruit or berries like wild canids do. They feed primarily on rabbits, usually cottontails, and tend to be most common where rabbits are abundant. They also feed on small mammals, game birds, deer, and Porcupine. Like Fishers and Cougars, Bobcats usually kill Porcupines by attacking them on the nose. They consume nearly everything but the skin, which may be left nearly intact. Bobcats ambush deer in their beds and kill with a bite to the throat. They often eat the hindquarters first, opening a round hole that expands as they feed. Like Coyotes, Bobcats can bite through deer ribs but not leg bones. But unlike a Coyote's carnassial teeth alone, the Bobcat's raspy tongue can completely clean the bones of meat.

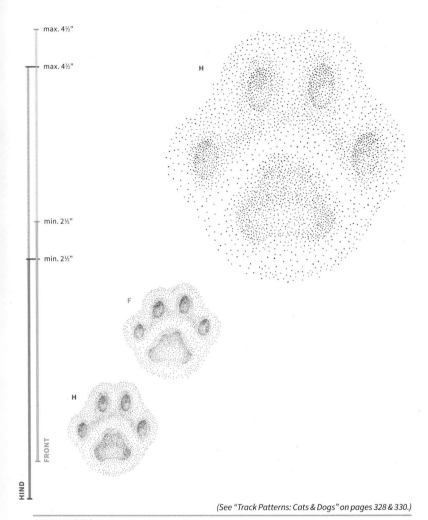

max. 4½"

max. 4½"

min. 2½"

min. 2½"

H

F

H

FRONT

HIND

(See "Track Patterns: Cats & Dogs" on pages 328 & 330.)

QUICK ID TIPS

- Typical felid track form but often blurred by thick fur.
- In deep snow, toes often spread to leave a cross-shaped compression.
- Large tracks relative to stride length.

Lynx
Lynx canadensis

TRACKS

Lynx have exceptionally large feet for their body size, serving as natural snow-shoes. Indeed, we most often encounter Lynx tracks in snow. The bottoms of Lynx feet are covered with dense fur that makes their toes and palms appear smaller and less defined than those of other felids, with rounder edges and smoother curves. Like other cats, Lynx show four asymmetrically arranged toes and a trapezoidal-shaped palm pad in each track. Due to the thick fur, the negative tends to be larger than in other felids but is still generally C-shaped. Sharp, retractable claws rarely show. The way the toes are arranged around the palm gives the leading edge of many tracks a stepped appearance, and compressions in deep snow often have a distinctive cross shape. Tracks measure 2½"–4½" long x 2½"–5" wide.

- Front tracks are round and more asymmetrical than hinds, with the middle toe (toe 3) set the farthest forward. The thumb (toe 1) and heel pad rarely register.
- Hind feet are more symmetrical than front and have longer toes. When unsplayed, hind tracks are smaller and narrower than fronts. When toes are extended, hind tracks are often wider and larger overall.

Tracks in the snow

TRACK PATTERNS & GAITS

Walks leaving a direct-register pattern of relatively shallow, cross-shaped compression in deep snow. On firm surfaces, usually leaves an overstep pattern. Often chases Snowshoe Hare through deep snow in a bound. Like other cats, Lynx sometimes trot, lope, or gallop. Because they have such large feet for their body size, Lynx sink less in deep snow than other animals that leave similarly sized tracks and trails.

HABITAT

Northern coniferous forests with deep winter snowpack. Generally absent from densely populated areas. Preys almost exclusively on Snowshoe Hare and occupies the same habitats.

OTHER SIGN

Scat

Scat: Long, cylindrical scat, usually segmented, with blunt ends and no twisting. Measures about ½"–1" in diameter and 3"–10" long. Adults rarely cover their scat, which is often left in exposed or slightly elevated areas. Strict carnivores, Lynx leave scat consisting exclusively of animal matter and occasional bits of grass. Bones are usually encased in scat and do not protrude.

Scratching Posts: Lynx sharpen their claws by scratching trees, logs, and stumps. Claw marks are generally 3'–4' off the ground or above peak winter snowpack.

Spray/Scent Posts: Lynx spray urine onto stumps, rocks, and low branches for communication. These posts can usually be seen only in winter, when the urine colors the snow a telltale yellow, but have a distinctive "litter box" smell that can be detected at any time of year.

ACTIVITY

Active year-round. Predominantly crepuscular and nocturnal. Usually rests during the day under shelter or on a tree limb.

SIMILAR TRACKS

Other felids and **canids** sink much farther into deep snow and take longer strides relative to their track size. Those with similarly sized tracks have much less fur on the bottoms of their feet, and their toe and palm pads register more clearly.

NOTES

Lynx are animals of the far northern forests and are highly adapted to cold weather and deep snow. Lynx are more prey-specific than their cousin the Bobcat, feeding almost exclusively on Snowshoe Hare. Not only do the Lynx's range and habitat mirror those of the Snowshoe Hare, their populations rise and fall together in roughly 10-year cycles. When hare populations are high, Lynx populations grow in response to the abundant food. Increased predation from the growing Lynx population causes hare populations to decline. As food becomes scarce, Lynx populations decline. Hare populations then grow again, continuing the cycle. During periods of declining hare populations, Lynx may disperse in search of food and turn up far outside of their normal range.

Lynx generally walk while hunting and tend to stick to cover. They cross open and exposed areas but often speed up to a trot to do so. They are more apt than other cats to follow trails and little-used roads, and they are killed on roads more commonly than other cat species.

Lynx do not generally kill large prey, and their caching behavior is less developed than in other Midwestern cats. Like other cats, Lynx are solitary, except for the young, who usually stay with their mother through their first winter.

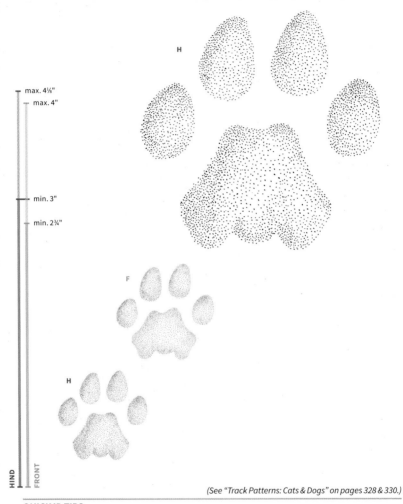

max. 4⅛"
max. 4"
min. 3"
min. 2¾"

H

F

H

HIND
FRONT

(See "Track Patterns: Cats & Dogs" on pages 328 & 330.)

QUICK ID TIPS

- Round, asymmetrical tracks the size of a baseball or softball.

- Typical felid form with four toes, a trapezoidal palm, and claws that rarely show.

- Front palm pad often larger than all four toe pads combined.

Cougar
Puma concolor

TRACKS

Cougar tracks are dominated by a large, trapezoidal palm showing two leading lobes and three trailing lobes. Four toes are arranged in an asymmetrical arc around the front of the palm, with the middle toe (toe 3) set farthest forward. Toes appear oval or teardrop-shaped—blockier in mature males and more tapered in females. Tracks are flat, with toe and palm pads registering at the same depth. Sharp, strongly curved retractable claws rarely register.

- Front tracks are larger, wider ,and more asymmetrical than hinds, with a slimmer negative space. The palm often makes up most of the area of the track and is usually larger than all four toe impressions combined. The C-shaped negative space is narrower in males than in females. A clawed thumb (toe 1) and single heel pad rarely register. Cougars often flick their front feet as they walk, slightly blurring the tracks. Front tracks measure 2¾"–4" long x 2¾"–4¼" wide.

- Hind tracks are smaller, more symmetrical, and typically narrower than fronts, with a smaller palm pad. The negative space is taller than in fronts and may appear C- or H-shaped. Hind tracks measure 3"–4⅛" long x 2½"–4¾" wide.

TRACK PATTERNS & GAITS

Usually walks leaving an overstep pattern on firm surfaces and a direct register in deeper substrates such as snow. Tends to wind across the landscape while hunting and follow a straighter path when traveling. Occasionally trots or lopes. Speeds up into bounds and gallops.

HABITAT

Lives in a wide range of habitats, generally mirroring habitats of deer, their primary food source. Generally stays on steep terrain or close to cover but crosses exposed areas when traveling. Makes heavy use of exposed ridges because of the safety, sun, and view of terrain they provide.

OTHER SIGN

Scat

Scat: Long, cylindrical scat, usually segmented with no twisting, and often with blunt ends. Measures about ¾"–1½" in diameter and 6"–17" long. May be found on a scrape, near a den, lay, or kill site, or along a trail. Sometimes covered. Cats are stricter carnivores than dogs, and their scat consists almost exclusively of animal matter. Bones are usually encased inside the scat and do not protrude.

Scratching Posts: Cougars sharpen their claws by scratching on trees, logs, and stumps; claw marks are generally about 5' off the ground.

Scrapes: Cougars mark their presence by scraping up mounds of dirt and debris with their hind feet and depositing urine or scat on top. Scrape marks generally measure 8"–12" wide; Bobcat scratches are usually less than 8" in width.

Cached Kills: Typical Cougar prey is too large for the animal to eat at one time and is generally covered and consumed over several days. Like other cats, Cougars cover their kills by using their front paws to rake dirt and debris toward the kill from many directions. Rake marks usually range from 1½' to 3' long (Bobcat rake marks are usually 1'–1½').

ACTIVITY

Active year-round. Predominantly nocturnal but sometimes active in daytime or at twilight.

SIMILAR TRACKS

Domestic Dog tracks are usually more symmetrical, with larger toes and a smaller, triangular palm pad. Their palm is rarely larger than two or three toe pads combined and has a round rather than bi-lobed leading edge. If claws show, they are stout rather than thin and sharp. **Bobcat** tracks are smaller and tend to show a taller negative space in the hind track. **Lynx** tracks may be the same size but have smaller palm pads and usually appear less distinct. Lynx take shorter strides and do not sink as far into deep snow. **Black Bear** tracks can be mistaken for those of Cougars when only four toes register. Bears have larger, wider, kidney bean–shaped palm pads, and their toes are arranged in a straighter line.

NOTES

Cougars have the largest natural range of any North American mammal and once roamed across all of the Lower 48. In the 1800s, predator-control programs wiped Cougars out of the eastern U.S. except for a small population in southern Florida. Today, the only breeding populations in the Midwest are in far western Nebraska and South Dakota.

Few animals elicit such strong emotions as Cougars. Reports of sightings often stir awe and frequently make the local news. Upon careful investigation, however, the vast majority of trail camera images and track photos sent to Midwestern state DNR offices as evidence of Cougars prove to be of Bobcats, Domestic Cats, Coyotes, Domestic Dogs, or Black Bears. But not all: some reports remain inconclusive, while a few prove to be of Cougars. Young male Cougars may disperse hundreds of miles in search of territory and a mate. With no females to the east, bachelors may wander halfway across the continent, looking for love in all the wrong places. Every state in the Midwest except for Ohio and Kentucky has confirmed at least one Cougar sighting since 2010. Such sightings are exceedingly rare. Dispersing Cougars may linger for weeks in one area but will inevitably move on. While traveling, Cougars are more likely to cross roads and trails than to follow them.

Cougars are primarily large-game hunters, feeding mainly on deer. Cougars can sprint faster than deer but can't endure a prolonged chase, and they prefer to stalk to within 20'–30', then pounce, killing with a bite to the neck. They usually drag the carcass to a sheltered area, such as a ravine or a thicket, to feed. Cougars also eat Porcupines, Beavers, Raccoons, foxes, and Coyotes and may take livestock on rare occasions.

(See "Track Patterns: Cats & Dogs" on pages 328 & 330.)

max. 1⅝"

min. 1"

FRONT

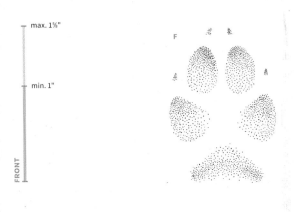

max. 1⅝"

min. 1"

HIND

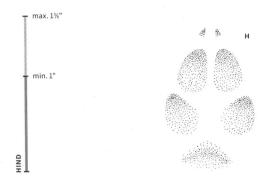

QUICK ID TIPS

- Smallest wild canid track in the Midwest.

- Palm pads usually register lightly and may not show at all.

- Feet are sometimes covered with thick fur, obscuring track details.

Swift Fox
Vulpes velox

TRACKS

Swift Foxes leave the smallest tracks of any wild canid in the Midwest. Tracks are symmetrical, with four prominent toes and a small, triangular palm. The toes register more deeply than the palms, which sometimes barely show at all. Small claws often register. The bottoms of Swift Fox feet are furred, with the amount of fur varying among individuals. The toes and palm are often somewhat blurred, and the negative space usually appears large. Swift Foxes with heavily furred feet may leave tracks resembling a miniature Red Fox's, with small toe impressions and a callused ridge forming a "bar" across the palm.

- The front track is nearly round and may be wider than long. The palm is broad, but sometimes appears short, like a boomerang. The negative space is also broad and may appear more H-shaped than X-shaped. A thumb (toe 1) and single heel pad sit high on the foot and rarely register. Front tracks measure 1"–1⅝" long x ⅞"–1½" wide.

- Hind tracks are smaller, narrower, and more elongated than front. The negative space is X-shaped. Hind tracks measure 1"–1⅝" long x ⅞"–1¼" wide.

TRACK PATTERNS & GAITS
Often travels in a rocking-horse lope. Also trots leaving direct-register and side-trot patterns. Slows to a walk when investigating and speeds up into a gallop.

HABITAT
Arid lands including shortgrass prairie and open shrubland.

OTHER SIGN

Scat: One or more long droppings ranging from ³⁄₁₆" to ⅝" in diameter and 2" to 4½" in length, often containing bone fragments encased in hair. Always consists of animal remains. Other foxes may deposit fruit scat in season. Often deposited in latrines at the base of prominent shrubs.

Burrows: Swift Foxes inhabit burrows year-round. Entrances measure about 8" wide and are often keyhole-shaped. Each fox uses multiple burrows, and each burrow typically has two or three entrances. Each burrow's main entrance often has an obvious mound of excavated dirt in front of it. Tracks, hair, and bones may be evident in the disturbed soil near the entrance.

Urine: Swift Fox urine has a pungent odor reminiscent of skunk or Red Fox urine.

ACTIVITY
Active year-round. Mostly nocturnal but sometimes active during the day.

SIMILAR TRACKS
Gray Fox tracks are usually larger but overlap in size. Gray Foxes have less fur on the bottoms of their feet, typically register their palm pads more clearly, and are less likely to show claws. Gray Foxes are uncommon in the open, arid country that Swift Foxes prefer. **Red Fox** tracks are larger. **Small domestic dogs** often show stout nail marks, usually register their palms as deeply as their toes, and tend to leave more-irregular track patterns.

NOTES

The Swift Fox is the smallest wild canid in the Midwest and leaves the most delicate tracks and trails. An animal of the arid grasslands, it is also our most carnivorous fox; its diet consists primarily of small mammals, rabbits, birds, insects, and lizards. Only a small fraction of its diet consists of plant material, which is not usually evident in scat. In the winter, Swift Foxes cache excess food under the snow.

Once widespread in the West, the Swift Fox has suffered from habitat loss, hunting, and trapping. Less wary than other foxes, and just as curious, it is especially vulnerable to human hunters. With recent conservation efforts and the collapse of the fur industry, Swift Foxes' range is expanding again. They have been reintroduced to the grasslands in the western portion of our region, but they remain an endangered species.

Swift Foxes inhabit their dens year-round, using them as shelter from the weather and from predators. Each fox has several dens in its home range, and each den has several entrances. Swift Foxes are remarkably fast for such a small animal, hence their common name. Nonetheless, they are vulnerable to both Coyotes and Domestic Dogs on the open prairie, and they usually try to escape underground when threatened.

Swift Foxes often pair for life but travel and hunt individually. Litters of three to six young are born in an underground chamber in the den in late winter or early spring. Pups stay in their den for the first month, are weaned at three months, and disperse by the end of summer.

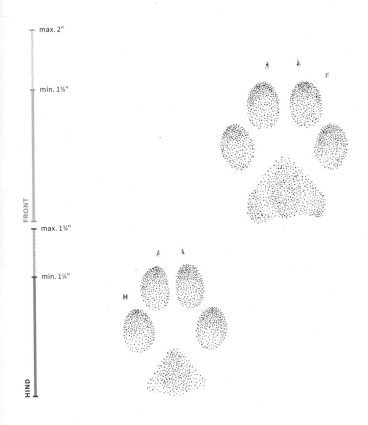

max. 2"

min. 1⅜"

FRONT

max. 1¾"

min. 1¼"

HIND

F

H

(See "Track Patterns: Cats & Dogs" on pages 328 & 330.)

QUICK ID TIPS

- Small canid tracks with four symmetrically arranged toes and a triangular palm.

- Semi-retractable claws often do not register.

- Prints may appear feline and are often confused with Domestic Cat tracks.

Gray Fox
Urocyon cinereoargenteus

TRACKS

Gray Fox tracks have a typical canid form: they are symmetrical with four large toes and triangular palms. The tracks are usually sloped, especially the hinds. Toes tend to register more deeply than palms, and the leading tips of the toes tend to register more deeply than the trailing edge. There is little fur between the toes, and pads register crisply in good substrate. The tracks also have some feline characteristics and are often mistaken for Domestic Cat tracks. Semi-retractable claws often do not show in the tracks. Front tracks may appear round and have relatively large palms for a wild canid.

- Front tracks are larger and rounder than hinds and sometimes appear circular. The palm pad is typically the size of two to three toe pads combined and often shows prominent lobes along the trailing edge. The negative space is typically H-shaped. Front tracks measure 1⅜"–2" long x 1⅛"–1¾" wide.

- Hind tracks are smaller and narrower than fronts and have a taller, X-shaped negative space. The palm often registers lightly. It may appear triangular but frequently shows as an oval about the size of one of the toes, or as an oval with two small "wings." Hind tracks measure 1¼"–1¾" long x ⅞"–1⅜" wide.

TRACK PATTERNS & GAITS

Travels in a trot, often leaving a slight understep indirect register, with the toes of the front foot visible just in front of the hind track. Also uses a straddle trot but rarely a side-trot. Avoids deep snow when possible, readily taking to compacted trails.

HABITAT

Wooded areas, brushland, and fragmented landscapes. Prefers areas with more cover than the Red Fox does. Adapts to suburban landscapes if there is sufficient cover.

OTHER SIGN

Scat: Typically one or more long droppings ranging from ⅜" to ¾" in diameter and 3" to 6" long. Structure varies with diet and often contains bone fragments. In summer, scat may include grasses, fruit or berry seeds, and insect remains. Often deposited at trail junctions or on raised surfaces. Easily confused with smaller Red Fox or Coyote scat.

Dens: Gray Foxes typically use natural cavities as dens; entrances vary in size and shape and are sometimes marked by hair, small bones, or scraps. When pups begin to emerge from the den, the ground becomes packed down from continuous play and feeding and is littered with tiny scat.

Caches: Buries excess food, typically covering it with loose dirt, turf, or moss. Excavated caches are wide, shallow depressions.

ACTIVITY

Active year-round but may hole up for many days at a time when snow is deep and soft. Predominantly nocturnal or crepuscular but sometimes active during the day.

SIMILAR TRACKS

Domestic Cat tracks are asymmetrical, with smaller toes and a more C-shaped negative space. Cats' palms are larger and trapezoidal rather than triangular. Their tracks are usually flat, with the toes and palm registering at the same depth. **Red Fox** tracks are typically larger. The dense fur on the bottoms of their feet usually makes their toes and palm appear smaller and less sharply defined. A bar is often visible across the palm of the front track. Claws register much more often. **Swift Fox** tracks may appear similar if the foot is not heavily furred. They are usually more oval, show claw marks more often, and have a smaller front palm pad. They show little overlap in range and habitat with Gray Foxes.

NOTES

Gray Foxes possess cat-like agility. Their trails often travel up angled tree trunks and along logs, walls, and fences, and may even disappear into the branches of shrubs and trees. Adept climbers, they sometimes forage, or even bed, in shrubs and trees. Gray Foxes are less likely than larger canids to bed in the open, preferring to find natural cover. They are also less adapted to the cold, and their shorter legs are less suited for moving through snow. They prefer to avoid deep snow and will usually seek packed trails to travel on, including roads.

Like most other canids, Gray Foxes primarily hunt smaller mammals. Rabbits make up about half of their diet, with mice, voles, and birds composing most of the rest. Red Foxes, by contrast, typically rely more on voles and mice than on rabbits. Gray Foxes are also more omnivorous than many canids and may eat large quantities of fruit, berries, and large insects in season. These supplementary foods may compose nearly 10% of their annual diet.

Gray Foxes typically travel alone or in pairs. Litters of one to seven young are born in a natal den in March, April, or May. The male helps raise the young but doesn't occupy the den. Pups are weaned at three months and travel with the mother before dispersing in late fall or early winter.

Gray Foxes are occasionally preyed on by Coyotes or Bobcats but are more likely to fall victim to humans or Domestic Dogs. As with Red Foxes, rabies and distemper are common in Gray Fox populations.

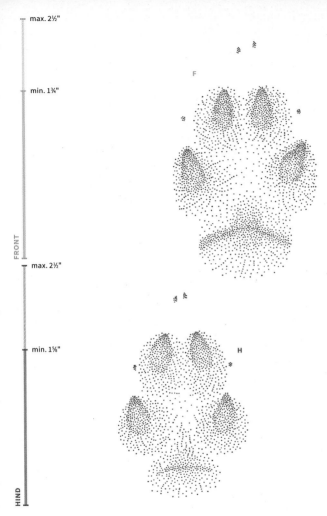

max. 2½"

min. 1¾"

F

FRONT

max. 2½"

min. 1⅝"

H

HIND

(See "Track Patterns: Cats & Dogs" on pages 328 & 330.)

QUICK ID TIPS

- Typical canid track showing four toes, a triangular palm, and an X-shaped negative space.
- Thick fur affects track appearance, often blurring pads and exaggerating the negative space.
- Shows a distinctive bar across the palm pad of the front track.

Red Fox
Vulpes vulpes

TRACKS

Red Fox feet are large for their body size and covered with dense fur, which is thickest in winter. Tracks show typical canid form, with four symmetrically arranged toes and a small, triangular palm. The track is usually slanted, with toes registering deeper than palms. Fur covers much of the toe and palm pads, often reducing their size and blurring their edges. The X-shaped negative space is often, but not always, exaggerated by the fur and may look like a rounded, domed rectangle in the middle of the track. A thin, callused ridge on the palm can appear as a "bar" in the track. The unfurred tips of the toe may be visible as teardrop-shaped impressions and are sometimes the only part of the toes that register. Fine claws often register but may be subtle or absent.

- Front tracks are oval to nearly round. The palm is about the size of one or two toe pads. The "bar" across the palm, which is diagnostic, is usually visible but may be subtle. Front tracks measure 1¾"–2½" long x 1⅜"–2¼" wide.

- Hind tracks are smaller and narrower than fronts, with a smaller palm. The outer toes (2 and 5) often tuck partly behind the middle toes (3 and 4), leaving a tall, narrow negative space. The palm "bar" may be visible. Hind tracks measure 1⅝"–2½" long x 1⅜"–1⅞" wide.

Track in mud

TRACK PATTERNS & GAITS

Red Fox trails usually appear narrow, precise, and elegant. They most often trot, leaving a direct-register or side-trot pattern. Short stretches of straddle trot patterns are also common. Direct-register trot patterns can be extremely narrow, with tracks forming a nearly straight line. Red Foxes use rocking-horse lopes and even gallops frequently, and they walk when moving slowly. They usually walk in deep snow, leaving a direct-register pattern or a bound leaving a series of 2x2 whole-body imprints.

HABITAT

Prefers a mixed habitat of brushland and fields. Adapts readily to human presence and is common in croplands, suburban areas, and even urban areas with enough brush or woods. Uncommon in continuous forest.

OTHER SIGN

Scat

Scat: One or more long droppings ranging from ⅜" to ¾" in diameter and 3" to 6" long. Structure varies with diet. Often contains bone fragments. In summer, scat may include grasses, fruit seeds, and insect remains. Often deposited at trail junctions or on raised surfaces. Easily confused with Gray Fox or Coyote scat, though Coyote scat is usually longer. Odor may be distinctive.

Dens: Found on open ground or areas with sparse cover and a good view of the surroundings, dens are often enlarged Woodchuck or Badger dens. The main entrance measures about 8"–9" in diameter and is usually marked with a fan of excavated earth. Tracks, hair, and a distinctive Red Fox odor are usually evident near the main entrance.

Odor: Red Fox urine has a distinctive, pungent odor similar to a skunk's spray.

ACTIVITY

Active year-round. Predominantly nocturnal, sometimes crepuscular. Occasionally active during the daytime, especially in winter.

SIMILAR TRACKS

Other **similarly sized canids** have much less fur on the bottoms of their feet. Their toes and palms usually register more crisply and often appear larger in the track. None shows the distinctive bar across the palm. **Coyote** tracks are usually larger. **Gray Fox** tracks are usually smaller. **Bobcat** tracks are asymmetrical, with smaller toes and a larger, trapezoidal palm. Their claws rarely register.

NOTES

Well adapted to human habitation, Red Foxes were the most abundant wild canid in most of our region until recently. Today they are being outcompeted by Coyotes across much of their range. Red Foxes are still common in many rural and suburban areas, and they can even be seen in some of our largest cities. Like all foxes, they are quite agile. While they do not climb, they commonly walk along fallen logs or up angled tree trunks.

Red Foxes stalk prey more than other canids do. Their hearing is uniquely sensitive to low frequencies, enabling them to hear small animals digging beneath grass, snow, or leaves. Once they locate their prey, they pounce. They primarily hunt voles, mice, and rabbits, supplemented with occasional birds, large insects, and, seasonally, fruits and berries. Birds are usually sheared of their feathers. Foxes consume voles and other small prey whole and carry larger animals off, caching whatever they do not eat immediately. They sometimes kill shrews but rarely eat them. They will also feed on carrion and may raid garbage cans.

Red Foxes form long-term pair bonds and frequently mate for life. They hunt and forage individually, but both parents care for young. Litters·of 4–10 pups are born March, April, or May in an underground den and stay with their parents until fall. Males disperse widely. Females usually stay closer, sometimes returning to their maternal den to help their parents raise the next year's litter. Dens are abandoned in the fall, and the foxes spend the winter in solitude. While they have few natural enemies, Red Foxes generally do not compete well with Coyotes. Common causes of mortality are vehicle traffic and disease. Red Foxes are one of the most common vectors for rabies, and populations frequently suffer from distemper and mange.

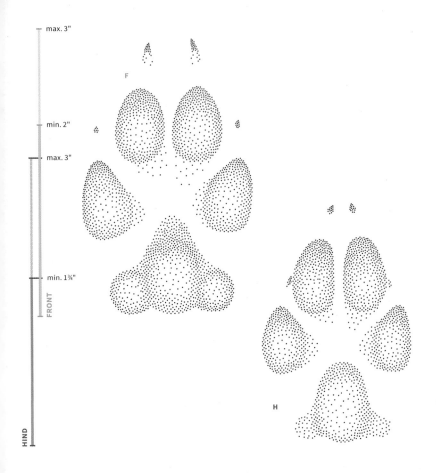

max. 3"

min. 2"

max. 3"

min. 1¾"

FRONT

HIND

F

H

(See "Track Patterns: Cats & Dogs" on pages 328 & 330.)

QUICK ID TIPS

- Classic canine track showing four large toes, a triangular palm, and an X-shaped negative space.

- Sharp claws usually point straight ahead or angle in toward the midline of the track.

- Hind tracks usually narrow, with inner and outermost toes nearly tucked behind the middle toes.

Coyote
Canis latrans

TRACKS

Coyote tracks have a typical canid form, with four large toes, a small palm, and an X-shaped negative space. Tracks are symmetrical, oval, and usually slanted, with toes registering deeper than palms. Toes usually point forward but may splay in soft substrate. Widely splayed tracks can appear nearly round, similar to those of many Domestic Dogs. Thin, sharp claws usually register. Claws on the middle toes (3 and 4) usually point straight ahead or in toward each other. The outer claws (on toes 2 and 5) register less reliably and often so close to the middle toes (3 and 4) as to be obscured.

- Front tracks are larger, wider, and more robust than hinds. The outer lobes of the triangular palm often extend farther back than the center, making the trailing edge of the pad concave. The clawed thumb (toe 1) and heel pad rarely register. Front tracks measure 2"–3" long x 1½"–2½" wide.

- Hind tracks are narrower than fronts, with the outer toes (2 and 5) often tucked partly behind the middle toes (3 and 4). The palm often registers lightly and may appear as an oval about the size of one of the toes. When the outer lobes register, they are typically fainter and may look like small "wings" at the base of the oval. Hind tracks measure 1¾"–3" long x 1⅜"–2⅛" wide.

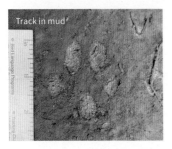
Track in mud

TRACK PATTERNS & GAITS

Coyotes display a wide range of symmetrical gaits. They usually trot while traveling and also walk frequently, most commonly leaving direct-register trot, side-trot, and overstep-walk track patterns. Direct-register trot patterns may be very narrow, with tracks registering in a nearly straight line. Coyotes gallop at speed, usually in a rotary sequence, and occasionally lope. They usually walk in deep snow, leaving a direct-register pattern, and sometimes bound, leaving a series of 2x2 whole-body imprints.

HABITAT

Prefers open brush, forest edges, and open farmland, but highly adaptable.

OTHER SIGN

Scat

Scat: One or more long droppings range from ⅜" to 1¼" in diameter. Similar to Red Fox scat in composition but can be much larger. Structure varies with diet. Often contains small bone fragments. In summer, scat may include grasses, fruit or berry seeds, and insect remains. Often deposited at trail junctions or on prominent, raised surfaces.

Natal Dens: Entrances measure about 12"–24" in diameter, larger than the entrances of fox dens but smaller than those of most Wolf dens. Dens typically have two entrances, with the main entrance often having a mound of dirt in front. Tracks and hair are usually evident in disturbed soil near the entrance.

ACTIVITY

Predominantly crepuscular but may be active at any time.

SIMILAR TRACKS

Domestic Dogs generally leave rounder tracks with more-splayed toes, larger palms, and a more H-shaped negative space. Dogs' palms tend to be proportionally wider and their tracks flatter, with palms registering about as deep as toes. Their claws are typically more stout, angle out more, and may be worn or trimmed. Their track patterns tend to be wider and less precise, while their trails tend to be more erratic. Some tracks and trails are remarkably similar.

Red Fox tracks are usually smaller. Fox feet are heavily furred, and their pads often appear smaller and less distinct. A bar is often visible across the front palm. Red Foxes are also lighter and do not sink as deeply into snow. **Bobcat** tracks are asymmetrical, with proportionally smaller toes, larger palms, and a thinner negative space. Bobcat tracks are usually smaller and rarely show claw marks. **Wolf** tracks are larger, with stouter claws and more-robust pads.

NOTES

Coyotes have adapted extremely well to modern human land use. Coyotes do not compete well with Wolves but are more resilient in the face of widespread predator control. While decades of carnivore-extermination policies extirpated Wolves from most of the Midwest, Coyote populations actually grew and expanded. Once almost exclusively a western species, Coyotes are now common throughout the Midwest. They have moved into many suburban and some urban habitats and can be found in green corridors in most of our largest cities. Coyotes often harass or exclude Red Foxes, and fox populations have declined as Coyotes have become more common.

Coyotes primarily hunt small mammals. Rabbits typically make up more than half of their diet, with mice and voles accounting for much of the rest. Opportunistic foragers, they also eat carrion, game birds, various other animals, and, seasonally, fruits and berries. Coyotes rarely kill large mammals but readily feed on animals that have died of other causes, including roadkill. They occasionally kill fawns or even adult deer that have been severely weakened.

The most common social structure for Coyotes is a mated pair or a small family group of three to five, though solitary individuals aren't rare. Coyotes may also form packs, which have a complex social structure similar to that of a Wolf pack. Groups usually disperse to hunt and forage, engaging in group yip howls before separating and after reuniting. Coyotes living in suburban and urban areas rarely howl but may bark instead.

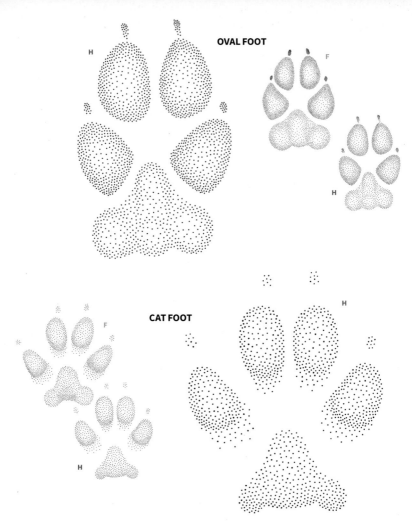

OVAL FOOT

H

F

H

CAT FOOT

F

H

H

(See "Track Patterns: Cats & Dogs" on pages 328 & 330.)

QUICK ID TIPS

- Ubiquitous and variable: the single most commonly misidentified animal track.

- Large toes make up most of the area of the track.

- Oval and symmetrical, with stout claws often but not always showing.

Domestic Dog
Canis familiaris

TRACKS

Domestic Dog tracks come in many shapes and sizes, with some closely resembling those of wild canids. Nearly all show the familiar canid traits of four large toes and a roughly triangular palm. Tracks range from oval to round and may show an X-, H-, or even C-shaped negative space. Most are symmetrical, but some show slight asymmetry. The outer toes (2 and 5) and claws splay more often than in wild canids. Palm pads are often larger and proportionally wider than in similarly sized wild canids. Tracks often register flat or only slightly slanted, with palms registering nearly as deep as toes. Claws usually register prominently and are usually thicker than in foxes and Coyotes. Worn or trimmed claws may appear blunt, register lightly, or be absent entirely. Track sizes of various breeds range from smaller than those of Swift Foxes to larger than those of Wolves.

- Front tracks are generally larger and rounder than hinds, with larger palm pads, but the difference is sometimes less pronounced than in wild canids. The trailing edge of the palm often appears straighter and less distinctly lobed than in many wild canid tracks.

- Hind palms usually register completely, with the outer lobes registering the same depth as the center. But there are exceptions.

TRACK PATTERNS & GAITS

Different breeds of dog have different body proportions and different preferred gaits. As a species, Domestic Dogs exhibit a wider range of gaits than any wild canid, including not just walks and trots but also ambles and running paces. Their track patterns are equally diverse. Dogs typically walk or trot, usually leaving an indirect-register or overstep pattern. Side-trots are common. Many also lope and gallop frequently, most often in a rotary sequence. Domestic Dogs tend to place their feet less precisely and change gaits more often than wild canids, leaving sloppier, less consistent track patterns. Their trails often look more erratic or distracted ("squirrel!"). But there are exceptions, and the dogs most likely to leave clean, precise, consistent trails are often the ones that show up in the most remote areas.

SIMILAR TRACKS

Domestic Dogs share a recent ancestor with Wolves and Coyotes, and some dog tracks are extremely similar to those of their wild cousins. It is often not possible to distinguish a wild canid from a dog based on just a few tracks. Use multi-factor analysis, taking habitat, behavior, and track patterns into account.

Coyote tracks are more elongated than those of most medium-sized dogs. Some dogs' hind tracks resemble Coyote fronts, and a few dogs leave similar fronts and hinds. Coyote claws usually appear narrower, sharper, and closer to the midline of the track. The outer claws (on toes 2 and 5) often hug the middle toes (3 and 4), while the middle claws often point slightly inward, particularly in the hind track. Coyote tracks tend to slant more, with palms registering more lightly than toes. Coyote palms are usually narrower and often more distinctly lobed. The hind palm more often registers as an oval or a "dot with wings" rather than a full triangle. Coyote tracks and trails tend to have a cleaner, more consistent appearance. Track patterns tend to show a consistent stride and trail width, and trails tend to be straight rather than meandering.

Wolf tracks are usually larger, but some dogs leave Wolf-size tracks. Where size overlaps, Wolf tracks are often narrower and have proportionally small palm pads that register more lightly than the toes, particularly in the hind track. Wolf claws are stout like those of Domestic Dogs but typically sharper. Claws tend to point forward even when toes splay. When toes splay, they usually splay evenly, preserving the track's symmetry. Wolves generally take longer strides than large dogs, and stride lengths of over 40" for a walk or 48" for a trot are good evidence of a Wolf. Note that Wolves' long, supple legs and slightly turned-out feet give some of their track patterns a variable appearance that can superficially resemble the sloppy track patterns of many

Domestic Dogs. Even though foot placement may appear inconsistent, individual Wolf tracks usually appear quite crisp, with the negative space often drawn into a sharply defined mound.

Cougar tracks are asymmetrical, with proportionally smaller toes and larger palm. Claws rarely register and appear much narrower and sharper if they do.

NOTES

The Midwest is home to roughly 21 million Domestic Dogs, making them far more common than any similarly sized wild mammal. Though restricted in some parks, reserves, and wilderness areas, "man's best friend" eventually shows up everywhere people go. Anywhere we find tracks, we may encounter dog tracks. Dogs were the first animal domesticated by humans, and today's diversity is the result of 10,000 years of selective breeding. There are over 400 recognized breeds, ranging from 4-pound Chihuahuas to 200-pound Mastiffs, showing a variety of body and foot shapes. Because dogs are so common and so varied, Domestic Dog tracks are misidentified more often than those of any other species. Most track photos sent to natural resource officials as evidence of Cougar, Wolf, or Black Bear turn out to show the tracks of a Domestic Dog.

Breeders recognize three specialized foot types in Domestic Dogs: cat feet, hare feet, and webbed feet. These are in contrast with oval feet, which have proportions similar to wild canines. Cat feet are compact and sturdy, with short toes that provide good grip and are less prone to injury. Cat-footed dog tracks may be nearly round, with the toes wrapping closely around the palm. Toes and claws usually appear splayed, and the negative space is often H-shaped or even C-shaped. Webbed feet have the same shape, plus a membrane between the toes which does not show in tracks. Many of the most popular dog breeds, including most Retrievers, Spaniels, Terriers, Great Danes, and Mastiffs, have these foot types. Most Domestic Dog tracks are this type, which is why most dog tracks appear rounder and more splayed than the tracks of most wild canids.

Hare feet, specialized for short bursts of high speed, are the least common. Hare feet are long and narrow, with elongated toes. The palm is typically wider than in wild canids. Greyhounds and Whippets have this foot type.

The toes of oval-footed dogs generally point forward, and these tracks are the ones most likely to resemble those of a Coyote or Wolf. Most oval-footed dog tracks still have broader palms and less negative space than those of most wild canids, but some are remarkably similar. Huskies, German Shepherds, Poodles, Irish Wolfhounds, and Alaskan Malamutes have oval feet.

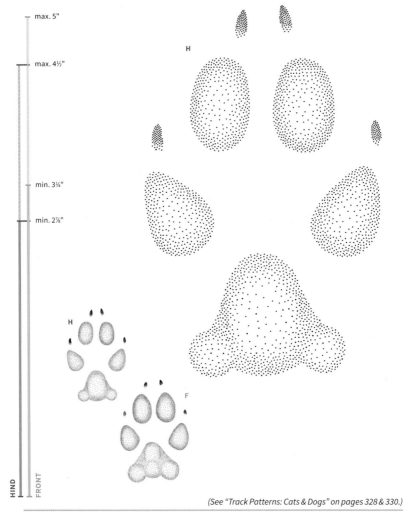

max. 5"

max. 4½"

min. 3¼"

min. 2⅞"

H

H

F

HIND   FRONT

(See "Track Patterns: Cats & Dogs" on pages 328 & 330.)

QUICK ID TIPS

- Largest wild-canid tracks—unlikely to be mistaken for anything other than a large dog.

- Tracks show four large toes, stout claws, and a triangular palm.

- Tracks appear crisp, and claws usually point forward even if toes splay.

Gray Wolf
Canis lupus

TRACKS

Wolves leave large, oval canid tracks, with four large toes, a triangular palm, and stout claws. Tracks usually appear crisp, and the central negative space is often drawn into a small dome. Claws are thicker and register more reliably than in other wild canids. Tracks may show slight asymmetry, with the middle toe (toe 3) registering slightly ahead of the ring toe (toe 4) and the palm slightly angled, particularly the front track.

- Front tracks usually show an H-shaped negative space and may appear nearly round when splayed. Claws tend to point forward, even when toes splay. The robust palm pad has a single leading lobe and three trailing lobes. The two outer lobes are usually set farther back, giving the trailing edge of the palm a concave, bi-lobed profile. A clawed thumb (toe 1) and heel pad rarely register. Front tracks measure 3¼"–5" long x 2⅝"–4½" wide.

- Hind tracks are narrower than fronts, show an X- or star-shaped negative space, and usually slope more, with toes registering deeper than palms. The outer lobes on the palm are small and may register lightly. Though usually triangular, the palm may have a Coyote-like "dot with wings" appearance. Hind tracks measure 2⅞"–4½" long x 2¼"–3⅜" wide.

TRACK PATTERNS & GAITS

Uses a wide variety of gaits. Typically travels in a trot, leaving direct-register or side-trot patterns. Side-trot patterns are more variable than Coyotes', and hind tracks may register in different relations to fronts from one stride to the next. Sometimes walks leaving overstep patterns or direct-register patterns. Front tracks sometimes appear turned outward (duck-footed). Speeds up into lopes and gallops, sometimes while traveling. Occasionally bounds in deep snow.

HABITAT

Historically found in nearly all habitats. Today in the Midwest, Wolves live primarily in sparsely populated, forested areas with robust White-Tailed Deer, Elk, or Moose populations.

OTHER SIGN

Scat

Scat: One or more long droppings ranging from ½" to 1⅞" in diameter and 6" to 18" in length. Frequently deposited along travel routes and near kill sites. Overlaps in size considerably with Coyote scat. Consistency depends on diet. Scat deposited after feeding on organ meat is dark, smooth, wet, and often poorly formed. Scat deposited after consuming hair and bone is firmer, lighter in color, and persists much longer.

Dens: Natal dens typically have two or more entrances that measure about 20"–25" in diameter. The main entrance usually has an obvious mound of excavated dirt in front of it. If left undisturbed, a pack may use the same den for many years.

ACTIVITY

Active year-round. Mostly crepuscular or nocturnal but may be active during the day. Often travels long distances at night when hunting.

SIMILAR TRACKS

Some **large Domestic Dog** tracks appear quite similar, and it may be impossible to distinguish them based on tracks alone. Use multi-factor analysis, taking habitat, behavior, and track patterns into account. Most large dogs leave rounder tracks, especially hind tracks, with larger palm pads that tend to register at the same depth as the toes. Nearly all large dogs take shorter strides and stride lengths over 40" for a walk or 48" for a trot are most likely Wolf. Domestic Dog claws are often trimmed or worn down and often splay to the sides. Wolf claws tend to point more or less forward even when toes splay. It is rare that large Domestic Dog tracks register as crisply as Wolf tracks or show the domed negative space often seen in Wolf prints. **Coyote** tracks are smaller and usually more elongated, and have finer claws. **Cougar** tracks are asymmetrical, with smaller toes and a larger, trapezoidal palm pad. Claws rarely show; if they do, they appear thin and sharp.

NOTES

The Gray Wolf was one of the most widely distributed land animals in the world, ranging across most of northern Asia, Europe, and North America. Heavily persecuted in the United States until the 1960s, Wolves were nearly wiped out in the Lower 48. Under the Endangered Species Act, Wolves rebounded, and today there are stable populations in the northern forests of Minnesota, Wisconsin, and Michigan.

Wolves are highly social, and most live in packs averaging five to seven individuals. Packs establish territories which they defend against other Wolves with deadly force. Territories do not overlap, range from 20 to 250 square miles, and are marked with scat and urine along major travel routes, including roads. Packs generally avoid one another. Coyotes and lone Wolves tend to travel in between marked territories and may be harassed or killed if they encroach on a pack. Foxes are generally tolerated. When prey is abundant, packs can maintain stable territories for generations. Lone Wolves are typically transient and may wander great distances. Since 2010, at least one Wolf from the Great Lakes population has been confirmed by DNA testing in every state in the Midwest except Ohio.

Wolves may travel farther and more often than any other land animal in the world. They are both masters of efficiency and remarkably strong. Packs often cover 25 miles each night, making use of smooth travel routes such as roads, packed trails, and frozen lakes. When traveling in snow, they often line up single-file and walk exactly in each others' footsteps. Their strong toes leave clean, consistent tracks and often pull the soil between them up into a small dome.

Wolves may eat Beavers, small mammals, and occasionally birds, fish, insects, and berries, but most specialize in hunting large ungulates. Despite eating mostly deer, Wolves have little impact on their populations. Even in Wolf-rich northern Minnesota, Wolves kill only about one-quarter as many deer as hunters do.

Hoofed animals, or ungulates, walk on the tips of their toes, which have evolved into sturdy hoofs. Ungulates are the most abundant large animals in most terrestrial habitats and important sources of food, materials, and labor for cultures across the world. All large domesticated animals are ungulates. The Midwest is home to eight native ungulates: the Pronghorn *(Antilocapra americana);* three species in the family Bovidae, including the iconic American Bison *(Bison bison);* and four species in the deer family, Cervidae. All are ruminants: large grazers or browsers that chew their cud. Europeans introduced domestic cows (*Bos taurus*), which are ruminants closely related to Bison; pigs (*Sus scrofa*); and horses (*Equus caballus*). White-Tailed Deer are the only wild ungulate common across most of the Midwest, but all of these species can be found in some areas. This section also includes the Nine-Banded Armadillo (*Dasypus novemcinctus*)—which is not closely related to any other Midwestern mammal—because its unusual tracks sometimes appear hoof-like.

TRACKS

Clear ungulate tracks show three components: a rigid hoof wall, or *unguis;* an area of *subunguis* inside the hoof wall; and a callused pad. The shape of the hoof wall, amount of subunguis, and shape of the pad each help with identification. Ruminants and pigs walk on the tips of toes 3 and 4, sometimes called *cleaves,* which together form a cloven hoof. In most tracks, the outer cleave (toe 4) is slightly larger and set slightly farther forward than the inner cleave (toe 3). In all species but the Pronghorn, toes 2 and 5 are present as dewclaws that sometimes register. Toe 1 is completely absent. Horses walk on the tip of toe 3, leaving a single, round hoofprint. All other toes are absent. Armadillos have four toes on their front feet and five on their hind, but often only the central toes register. The resulting two-toed front tracks can resemble tiny hoofprints, while three-toed hind tracks may appear bird-like.

TRACK PATTERNS & GAITS

Most ungulates travel in a walk, speeding up into trots, lopes, bounds, and gallops. Most species have long legs and take long strides relative to their track size. Many species leave distinctive track patterns at least some of the time, which can help with identification.

HOOFED & HOOF-LIKE

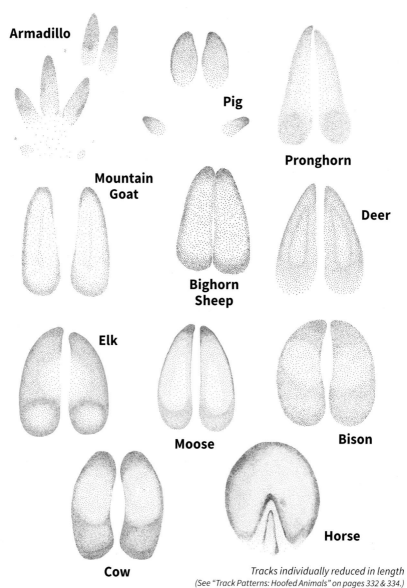

Armadillo

Pig

Pronghorn

Mountain Goat

Bighorn Sheep

Deer

Elk

Moose

Bison

Cow

Horse

Tracks individually reduced in length
(See "Track Patterns: Hoofed Animals" on pages 332 & 334.)

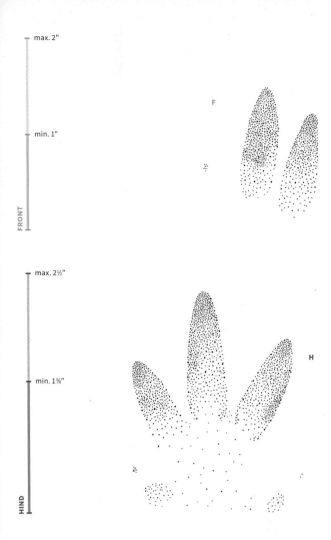

max. 2"

min. 1"

FRONT

F

max. 2½"

min. 1⅜"

HIND

H

(See "Track Patterns: Flat-Footed Walkers & Armadillos" on pages 324 & 326.)

QUICK ID TIPS

- Tracks have a bird-like appearance unique among North American mammals.
- Front tracks show two toes; hind tracks show three.
- Stout, blunt claws register prominently.

Nine-Banded Armadillo
Dasypus novemcinctus

TRACKS

Armadillos have four toes on their front feet and five on their hind. The inner and outermost toes are short, set higher on the foot, and often do not register. The resulting tracks have a unique two- or three-toed appearance that is unlike any other Midwestern mammal's. Large, blunt nails register prominently as extensions of the cigar-shaped toes. Palms rarely register, and heels never do. The nails and tips of the outermost toes occasionally register near the rear of the tracks.

- Front tracks reliably show two toes and may resemble a tiny hoofprint. The outer toe (toe 4) is longer than the inner toe (toe 3), making the track asymmetrical. Front tracks measure 1"–2" long x ½"–1" wide.

- Hind tracks reliably show three toes and often appear bird-like. The central toe (toe 3) is the longest, and the toes are arranged symmetrically. Larger than front tracks, hind tracks measure 1⅜"–2½" long x 1½"–2" wide.

TRACK PATTERNS & GAITS

Walks while foraging, often leaving an overstep track pattern. Faint tail drag is sometimes visible. Travels in a gentle lope. Speeds up into a gallop.

HABITAT

Wooded areas, fields, and brushland. Prefers areas with soft, sandy soils and abundant downed wood. Less common in areas with clay soils, where digging is more difficult.

OTHER SIGN

Scat: Armadillos dig for insects and consume a large quantity of soil as they forage. Scat is round or oval and may resemble deer pellets but is composed mostly of clay. Individual pellets measure ½"–1" in diameter and ¾"–1½" in length. Armadillos usually bury scat but sometimes form exposed latrines.

Burrows: Armadillos are excellent diggers and may excavate large burrows. Entrances are 6"–8" in diameter, with a large mound of excavated earth usually evident. Burrows are commonly located along streambanks or in the root system of a large tree. Active burrows have abundant tracks in and out of the entrance and trails radiating from it.

Nests: Armadillos usually nest in borrows, but in areas subject to flooding they will rest in aboveground nests, which resemble miniature haystacks.

Feeding Sign: Armadillos root for ground-dwelling insects and also break apart anthills. Digs often have a triangular shape but may look similar to skunk or even Raccoon activity.

ACTIVITY

Active year-round. Changes its periods of greatest activity with the seasons to avoid exposure to extreme heat and cold. Predominantly nocturnal during hot summer weather and diurnal during cold winter weather.

SIMILAR TRACKS

Tracks are unlike those of any other North American mammal. They often appear bird-like and may resemble **crow** or **raven** tracks.

NOTES

Armadillos were named by the Spanish conquistadors, who called this unusual animal the "little man in armor." They are the only mammal found in North America that is covered with heavy, bony plates, and the only representative of the order Cingulata found north of Mexico. The Armadillo's U.S. range once covered only southern Texas, but in the past century, Armadillos have been introduced to Arkansas and Florida, and they have considerably expanded their range northward into the southern parts of the Midwest.

Though they appear clumsy, Armadillos are surprisingly swift. They will generally run when threatened and have a habit of jumping straight up in the air when startled. If cornered, they will curl their bodies to protect their soft underparts, but they do not roll into a ball. They are excellent diggers and can disappear into loose soil quite quickly. Armadillos are capable swimmers and gulp air to increase buoyancy. They are also known to walk along the bottom of streams and ponds for short distances.

Armadillos are generally solitary but not territorial. They are nearsighted and can often seem oblivious to their surroundings. They spend much of their time rooting for insects, which are their primary food. They also eat crayfish, amphibians, reptiles, eggs, fruits, and carrion.

In addition to their unusual habits and appearance, Armadillos exhibit another distinctive trait: each year females give birth to a single litter of identical quadruplets. The young are born well developed, but with soft armor that hardens over time. When traveling, the babies trail behind their mother like piglets.

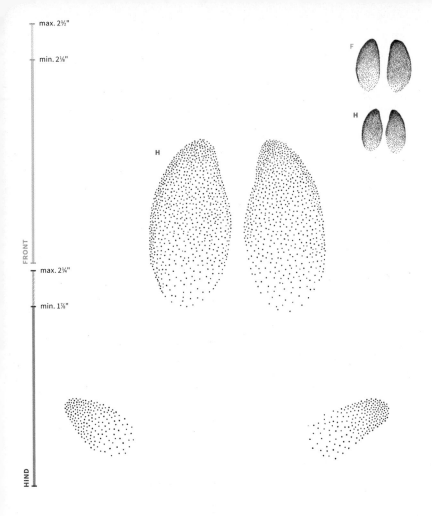

max. 2½"

min. 2⅛"

FRONT

max. 2¼"

min. 1⅞"

HIND

F

H

H

H

(SSee "Track Patterns: Hoofed Animals" on pages 332 & 334.)

QUICK ID TIPS

- Round hoofprints are nearly as wide as they are long.
- Cleaves are usually separated by a prominent ridge.
- Large dewclaws often register wider than the cleaves.

Feral Pig
Sus scrofa

TRACK
Feral Pigs leave round hoofprints similar in size to deer tracks. The cleaves (toes 3 and 4) typically appear blunt and rounded, though they may appear pointed in juveniles. The cleaves are generally separated more than in deer, with a distinct ridge between them. The dewclaws (toes 2 and 5) are long, large, and set low on the leg. They frequently show in tracks and often register wider than the cleaves. When dewclaws are visible, their width is helpful for identification. Front tracks are larger than hind.

- Front tracks measure 2⅛"–2½" long x 2"–2½" wide.
- Hind tracks measure 1⅞"–2¼" long x 1⅞"–2¼" wide.

TRACK PATTERN & GAITS
Walks while foraging, leaving an indirect register or understep pattern. May trot while traveling and speed up into bounds and gallops.

HABITAT
Wide-ranging. Most common in brushy areas and wooded slopes and lowlands. Cannot tolerate regular winter snowfall. Leaves prominent signs when rooting for food. Turns up earth and does considerable damage to vegetation.

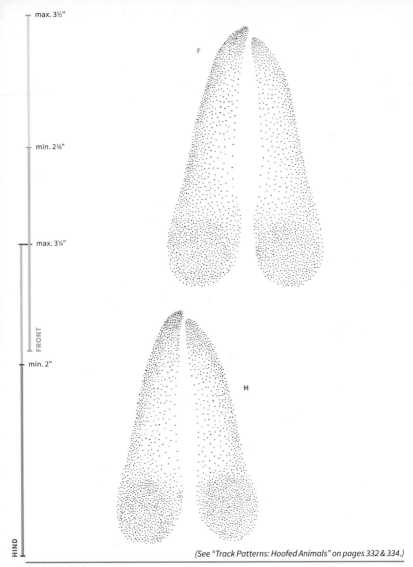

max. 3½"

min. 2⅛"

max. 3¼"

FRONT

min. 2"

HIND

F

H

(See "Track Patterns: Hoofed Animals" on pages 332 & 334.)

QUICK ID TIPS

- Narrow, heart-shaped tracks point in the direction of travel.
- Center of the track is often slightly raised.
- Lacks dewclaws, unlike members of the deer family.

Pronghorn
Antilocapra americana

TRACKS

Pronghorn leave narrow, heart-shaped tracks similar to those of deer, but more tapered. Tracks are widest close to the rear. The outer cleave (toe 4) is slightly larger than the inner cleave (toe 3) and usually extends slightly farther forward. Dewclaws are absent. Bulbous pads leave strong, often-circular impressions at the rear of each cleave. The outer hoof wall is straight or slightly concave mid-track. The center area of the track is often raised. Front and hind tracks are similar in size.

- Front tracks measure 2⅛"–3½" long x 1½"–2½" wide.
- Hind tracks measure 2"–3¼" long x 1⅜"–2¼" wide.

TRACK PATTERNS & GAITS

Usually walks, often leaving an overstep-track pattern. The overstep pattern is diagnostic for Pronghorn but may resemble the understep track pattern of a deer. Speeds up into trots, lopes, and gallops.

HABITAT

Open prairie and brushland with high visibility. Requires low, broken vegetation for birthing.

OTHER SIGN

Scat: Varies by season. The typical form is an oval pellet measuring ¼"–½" in diameter and ⅜"–¾" long, with a dimple on one end and a small point on the other. In winter, pellets are typically dry and fibrous. In spring and summer, when Pronghorn feed on more-succulent browse, pellets are very soft and may clump together into a single large mass.

Territorial Mark: Males urinate and deposit scat to mark territory boundaries, often after scraping the ground with their hooves. Urine or scat may be on top or next to scrapes, which are made in all seasons but are most frequent during the fall rut and in spring as territories are established.

ACTIVITY

Active year-round. Predominantly diurnal. Often grazes in mornings and evenings but may be active any time.

SIMILAR TRACKS

Deer tracks are wider in the forward half of the track and have a convex outer edge. Their tracks are flatter, lacking the round pad compressions and raised center area commonly seen in Pronghorn tracks. Deer may show dewclaws in deep substrate or when running and never show an overstep walk, though understep walks are common.

NOTES

The Pronghorn is a species of the open plains. An unusual animal, it is the only representative of its family in the world. Once abundant across the West, their distribution is now spotty. Perhaps the most athletic land animal on Earth, Pronghorns have huge hearts and lungs, which, together with an elevated hemoglobin level, allow them to run at high speeds for longer periods than any other animal. Pronghorn cruise at 35–40 mph for miles on end and sprint near 60 mph. No North American predator comes close. Pronghorn appear to know this and seem to playfully flaunt their speed, racing one another and sometimes even cars on the highway. Despite their athleticism, Pronghorn can't jump, and fences on rangeland have seriously inhibited their migration.

Most of the year, Pronghorn are found in small bands of females and fawns. In the spring, dominant males associate with these bands and establish territories that they defend through the fall rut. Fawns are born in May and June and are vulnerable for their first month of life, until they can run with the herd. Fawns are preyed upon by Coyotes and Golden Eagles. Dominant males defend fawns against Coyotes and can usually drive off a lone Coyote. Young are weaned by 12 weeks, and males usually leave their mother to join a bachelor herd at this time. Bachelors may test the dominance of territorial males, and serious fights resulting in injuries or fatalities are not rare. Such territorial aggression increases with population density. During the winter, large herds form, with little aggression evident. Dominant males usually avoid contact with these herds. Adults are generally safe from predators, and most adult mortality is due to winter starvation. Poorly adapted to snow, Pronghorn require nearly open ground to access winter browse.

Pronghorn get their name from their unique horn, which bears a pronged sheath of keratin (the material that makes up hooves and human fingernails). The sheath is shed each year shortly after breeding, but the bony core is retained—making the structure a true horn, not an antler.

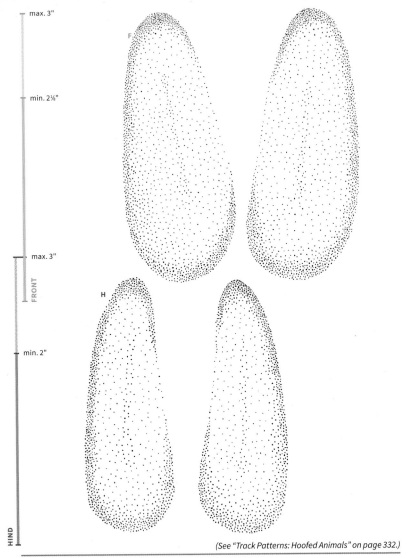

max. 3"

min. 2⅛"

F

max. 3"

FRONT

H

min. 2"

HIND

(See "Track Patterns: Hoofed Animals" on page 332.)

QUICK ID TIPS

- Wide, blocky hoofprints may appear nearly rectangular.
- Front tracks often splay widely.
- Exceptional climbers at home in steep, rocky terrain.

Mountain Goat
Oreamnos americanus

TRACKS

Mountain Goats leave nearly rectangular hoofprints similar in size to deer tracks. The cleaves (toes 3 and 4) are blocky, with rounded tips. The rounded point of each cleave falls near the midline of the toe rather than toward the center of the track as in deer. The outer hoof wall is straight or slightly convex. The inner hoof wall is fairly straight. A large, soft pad fills the interior of each cleave. Dewclaws (toes 2 and 5) may show in deep snow or mud, registering about as wide as the cleaves. The front track is slightly larger than the hind, is usually blockier, and often splays widely.

- Front tracks measure 2⅛"–3" long x 2"–3" wide.
- Hind tracks measure 2"–3" long x 1¾"–2¾" wide.

TRACK PATTERN & GAITS

Usually walks leaving a direct-register or slight indirect-register pattern. Bounds to navigate steep terrain.

HABITAT

An isolated population lives among the Ponderosa Pines, granite spires, meadows, and ridges around Custer State Park, the Crazy Horse Memorial, Mount Rushmore, and nearby canyons between 4,000' and 7,250' elevation.

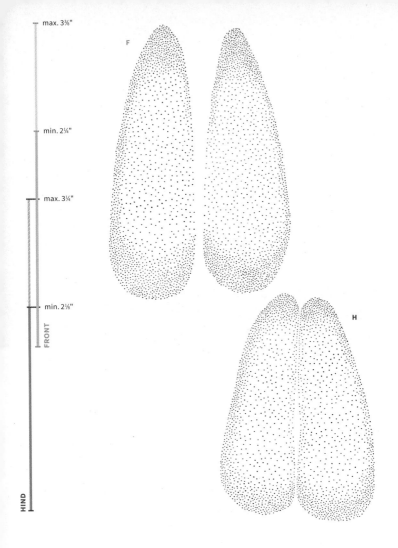

max. 3⅜"

min. 2¼"

max. 3¼"

min. 2⅛"

FRONT

HIND

F

H

(See "Track Patterns: Hoofed Animals" on page 332.)

QUICK ID TIPS

- Found on or near steep, rocky slopes.
- Similar to deer tracks but usually blockier, with more-rounded tips.
- Often leaves an overstep track pattern when walking.

Bighorn Sheep
Ovis canadensis

TRACKS

Bighorn Sheep tracks range from heart-shaped prints that closely resemble those of deer to blocky, nearly rectangular prints. The cleaves (toes 3 and 4) taper toward the tips, which are usually rounder than in deer. The outer hoof wall is straight or slightly convex, but usually straighter than in deer tracks. The inner hoof wall is slightly concave. A pad usually registers clearly at the rear of each cleave, filling roughly the rear quarter of the track. The center of the track is often raised, particularly in soft substrates. Front tracks are larger and blockier than hind, especially in mature males. Hind tracks often look most similar to those of deer.

- Front tracks measure 2¼"–3⅜" long x 1⅜"–2⅝" wide.
- Hind tracks measure 2⅛"–3¼" long x 1¼"–2½" wide.

TRACK PATTERN & GAITS

Usually walk in rough terrain, often leaving an overstep pattern. Often trot while traveling on level ground. Speed up into lopes and gallops.

HABITAT

Rough, steep, rocky terrain close to areas of open grassland and brushland.

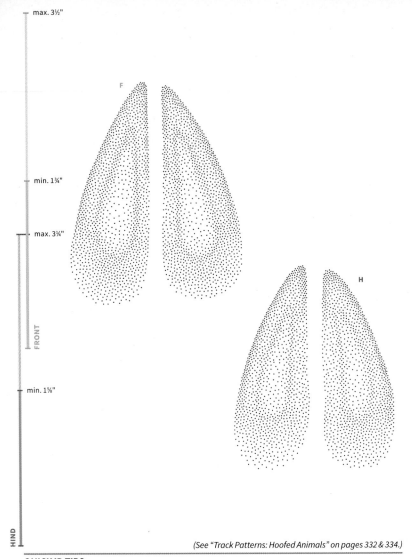

max. 3½"

min. 1¾"

max. 3¼"

F

FRONT

min. 1⅝"

H

HIND

(See "Track Patterns: Hoofed Animals" on pages 332 & 334.)

QUICK ID TIPS

- Distinctive heart-shaped tracks point in the direction of travel.

- Dewclaws often register in soft substrate or at speed.

- Cleaves may splay widely.

White-Tailed Deer & Mule Deer
Odocoileus virginianus and *Odocoileus hemionus*

Mule Deer also ▨

TRACKS

Deer leave familiar heart-shaped tracks that point in the direction of travel. Two cleaves often register close together, separated by a thin line, but may splay widely. The tips of the cleaves splay wider than the bases, and front tracks usually splay more than hind. The outer cleave (toe 4) is usually, but not always, slightly larger and set farther forward than the inner cleave (toe 3). The outer track wall is straight or slightly convex. On hard surfaces, the outer hoof wall is sometimes all that registers. The inner track wall is straight or slightly concave. The subunguis is narrow and often indistinguishable from the pads that fill most of the cleave. The pads slope upward at the rear, and the trailing edge of the track is often poorly defined. Dewclaws (toes 2 and 5) often register in deep substrates or when the animal is moving fast.

- Front tracks are larger and wider than hind, with the difference most pronounced in mature males. The dewclaws sit closer to the cleaves and register nearly perpendicular to the direction of travel. Front tracks measure 1¾"–3½" long x 1½"–2½" wide.

- Hind tracks are smaller. The dewclaws are higher on the leg and register parallel to the cleaves. Hind tracks measure 1⅝"–3¼" long x 1⅜"–2⅜" wide. Fawn tracks may measure less than 1".

TRACK PATTERNS & GAITS

Usually walks leaving a direct-register or indirect-register track pattern. Understep patterns are also common. Drags its feet in snow, regardless of depth. Leaves hoof-tip drag marks between tracks in shallower snow and parallel troughs in deeper snow. Occasionally trots when agitated. White-Tailed Deer speed up into lopes, bounds, and gallops, commonly bounding into cover when startled. Mule Deer flee in a *pronk,* unique to this species.

HABITAT

White-Tailed Deer prefer edge habitat and are especially abundant in some human-altered habitats, including parks, suburban greenways, and woods adjacent to farmland. Mule Deer are adapted to arid conditions such as sagebrush country. Where ranges overlap, Mule Deer tend to occupy the drier habitats. Both species are uncommon in continuous dense woods and open grasslands with no tree cover.

OTHER SIGN

Scat: Varies by season. The typical form is an oval pellet less than ½" in diameter, with a dimple on one end and a small point on the other. In winter, pellets are typically dry and fibrous. In spring and summer, pellets are soft and may clump in a single large mass.

Beds: Deer rest most of the day and night in kidney bean–shaped beds found on dry, level ground with shelter and a view of the landscape.

Browse: Deer browse appears ragged rather than cleanly cut, and is typically found 1'–3' off the ground. In winter, deer may feed on bark, scraping upward with their lower incisors.

Rubs: Before mating season, bucks use their antlers to shred bark and break twigs on saplings, shrubs, and sometimes small trees, leaving conspicuous scars.

Scrapes: During mating season, White-Tailed Deer bucks scrape 1'–3' patches of ground down to bare soil with their front hoofs, then urinate in them. This behavior is not observed in Mule Deer. Scrapes are usually made under a low branch, which the deer rubs, licks, and chews to deposit more scent. Does investigate these scrapes, and bucks regularly refresh them, often leaving clear tracks in the disturbed soil.

ACTIVITY

Active year-round. Predominantly crepuscular, browsing primarily at dusk and dawn and retiring to beds for much of the night and day. Midday feeding is common in fall and winter.

SIMILAR TRACKS

Pronghorn tracks usually have a raised area in the center. The widest part of the track is farther back than in deer, and the outer edge is sometimes concave. Pronghorn lack dewclaws and often leave an overstep track pattern. **Feral Pig** tracks are rounder and usually more separated, and they often show dewclaws registering wider than the cleaves. **Elk** tracks are larger and rounder. **Moose** tracks are much larger.

NOTES

White-Tailed Deer *(Odocoileus virginianus)* are the most abundant large animal in North America, with current populations exceeding those at the time of European settlement. Different subspecies vary greatly in size, with adults ranging from 90 to 300 pounds or more. In the Midwest, White-Tailed Deer from Kansas, Nebraska, Iowa, and Missouri tend to be smaller than their northern and eastern kin. Mule Deer *(Odocoileus hemionus)* are close relatives of White-Tailed Deer, adapted to the dry habitats of the western Midwest.

Despite their size, deer are masters of stealth. They can stand motionless for long periods of time, move almost silently, and crawl through surprisingly small spaces. They are also remarkably fast and agile runners, able to sprint over 35 mph and jump 7' fences from a standstill. Deer typically travel on well-established runs, which become worn over time and are especially obvious in snow. Bucks are often solitary, especially in summer, but sometimes form small bachelor groups. Does usually travel with fawns and yearlings. Larger groups are most common in winter, after the mating season, as deer congregate in areas of shelter and winter browse. For most of the year, deer feed on herbs, grasses, fruits, acorns, mushrooms, corn, sedges, and ferns.

Human hunting is the largest cause of deer mortality, accounting for more than 50% of all deaths. Deer are also vulnerable to winter starvation and are preyed on by Coyotes, Bobcats, Lynx, Cougars, and Wolves. Many deer are also struck by cars, especially during the mating season between late October and early December. During the mating season, White-Tailed Deer bucks create scrapes, and both deer species create rubs to communicate dominance and attract mates. Bucks do not collect harems as bull Elk do, but follow a single doe until mating. Dominant bucks, however, mate with many females. Fawns are born in the spring or early summer and stay with their mother for a year.

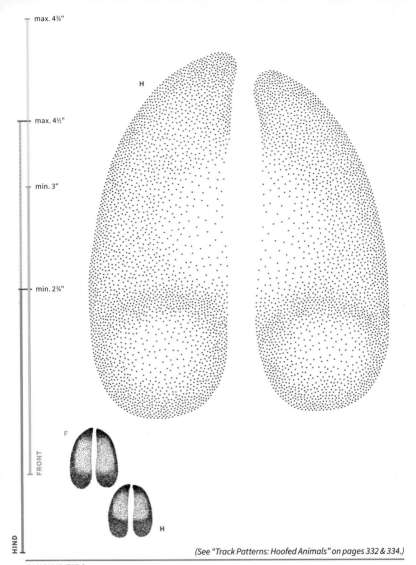

max. 4¾"

max. 4½"

min. 3"

min. 2¾"

H

F

H

FRONT

HIND

(See "Track Patterns: Hoofed Animals" on pages 332 & 334.)

QUICK ID TIPS

- Blocky tracks shaped like a rounded heart.

- Hoof wall is often more prominent than in other deer.

- Pad fills the rear quarter to third of each cleave.

Elk
Cervus elaphus

TRACKS

Elk leave blocky tracks shaped like a rounded heart. The cleaves are wide for most of their length, tapering less than in other deer. The outer cleave (toe 4) is slightly larger and farther forward than the inner cleave (toe 3), particularly in the front track. Toes 2 and 5 are dewclaws, which register in soft substrate or when the animal is moving fast. The outer hoof wall is straight or slightly convex and usually registers prominently. The pads are limited to the rear of the cleaves, and the center area of the track is often raised.

- Front tracks are larger and wider than hinds. The cleaves taper closer to the tip, giving front tracks an even blockier appearance. The pads fill the rear quarter of each cleave. Dewclaws are closer to the cleaves than on the hind, register more often, and register angled outward. Front tracks measure 3"–4¾" long x 2¾"–4½" wide.

- Hind tracks are smaller, more symmetrical, and more gradually tapered than fronts. The pads fill the rear third of each cleave. Dewclaws are higher on the leg and register parallel to the cleaves. Hind tracks measure 2½"–4½" long x 2½"–4" wide.

TRACK PATTERNS & GAITS

Typically walks leaving an indirect-register or direct-register pattern. Drags its feet while walking in snow, leaving two parallel troughs. Trots leaving direct-register and straddle track patterns. Speeds up into lopes and gallops.

HABITAT

Found primarily in open forest, young conifer stands, young aspen stands, farmlands, prairies, and river corridors. Prefers edge habitats with open fields for browse and some cover.

OTHER SIGN

Scat

Scat: Varies from season to season as diet changes. The typical form is an oval pellet ½"–¾" in diameter and ½"–1" long, with a dimple on one end and a small point on the other. In winter, pellets are dry and fibrous. In spring and summer, pellets are soft and may clump together in a single large mass, sometimes appearing as a formless plop about 6" in diameter.

Beds: Elk rest most of the day in kidney bean–shaped beds measuring 39"–52" long. These are usually found on dry, smooth ground, with a good view of the surroundings.

Browse: In grasslands, Elk are primarily grazers. Where abundant grass and herbs are sparse, they browse woody plants, particularly young aspen. Elk also scrape tree bark with their lower incisors when browse is scarce.

Rubs: Prior to the rut, bulls rub their antlers and foreheads against small trees, tearing the bark, breaking small branches, and depositing scent. Similar to deer rubs but generally higher off the ground and on larger trees.

Wallows: Bull Elk scrape shallow depressions with their hooves and antlers, urinate or defecate in them, and then roll or wallow in the depression as part of the mating ritual.

ACTIVITY

Active year-round. Primarily crepuscular, retiring to beds for most of the day.

SIMILAR TRACKS

White-Tailed and Mule Deer tracks are smaller. **Moose** tracks are larger. Elk tracks are noticeably rounder and blockier than those of other members of the deer family. **Domestic calf** tracks can appear similar. Calves generally take much shorter strides, leave less-regular track patterns, and travel with mature cows.

NOTES

The Elk was once abundant throughout the U.S. and Canada but was extirpated from much of its former range by overhunting and habitat loss. Elk have been reintroduced in select areas around the Midwest, and a few of these populations are now thriving. Elk are also raised on private farms in many states. The best place to see Elk is in one of the areas where they have been reintroduced. But lone individuals, including escapees from farms, are occasionally seen in all corners of the Midwest.

Elk are herd animals. In the West, herds of cows and calves may grow to over 400 animals. In the Midwest, herds are a fraction this size. Bulls herd separately in small groups that may live on the outskirts of a cow–calf herd. Lone Elk, usually older bulls, are also common. Elk are the most polygamous species in the deer family in North America. During the rut, herd dynamics change as dominant bulls assemble and defend large harems of cows.

Elk are grazers, feeding primarily on grasses and herbs, but also browse when given the opportunity. Elk do particularly well after fires, which create favorable young browse and open up densely wooded areas. Elk are particularly fond of aspen and can do considerable damage to aspen stands.

Elk travel along regular corridors but are less likely than other members of the deer family to use the same exact trails. They walk when browsing and speed up to a trot when agitated. When mildly alarmed, Elk frequently move in a stiff-legged, overstep straddle trot with head erect, scoping for danger.

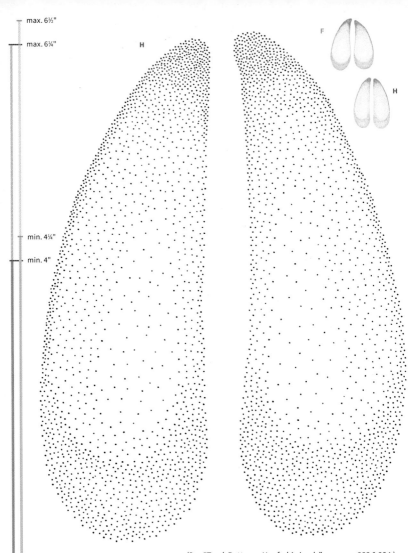

max. 6½"

max. 6¼"

min. 4¼"

min. 4"

H

F

H

HIND   FRONT

(See "Track Patterns: Hoofed Animals" on pages 332 & 334.)

QUICK ID TIPS

- Distinctive heart-shaped tracks point in the direction of travel.

- Large size makes tracks nearly unmistakable in our region.

- Dewclaws may register in deep substrate or at speed.

Moose
Alces alces

TRACKS

Moose tracks look like enormous deer tracks. Two large cleaves form a heart shape that points in the direction of travel. The tips of the cleaves are pointed but tend to round with age. The outer cleave (toe 4) is slightly larger and forward of the inner cleave (toe 3). The outer track wall is straight or convex. The inner track wall is usually slightly concave in the forward half of the track. The subunguis is narrow and often indistinguishable from the pads that extend most of the length of the track. The cleaves tend to register farther apart than in other deer, even when not splayed, often leaving a prominent ridge between them. The track floor is generally flat or sloped slightly tip-down. Dewclaws (toes 2 and 5) register in deep substrates and when the animal is moving fast.

- Front tracks are larger and wider than hind. The dewclaws sit closer to the cleaves and angle outward. Front tracks measure 4¼"–6½" long x 3¾"–5" wide.

- Hind tracks are smaller and more symmetrical than front. The dewclaws are higher on the leg and register parallel to the cleaves. Hind tracks measure 4"–6¼" long x 3½"–4⅝" wide. Calf tracks may measure 3".

TRACK PATTERNS & GAITS

Usually walks taking very long strides and leaving a direct-register or indirect-register pattern. Speeds up into trots, leaving both direct-register and straddle trot patterns. Lopes or gallops when alarmed or threatened. Walks in deep snow, dragging its feet much less than smaller members of the deer family.

HABITAT

Northern forests with lakes and swamps. Typically associated with willow growth throughout its range.

OTHER SIGN

Scat

Bed

Scat: Varies by season as diet changes. The basic form is an oval or block-like pellet ½"–⅞" in diameter and 1"–1¾" long. In winter, pellets are typically dry and fibrous. In spring and summer, when Moose feed on more-succulent browse, pellets are very soft and may clump together into a single large mass.

Beds: When not feeding, Moose often rest in beds, which have a roughly kidney bean shape. Beds measure 52"–75" long, much larger than White-Tailed Deer beds but overlapping with Elk beds in size.

Winter Browse: Moose scrape the bark and strip small branches from trees as high as they can reach, frequently 7'. Look for incisor scrapes on Red Maples and aspens, and for high browse on willows and Balsam Firs.

Rubs: Before mating season, bulls shred bark on small trees with their antlers, then rub their foreheads to deposit scent. These are similar to White-Tailed Deer rubs but much higher, ranging from 3' to over 7' off the ground.

Rut Pits/Wallows: Bulls make rut pits by scraping the ground with their front hooves, then urinating in the depression. Cows, and sometimes bulls, wallow in these pits as part of the mating ritual. Pits measure 1½'–4' long, 1'–4' wide, and 3"–6" deep.

ACTIVITY

Active year-round. Predominantly nocturnal and crepuscular but may be seen foraging at any time of day.

SIMILAR TRACKS

Other members of the deer family leave smaller tracks. **Moose calf** tracks tend to be rounder than adult tracks and may resemble Elk. **Elk tracks** still tend to appear blockier and more rounded at the tips. They often show a more prominent hoof wall and rounded pads that fill the rear quarter to third of each track. The pads on Moose hooves are less distinct and extend most of the length of the track.

NOTES

Animals of the boreal forest, Moose are well adapted to cold and snow. Their long legs allow them to walk unimpeded through snow up 28" deep, while their large bodies and dense hair keep them warm. Moose are so well adapted to cold that they need to expend extra energy to stay cool when temperatures rise above 55° F. Easily stressed by heat, Moose spend much of the summer on north-facing slopes and near water, browsing on willows and aquatic plants. Moose populations are declining in the Midwest, primarily due to climate change. Researchers predict that these magnificent animals could vanish from our region within the next 50 years.

Like other members of the deer family, Moose make prominent trails in the forest. Moose trails are wider and deeper than White-Tailed Deer or Elk trails, and Moose are more likely to detour around obstacles. Moose are primarily browsers, not grazers, and their browse sign can often be distinguished from that of deer by its height. Though generally solitary, Moose are not territorial and may congregate to feed during summer.

While Moose may look ungainly, they can run at up to 35 mph, move almost silently through the forest, and be fiercely unpredictable. Huge animals with strong legs and sharp hooves, they have no natural enemies except for Wolves, which specialize in hunting Moose in some areas. While generally shy and docile, rutting bulls and cows with calves have been known to attack not only people but cars and trucks as well. It is wise to be cautious when tracking Moose.

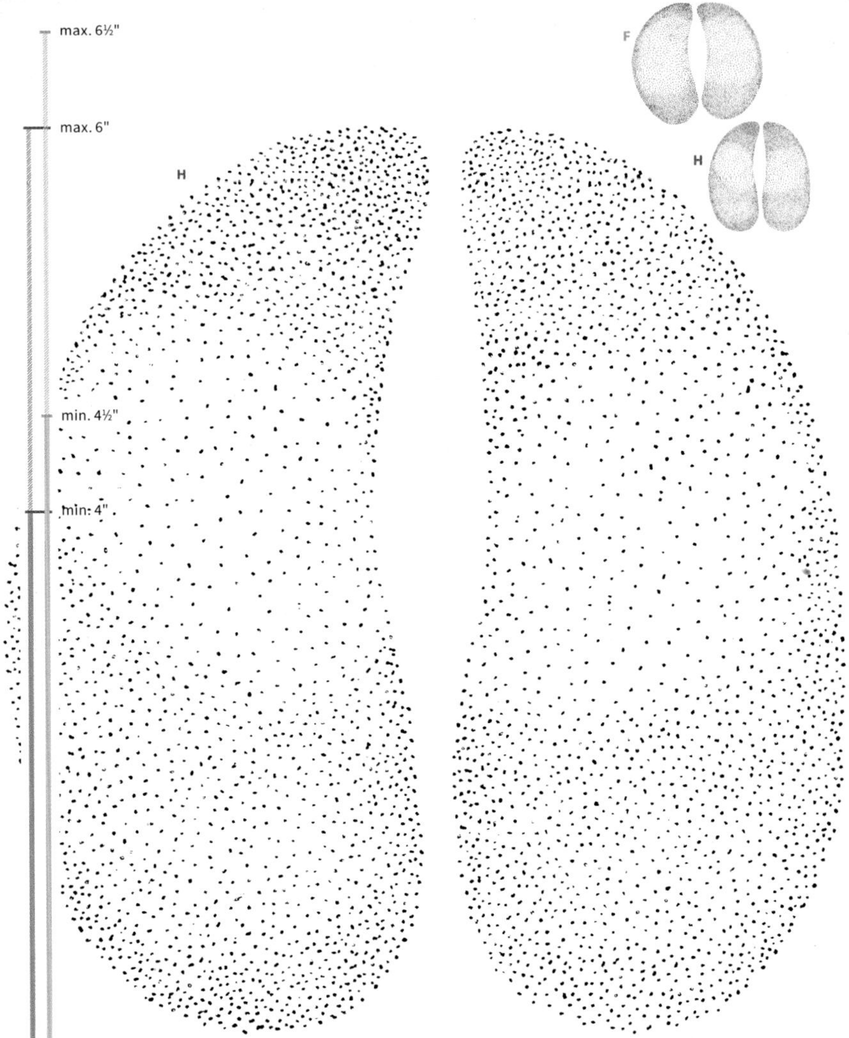

max. 6½"

max. 6"

H

min. 4½"

min. 4"

F

H

HIND

FRONT

(See "Track Patterns: Hoofed Animals" on pages 332 & 334.)

QUICK ID TIPS

- Enormous round hoofprints can be mistaken only for tracks of domestic cattle.
- Outer hoof wall shows prominently in tracks.
- Typically walks, leaving an understep track pattern.

American Bison
Bison bison

TRACKS

Bison leave large, nearly circular, two-toed hoofprints unlike those of any wild ungulate in the Midwest. Tracks of mature bulls are wider than those of juveniles and cows and may be wider than long. The outer cleave (toe 4) is slightly larger than the inner cleave (toe 3) and typically appears slightly farther forward. A pad filling the rear quarter of each cleave is well defined in clear tracks. Unlike in Elk, the leading edge of the pad appears distinctly concave or even notched. Two dewclaws (toes 2 and 5) may register in deep snow or mud.

- Front tracks are larger and wider than hind. The inner wall of each cleave is strongly convex, creating a wide negative space in the middle of the track. Front tracks measure 4½"–6½" long x 4½"–6½" wide.

- Hind tracks are narrower. The inner wall of each cleave is slightly convex, creating a narrower negative space than in the front track. Hind tracks measure 4"–6" long x 4"–6" wide.

TRACK PATTERNS & GAITS

Typically walks, leaving an understep pattern. Speeds up into trots, lopes, and gallops. Plows through remarkably deep snow.

HABITAT

Open grasslands; ventures into adjacent open forests.

OTHER SIGN

Scat

Wallow

Scat: Varies from season to season as diet changes. In summer, scat consists of large, amorphous patties measuring 10"–12" in diameter and nearly identical to cow patties, though usually larger. In winter, scat consists of piles or clumps of "chips," each measuring 3"–4½" in diameter.

Rubs: In wooded areas, Bison rub their horns and foreheads against trees, wearing the bark smooth and trampling the surrounding ground. Bison also rub against boulders on the open plains and against telephone poles.

Wallows: In open grasslands, Bison create large, dusty, saucer-shaped depressions 8'–10' across where they wallow to avoid biting insects. Bison sometimes urinate in these pits and then wallow, caking themselves with mud as protection from insects.

ACTIVITY

Active year-round. Predominantly diurnal. Most active grazing in the mornings and evenings but may be seen any time of day or night. Often rest in the open during the day, chewing their cud.

SIMILAR TRACKS

Domestic cow tracks are usually smaller but may be indistinguishable. **Moose** tracks are heart-shaped. All other cloven-hoof tracks are much smaller. **Bison calf** tracks may resemble an Elk's but are even rounder and will be found with prints of adults. Under some conditions, a Bison's interior hoof walls may not register clearly and tracks can superficially resemble those of a horse. Horses typically leave overstep rather than understep track patterns.

The Bison is the largest land animal in North America and was once the most abundant large animal on the continent and a fixture of the Midwestern plains. Bison numbered in the tens of millions when European settlers first arrived. In the 1800s, the great Bison herds were hunted to near extinction. By the early 1900s, fewer than 1,000 remained. Theodore Roosevelt, one of America's iconic outdoorsmen, wrote of the slaughter, "Never before in all of history were so many large wild animals of one species slain in so short a space of time." An emblem of the American West, the Bison was saved from extinction but no longer ranges in huge wild herds across the Great Plains. The best estimates are that Bison today occupy less than 1% of their historical range. The total wild Bison population is now estimated to be about 30,000 individuals, scattered across a few large national parks in the West. A much larger number of Bison—perhaps half a million—now live in commercial herds on private ranches. Only captive and range-restricted herds live in our region.

Bison normally travel in herds of 5–20, though lone animals are not rare. Males herd separately from females and calves. Where the animals still range freely, herds merge together during the breeding season and may become very large. The breeding season lasts from June to September, with a single calf born about nine months later. Calves can stand 30 minutes after birth, walk within hours, and join the herd after one or two days. Bison are hardy animals, well adapted to hard winters on the open plains. They are grazers, feeding on grass and herbs year-round. In the winter, Bison use their huge heads to plow even deep snows aside to feed on the plants underneath. Adult Bison are formidable, a herd even more so. Their primary defense is stampeding. In our region, Bison have no natural predators. In the West, only Wolves and Grizzlies are a threat, and even they prey only upon calves or sick individuals apart from the herd.

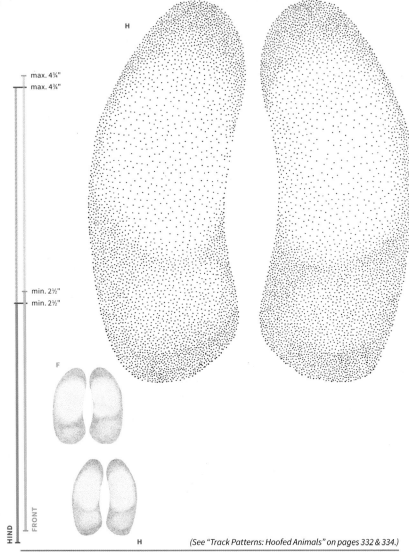

H

max. 4¾"
max. 4¾"

min. 2½"
min. 2½"

F

FRONT

HIND

H

(See "Track Patterns: Hoofed Animals" on pages 332 & 334.)

QUICK ID TIPS

- Large, rounded, two-toed tracks.
- Calf tracks may resemble those of adult Elk.
- Primarily found on private land in the Midwest.

Domestic Cow
Bos taurus

TRACKS

Cows leave large, round, two-toed hoofprints similar to Bison, but typically smaller. The outer cleave (toe 4) is slightly larger than the inner cleave (toe 3) and usually appears slightly farther forward, particularly in the front track. The inner wall of each cleave is convex, creating a distinct negative space that is widest mid-track. A pad fills the rear quarter of each cleave and is visible in clear prints. Unlike in Elk, the leading edge of the pad is indented. Two dewclaws (toes 2 and 5) may register in deep snow or mud. Front tracks are larger and wider than hind.

- Front tracks measure 2½"–4¾" long x 2¼"–5¾" wide.
- Hind tracks measure 2½"–4¾" long x 2¼"–4¾" wide.

TRACK PATTERNS & GAITS

Typically walks, leaving an indirect-register pattern. Speeds up into trots, lopes, and gallops.

HABITAT

Raised for meat and dairy on farms across the Midwest, and some public lands in western prairie states, domestic cows are common but generally fenced in.

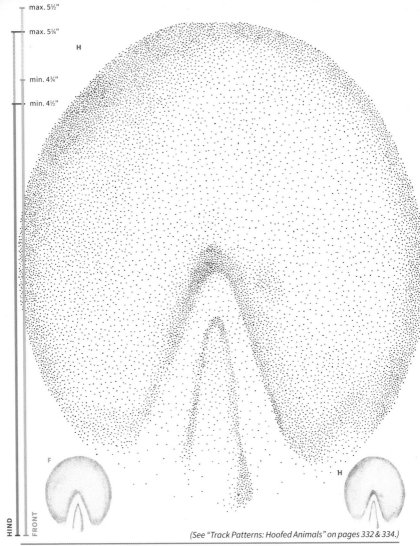

max. 5½"
max. 5¼"

H

min. 4¾"
min. 4½"

HIND   FRONT

F   H

(See "Track Patterns: Hoofed Animals" on pages 332 & 334.)

QUICK ID TIPS

- Large, round, single-toed tracks are unmistakable.
- Scat is usually evident along trails used by horses.
- Long strides and overstep track patterns can distinguish obscure tracks from those of Bison and cattle.

Wild Horse
Equus caballus

TRACKS

Horses are the only single-toed ungulate in the Midwest, making their large, round tracks unmistakable. The hoof wall forms a partial ring, wrapping about three-quarters of the way around the track. A triangular pad, known as a "frog," creates a wedge-shaped impression at the back of the track that can resemble a deer print. Horseshoes are often visible in tracks. These are typically the familiar U-shape, but some horses are shod with hoof boots that resemble modern sneakers. Front tracks are larger and rounder than hind.

- Front tracks measure 4¾"–5½" long x 4¼"–5¼" wide.
- Hind tracks measure 4½"–5¼" long x 4"–4¾" wide.

TRACK PATTERN & GAITS

On riding trails, horses usually walk, leaving an overstep pattern.

HABITAT

Live primarily on private, fenced pastureland. Accompanied by riders on designated trails, some rural roadways, and very limited suburban and urban locations. Small, free-ranging herds live in Theodore Roosevelt National Park (ND), the Black Hills Wild Horse Sanctuary (SD), and Flint Hills (KS).

The Midwest is home to a wide variety of reptiles and amphibians, collectively known as herpetiles or simply herps. Midwest herps all belong to one of four orders: frogs and toads (Anura); newts and salamanders (Caudata); snakes and lizards (Squamata); and turtles and tortoises (Testudines). Each of these major groups creates distinctive tracks and trails.

Herps have different hip, shoulder, and leg structures than mammals, causing many to shift side-to-side as they move, often twisting their feet and blurring their tracks in the process. Because of this, and the habitats they live in, clear tracks are less common than those of birds or mammals. Herp tracks can be difficult to identify beyond the order—but this is often enough. By getting to know the herps in a particular region and habitat, it is often possible to narrow tracks down to just a handful of species.

Frogs and toads frequently hop with their front feet facing in toward each other, and their much larger hind feet register wider, slightly farther back, and angled outward. On firm substrate, often only the tips of the toes of the hind feet register, forming a pair of "check marks." Toads have shorter, stouter toes than frogs and often walk as well as hop.

Salamanders and newts walk on land, leaving small trails of closely spaced tracks surrounding a prominent body or tail drag. Most species have four clawless toes on their front feet and five on their larger hind feet, though some toes may be very small.

Lizards typically walk, trot, or bound, leaving trails similar to those of comparably sized mammals but usually less distinct. Tracks typically show five long, slender toes on each foot, tipped with sharp claws. Many trails also include some trail drag.

Snakes, which are closely related to lizards, leave distinctive serpentine body marks without accompanying footprints.

Turtles and tortoises walk exclusively, leaving wide trails with short steps. Tracks tend to be round or wider than long, and show prominent claw marks. They have five toes on each foot, but the outermost toe on the hind foot is reduced in many species and may not register.

HERP TRACK GROUPS

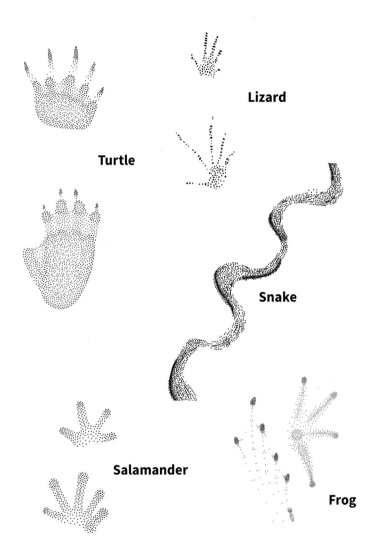

Lizard

Turtle

Snake

Salamander

Frog

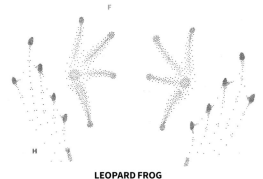

LEOPARD FROG

(See "Track Patterns & Gaits," opposite.)

QUICK ID TIPS

- Front feet point in toward each other, while larger hind feet angle out.

- Often only the tips of the hind feet register, forming a pair of "check marks."

- Toads walk and hop, while frogs hop almost exclusively.

Frogs & Toads
Order Anura

There are about 30 species of frogs and toads in the Midwest. We are most likely to see the tracks of a pond frog in the genus *Lithobates* or a toad in the genus *Anaxyrus*. It is often possible to distinguish frog and toad tracks, but identifying tracks to species is difficult except for the enormous Bullfrog.

TRACKS

- Front tracks show four thick, widely splayed toes radiating out from a small palm. Toads have shorter, thicker toes than frogs. Front tracks measure ¾"–1½" long x ⅜"–1" wide; Bullfrog front tracks measure over 1½" long

- Hind tracks show five long, slender, clawless toes connected by webbing. Toe tips may appear claw-like and may be the only thing to register in firm substrate. A pad at the base of the thumb (toe 1) may register, looking like a sixth toe. The ring toe (4) is the longest, and the tips of the toes usually form a check-mark shape. Hind tracks measure ⅝"–2" long x 5/16"–1¼" wide; Bullfrog hind tracks measure more than 2" long.

TRACK PATTERNS & GAITS

Most frogs hop almost exclusively. Toads hop or walk. When hopping, the front feet face inward and the hind feet register wider, farther back, and usually turned out slightly. Walking trails are wide and usually show an understep.

F

H

**TIGER
SALAMANDER**

EASTERN NEWT

(See "Track Patterns & Gaits," opposite.)

QUICK ID TIPS

- Small trails of closely spaced tracks with prominent tail drag.

- Usually found in mud near bodies of water.

- Most species have four toes on the front feet and five on the hind.

Salamanders & Newts
Order Caudata

Many of the 33 salamanders in the Midwest are aquatic, and the rest usually live under rocks or debris and sometimes underground. We are most likely to see salamanders or their tracks during spring and fall migrations. Our most widespread and recognizable salamanders belong to the genus *Ambystoma*, the mole salamanders. This group includes the large and attractive Tiger Salamander, found in every Midwestern state.

TRACKS

Tiger Salamanders have four clawless toes on their front feet and five on their hind. Toes are wider than in many species and have bulbous tips. The squat tracks often measure wider than long. Front tracks are symmetrical. Hind tracks are larger and less symmetrical: the thumb (toe 1) is the shortest and tends to splay less than the pinkie (toe 5). The Eastern Newt, which is a more typical size for our salamanders, has tiny outer toes that give its tracks a distinctive "trident" shape. Tracks measure about ¼" for most species up to ½" long x ¾" wide for the Tiger Salamander.

TRACK PATTERNS & GAITS

Salamanders usually walk, leaving an understep pattern. Feet tend to register pointing forward or slightly turned in. Tail drag is often evident.

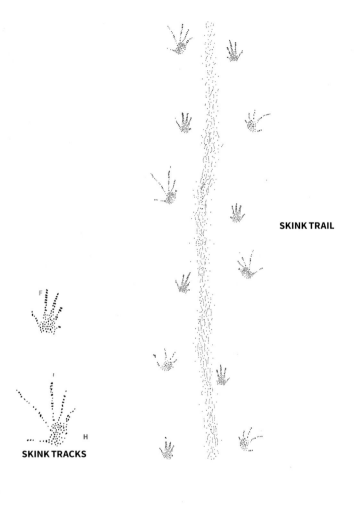

SKINK TRAIL

SKINK TRACKS

F

H

(See "Track Patterns & Gaits," opposite.)

QUICK ID TIPS

- Tracks are often less distinct than similarly sized mammal tracks.

- Trail patterns are similar to those of many small mammals.

- Many trails include belly or tail drag.

Lizards
Order Squamata (except Suborder Serpentes)

The Midwest is home to 18 species of lizards living in diverse and often specialized habitats. The most common and representatives are skinks in the genus *Eumeces*. Skinks are thick-bodied lizards with short legs and a low-slung posture. They are most active on warm, sunny days, foraging for insects.

TRACKS
Like most lizards, skinks have five long, clawed toes on each foot. The toes arch from the palm to the claw and rarely register their complete length. The middle toes (3 and 4) are the longest, and the thumb (toe 1) is the shortest. On the hind feet, the middle toes (3 and 4) are extremely long—up to double the length of the palm. The pinkie (toe 5) is set farthest back and splays the most. Front tracks tend to point forward or angle in slightly. Hind tracks usually register wider and strongly turned out. Front tracks measure ¼"–½" long and ¼"–½" wide. Hind tracks measure ½"–1¼" long x ⅜"–¾" wide.

TRACK PATTERNS & GAITS
Skinks usually walk by flexing their bodies side-to-side like a snake. Most trails show prominent, undulating body and tail drag—often more prominent than the footprints. Skinks sometimes trot, with their bellies off the ground, but usually only for short distances. Walk stride (and tail-drag wavelength): 1¾"–5"; trail width: 1"–2½".

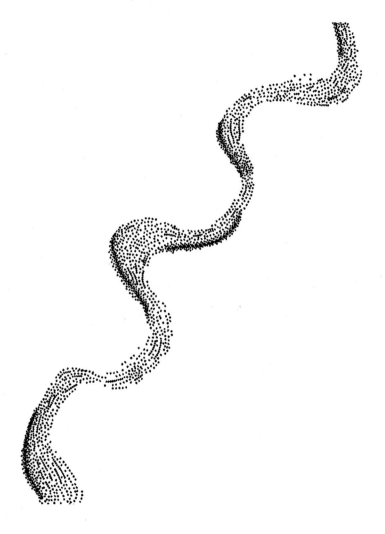

(See "Track Patterns & Gaits," opposite.)

QUICK ID TIPS

- Distinctive serpentine body marks without accompanying footprints.

- Trails are usually less consistent or proportionally wider than tail-drag marks.

- Trails range enormously in size, with the smallest resembling earthworm trails.

Snakes
Suborder Serpentes: Families Colubridae and Viperidae

Nearly 50 species of snakes in the Midwest showcase the diversity of this amazing group of reptiles. From the semiaquatic Water Snake to the Plains Rattlesnake of arid grasslands, they occupy almost every habitat. They range in size from the pencil-length Redbelly to the 6' Bullsnake and vary in shape from the stout Hognose to the reed-like Green Snake. There are six venomous species across our region. On balance, snakes are highly beneficial, helping keep pests from garden slugs to grain-store-raiding rodents in check.

TRAIL PATTERNS & GAITS
The sinuous movements of snakes have fascinated people since time immemorial. Snakes seem to glide effortlessly across nearly any surface—even up the trunks of trees. Snakes have a variety of gaits. The most common is lateral undulation in which the snake moves its body in a side-to-side wave. The resulting trail resembles a sine wave. Ridges of soil may form behind the outer edges of the wave, showing the direction of travel. Other snake gaits include belly crawling (or rectilinear locomotion), which produces nearly straight trails, and sidewinding, used on very loose substrate, which leaves a series of regularly spaced body prints perpendicular to the direction of travel.

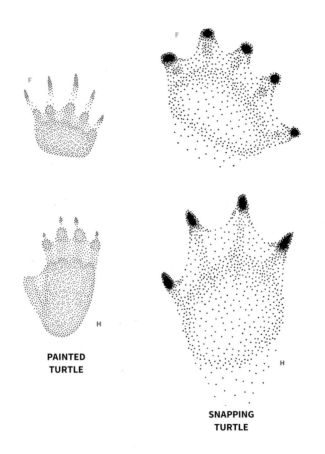

PAINTED TURTLE

SNAPPING TURTLE

(See "Track Patterns & Gaits," opposite.)

QUICK ID TIPS

- Walk exclusively, leaving wide trails with short steps.
- Tracks are usually round or wider than they are long, with prominent claws.
- Often only claws register clearly.

Turtles
Order Testudines

Most of the 17 species of turtles in the Midwest are aquatic, coming to land only to bask, lay eggs, and move between bodies of water. Box turtles in the genus Terrapene may inhabit woods and grasslands. The Painted Turtle (*Chrysemys picta*) and Snapping Turtle (*Chelydra serpentina*) are common in waterways across the Midwest. Turtles grow slowly and continuously over their long lives, and the size of their tracks varies much more than in mammals.

TRACKS
Most turtles have five webbed toes on each foot. All except for the hind pinkie (toe 5) have stout claws. The soles are covered with small scales, giving some tracks a pebbly appearance. In firm substrates, often only nail marks show. Front tracks are usually round or wider than long and may register straight ahead or turned in. Hind tracks are usually round or longer than wide. The pinkie (toe 5) is set farthest back and often does not register. Painted Turtle tracks measure ½"–1¼". Snapping Turtle tracks measure up to 3".

TRACK PATTERNS & GAITS
Turtles walk exclusively, leaving understep patterns. Painted Turtles often drag their shells as they walk. Snapping Turtles frequently leave tail drags.

Birding is one of the most popular pastimes in the United States, and with good reason: birds are beautiful, fascinating, and diverse. More than 500 species of birds representing 18 orders live at least part of their lives in the Midwest. Learning common bird tracks gives us additional insights into the presence and behavior of these feathered neighbors. It also adds richness to our tracking adventures, since birds are some of the most prolific track-makers in many tracking "hot spots," like muddy shorelines.

TRACKS

Birds have a different fundamental foot structure from mammals and leave distinct tracks. Most birds have four slender, clawed toes that radiate out from a small palm. As with mammals, we can number birds' toes 1–4, beginning on the inside. Toe 1, also called the *hallux,* points backward and is reduced or absent in some species. We can group most bird tracks in the Midwest into four main categories based on their overall shape.

Classic

Songbirds, doves, raptors, and herons leave **classic** bird tracks, with toes 2, 3, and 4 pointing forward and a long hallux pointing backward.

Zygodactyl

Woodpeckers and owls leave **zygodactyl** (meaning "paired toes") tracks, in which toes 2 and 3 point forward and toes 1 and 4 point backward. Owls can rotate toe 4 forward and back, and it often points straight to the side.

Game

Wading shorebirds and upland game birds leave **game** bird tracks, with three straight, forward-facing toes (2–4). The hallux is reduced or absent.

Webbed

Seabirds and waterfowl leave **webbed** tracks, with three forward-facing toes (2–4) and a small hallux that may or may not register. Webbing itself may not be visible, but unlike in game bird tracks, it causes toes 2 and 4 to curve inward.

MEASURING BIRD TRACKS

- Always include claws when they are visible, but not drag marks.

- Measure **classic** bird tracks from the tip of toe 1 to the tip of toe 3.

- Measure **zygodactyl** tracks from the tip of the rearmost toe to the tip of the foremost toe. In woodpecker tracks, toe 4 is usually the rearmost toe. In owl tracks, toe 2 is often the foremost toe.

- Measure **game** and **webbed** tracks from the base of the palm to the tip of toe 3. Do not include the hallux, as it registers inconsistently in many species.

BIRD TRACK GROUP

CLASSIC

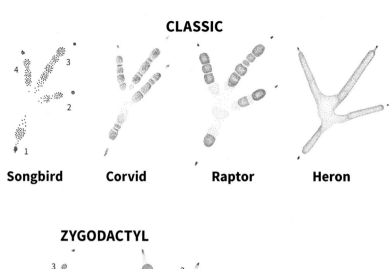

Songbird   **Corvid**   **Raptor**   **Heron**

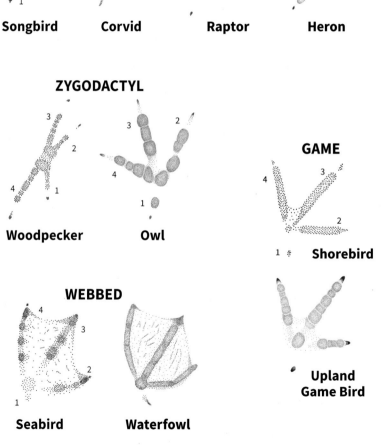

ZYGODACTYL

Woodpecker   **Owl**

GAME

Shorebird

Upland Game Bird

WEBBED

Seabird   **Waterfowl**

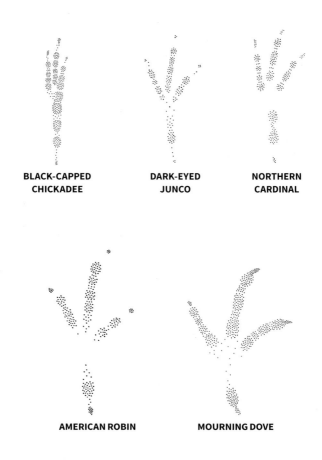

BLACK-CAPPED CHICKADEE

DARK-EYED JUNCO

NORTHERN CARDINAL

AMERICAN ROBIN

MOURNING DOVE

QUICK ID TIPS

- Note how the toes splay. Narrow or wide, straight or curved.
- Note the shape of the hallux.
- Note the track pattern. Some birds always hop, others always walk.

Songbirds & Doves
Orders Columbiformes and Passeriformes

Most small classic bird tracks we find are left by either a songbird in the order Passeriformes or a dove in the order Columbiformes. The Midwest is home to more than 200 species of songbirds and 3 species of doves, including many of our most familiar backyard species. Many small classic bird tracks look similar and can be challenging to identify.

TRACKS

Chickadees hop with short, 1"–5" strides. Their tracks are distinctively narrow and measure ⅞"–1⅛" long. **Titmouse** and **nuthatch** tracks are similar.

Juncos hop with 1"–6" strides. Their straight or slightly curved tracks measure 1¼"–1½" long. Most other **sparrow** tracks curve more.

Cardinals hop with 3"–12" strides. Tracks measure 1¼"–1½" long and have a broad hallux that looks like a plump inchworm. **Finch** tracks are similar.

Robins typically run, pausing frequently. Their tracks have a curved "peeling banana" shape and a prominent hallux, and measure 1¼"–1½" long.

Mourning doves typically walk, taking very short strides. Their short, wide tracks measure 1⅝"–1⅞" long. **Pigeon** tracks are similar but larger.

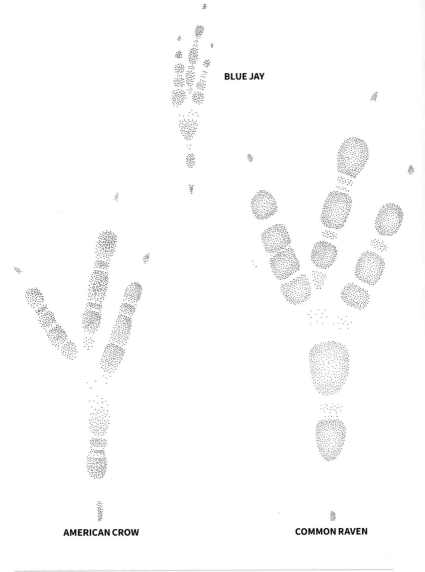

BLUE JAY

AMERICAN CROW

COMMON RAVEN

QUICK ID TIPS

- Toe 3 angles in, hugging toe 2 in the track.
- Thick toes have well-defined pads.

Corvids
Order Passeriformes: Family Corvidae

Corvids are large, vocal birds in the order Passeriformes. They include two of the most common Midwestern birds, the Blue Jay (*Cyanocitta cristata*) and the American Crow (*Corvus brachyrhynchos*). The Canada Jay (*Perisoreus canadensis*) and Common Raven (*Corvus corax*) range into our northern forests, while the Black-Billed Magpie (*Pica hudsonia*) and the occasional Pinyon Jay (*Gymnorhinus cyanocephalus*) occupy the western plains. All of our corvids are year-round residents and prolific track-makers. Their tracks are distinctive enough that most can be identified to species.

TRACKS

Corvids have stout toes with well-developed pads. Distinctively, their middle toe (3) angles to the inside and hugs the inner toe (2).

Jays hop with 6"–18" strides, except for Pinyon Jays, which walk. Their narrow, thick-toed tracks measure 1¾"–2¼" long.

Crows walk, hop, and skip. Their tracks measure 2¾"–3½" long. Magpie tracks resemble crow tracks in miniature.

Ravens also walk, hop, and skip. Their tracks, which appear more robust than those of crows, measure 3¾"–4¾" long. The base of their hallux often has a keystone shape, tapering away from the palm.

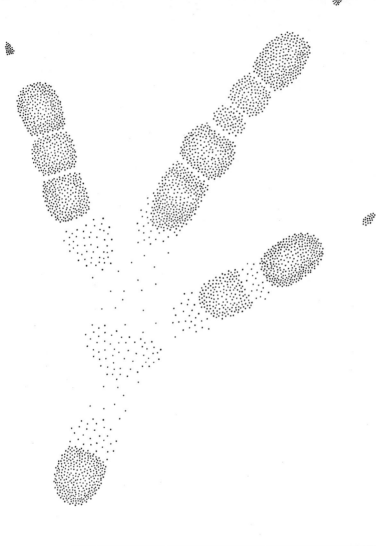

QUICK ID TIPS

- Robust toes have large, bulbous pads.
- Long talons register prominently.
- Palm often registers lightly or not at all.

Bald Eagles & Other Hawks & Eagles

Haliaeetus leucocephalus
Order Accipitriformes: Family Accipitridae

The Bald Eagle, the national symbol of the United States, nearly went extinct in the 1960s. Habitat destruction, poaching, and poisoning from the pesticide DDT reduced the population to 487 known nesting pairs. Under the Endangered Species Act and a ban on DDT, Bald Eagle populations have rebounded, and today this iconic raptor is a common sight in the skies over our region. The Midwest is home to eight genera and 15 species of hawks, eagles, and their relatives in the family Accipitridae, all of which have benefited from the protections afforded to eagles. Though many of these birds are now common, their tracks are not. If a hawk or eagle is on the ground, it is usually because there is food nearby. Bald Eagles feed on fish and carrion and will forage in trash. We may find their tracks on shorelines, near roadkill, and around garbage dumps.

TRACKS

Eagle tracks are among the largest classic bird tracks in our region. Their arching toes are covered with thick, bulbous pads that are pronounced in the tracks. The palm usually registers lightly or not at all while long, sharp talons are prominent. Eagles walk on the ground, taking 8"–22" strides. Tracks measure 6"–8" long.

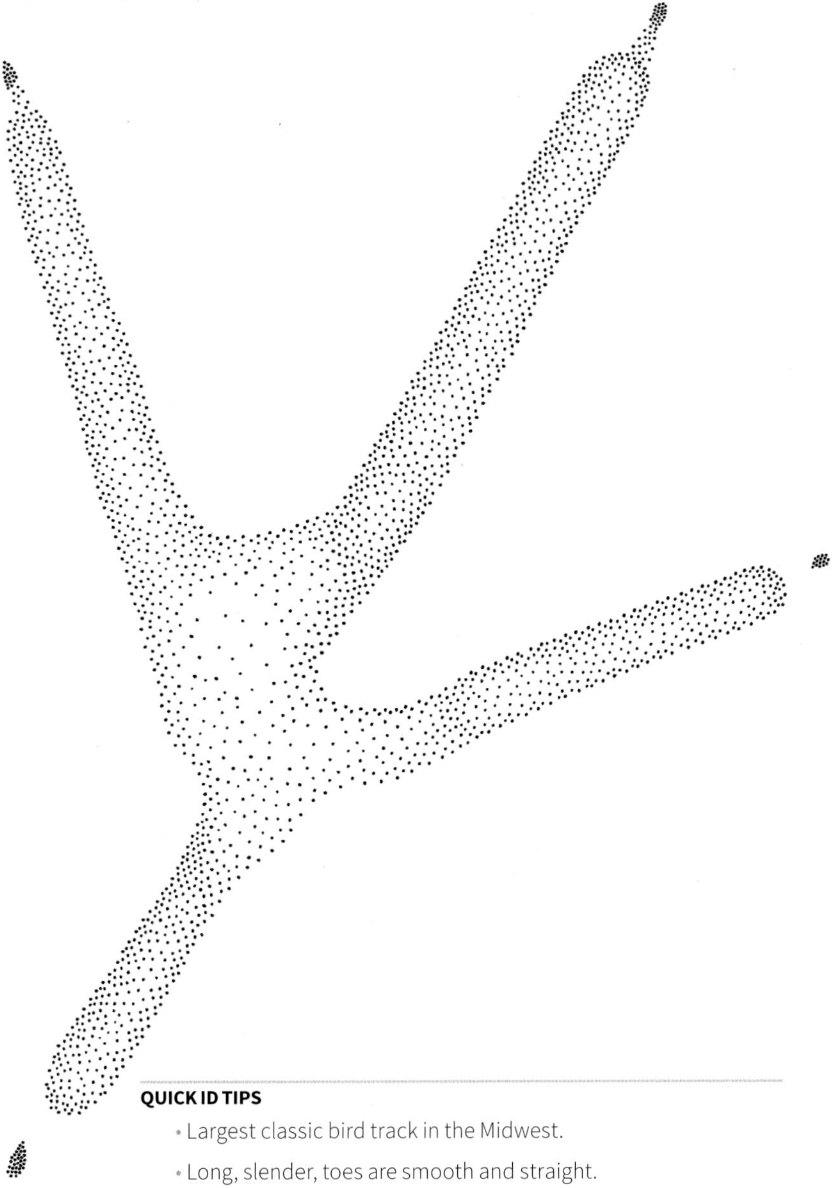

QUICK ID TIPS

- Largest classic bird track in the Midwest.
- Long, slender, toes are smooth and straight.
- Hallux is not aligned with the central toe (toe 3).

Great Blue Heron & Other Herons

Order Pelecaniformes: Family Ardeidae: *Ardea herodias* and others

Herons are medium-to-large birds with long legs, long bills, and long necks that they draw into a tight S-curve in flight. Wading birds that forage primarily in shallow waters, they are seen along wetlands and waterways throughout the Midwest. Five species of heron summer across most of our region. The Great Egret (*Ardea alba*) and Great Blue Heron (*Ardea herodias*) are both prolific track-makers. We may find occasional tracks of the mid-size Black-Crowned Night Heron (*Nycticorax nycticorax*) and the diminutive Green Heron (*Butorides virescens*), while the secretive bitterns (*Botaurus lentiginosus* and *Ixobrychus exilus*) stick to the reeds and rarely leave visible tracks.

TRACKS

Heron tracks have long, smooth, straight toes that register at a consistent depth. The outer toe (toe 4) often splays more than the inner toe (toe 2) and is connected at its base to the central toe (toe 3) by a small arc of webbing. The hallux (toe 1) is offset to the inside of the track and does not line up directly with the central toe (toe 3). Nails are narrow and short and may appear as a pointed extension of the toes. Great Blue Herons walk with typical strides of 20"–36", but may take much shorter strides while stalking. Their tracks measure 6½"–8½" long.

QUICK ID TIPS

- The only small zygodactyl tracks in our region.

- Narrow, K-shaped tracks with the long bar on the outside of the trail.

- Slender toes connect to a long palm.

Northern Flicker & Other Woodpeckers

Order Piciformes: Family Picidae: *Colaptes auratus* and others

Nine species of woodpeckers inhabit at least one corner of the Midwest. They range from the house sparrow–size Downy (*Picoides pubescens*), which is a frequent backyard visitor, to the crow-size Pileated (*Dryocopus pileatus*), known for carving large, oval cavities in snags. All are highly insectivorous, and most forage primarily on trees, sometimes leaving prominent and distinctive sign. Northern Flickers usually feed on the ground. Flicker tracks, beak probing sign, and ant-filled scat are fairly common in loose soil where ant mounds are abundant.

TRACKS

Northern Flicker tracks look like a narrow letter K, with four long, thin toes connecting to an elongated palm. Toes 2 and 3 are partially fused and point forward. Toes 1 and 4 point backward. Toes 3 and 4 are the longest, are located along the outside of the track, and often register in a straight line. Toes 1 and 2 are shorter and usually angle inward. Flicker tracks are almost symmetrical front to back, making it difficult to distinguish left from right and interpret what direction the bird was facing. Toe 4 is slightly longer than toe 3, and toe 1 is slightly shorter than toe 2, so the rear of the track shows the greater difference in length between its two toes. Flickers usually hop with their feet turned slightly inward and a stride of 3"–18". Tracks measure 1¾"–2½" long.

Other woodpecker tracks are similar.

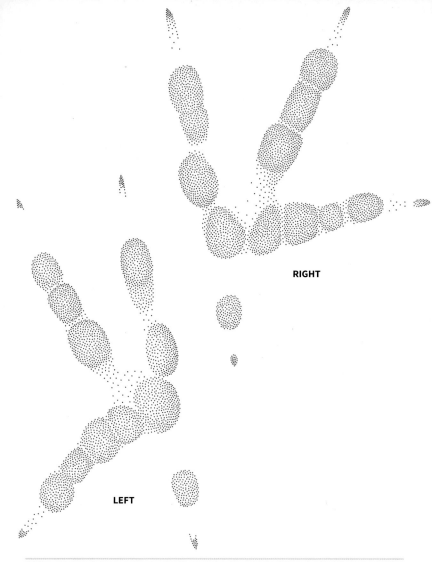

RIGHT

LEFT

QUICK ID TIPS

- Stout toes usually form a large letter K.
- The straight side of the K is along the inside of the track.
- Toe 4 is flexible and can change orientation from one track to the next.

Great Horned Owl & Other Owls
Order Strigiformes: Family Strigidae: *Bubo virginianus* and others

Most owls are solitary and nocturnal; we tend to hear them more often than we see them. A dozen species frequent at least part of the Midwest each year. Many are seasonal residents found in a few states. Three are widespread, year-round residents: the Eastern Screech Owl (*Otus asio*), Barred Owl (*Strix varia*), and Great Horned Owl (*Bubo virginianus*)—the largest and most wide-spread owl in North America. Most owls spend little time on the ground. The exceptions are the Burrowing Owl (*Athene cunicularia*), which nests on the open plains; the Snowy Owl (*Nyctea scandiaca*), which nests on the tundra and winters in our northernmost states; and the Great Horned Owl. Though certainly not common, owl tracks are not as rare as one might imagine. Finding them is always a treat, and their distinctive shape makes them easy to identify.

TRACKS
Great Horned Owl tracks are stout, with robust toes typically forming a large K. The hallux (toe 1) points backward and often makes a straight line with toe 2 along the inside of the track. Toe 3 points forward. Toe 4 most often points to the side but is highly flexible and can change orientation from one track to the next. This flexibility makes owl tracks more variable than those of many other birds. Great Horned Owls typically walk, taking 6"–22" strides. Tracks measure 3¼"–4½" long.

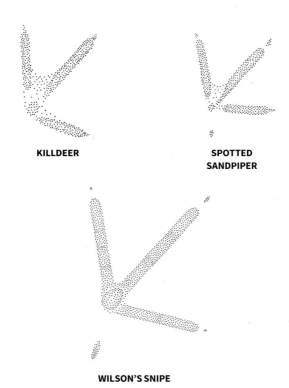

KILLDEER

SPOTTED SANDPIPER

WILSON'S SNIPE

QUICK ID TIPS

- Long, thin, straight toes radiate out from a tiny palm.
- Sandpiper tracks often show a tiny hallux; plovers' do not.
- Plover tracks are asymmetrical; sandpiper tracks splay evenly.

Shorebirds
Order Charadriiformes: Families Scolopacidae and Charadriidae

Shorebirds are long-legged birds that forage on the ground. Most live near water, but some frequent dry habitats. Five species summer across much of the Midwest, and another twenty migrate through or summer on the plains. Most are sandpipers in the family Scolopacidae, or plovers in the family Charadriidae. Spotted Sandpipers (*Actitis macularius*) forage along shore-lines and are prolific track-makers. Woodcocks (*Scolopax minor*) and Snipes (*Gallinago delicata*) are large sandpipers that often leave tracks and probing sign in mud puddles. Killdeer (*Charadrius vociferus*), our most common plover, are common on farmlands, ballfields, and similar open landscapes.

TRACKS
Sandpipers and plovers leave game bird tracks, with three long, thin, straight toes radiating out from a tiny palm. In most species, a tiny stretch of webbing connects the bases of the outer toes (3 and 4). Plovers lack a hallux and usually leave asymmetrical tracks, with the inner toe (2) splaying wider than the outer toe (4). Sandpipers leave more-symmetrical tracks and, with the exception of the Sanderling (*Calidris alba*), have a tiny hallux that often registers as a small dot; remember *spot* for "Spotted Sandpiper." Killdeer and Spotted Sandpiper tracks measure 1"–1¼" long; Woodcock and Snipe tracks measure 1⅜"–2" long.

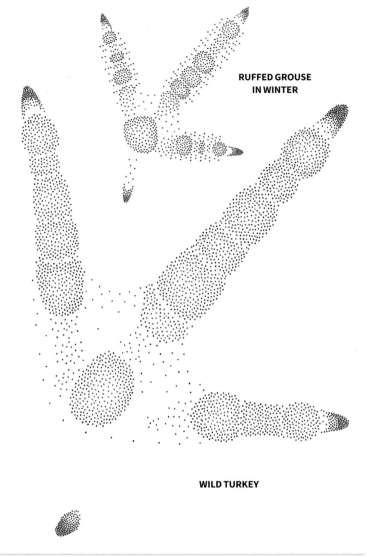

RUFFED GROUSE IN WINTER

WILD TURKEY

QUICK ID TIPS

- Three robust, bulbous toes extend out from a small, round palm.
- Broad nails usually register as extensions of the toes.
- The short hallux is often prominent.

Game Birds

Order Galliformes: Families Phasianidae and Odontophoridae

Game birds, or landfowl, are stocky, ground-dwelling birds in the order Galliformes, that includes quail, grouse, pheasant, and turkey. Long popular as food, several species have been domesticated for agriculture, including the turkey and domestic chicken. The Midwest is home to seven native species of wild game birds: the Northern Bobwhite (*Colinus virginianus*), four species of grouse (subfamily Tetraoninae), the Ring-Necked Pheasant (*Phasianus colchicus*), and the Wild Turkey (*Meleagris gallopavo*). Their tracks are common and nearly identical except for size. Turkeys travel in flocks most of the year and are especially prolific track-makers wherever they reside.

TRACKS

Game birds leave medium-to-large tracks, with three robust toes extending out from a round palm. Toes are distinctly bulbous and show a rough texture in good substrate. The round palm registers clearly in most tracks. The hallux (toe 1) is reduced but proportionally larger than in shorebirds, and it usually registers prominently. Small stretches of webbing, sometimes visible in the tracks, connect the bases of toes 2 and 3 as well as 3 and 4. The outer toe (toe 4) is longer than the inner toe (toe 2), and the hallux angles toward the inside of the trail. Ruffed Grouse (*Bonasa umbellus*) grow a comb-like fringe on their toes in winter that acts like snowshoes.

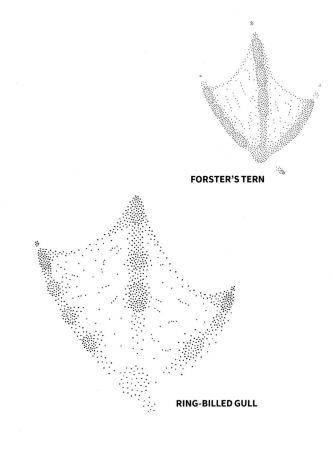

FORSTER'S TERN

RING-BILLED GULL

QUICK ID TIPS

- Three prominent toes connected by webbing.
- Outer toes curve inward.
- The hallux is often absent in gull tracks.

Gulls & Terns
Order Charadriiformes: Family Laridae

Gulls and terns are seabirds with feet adapted for swimming. They are related to shorebirds, but convergent evolution has led their feet, and thus their tracks, to resemble those of waterfowl. They are slow-maturing, long-lived birds that typically nest in large colonies, making them especially vulnerable to habitat disturbance. Many species are in decline, but a few have adapted well to modern human-transformed landscapes. Gulls and terns can be difficult to identify to species when seen live, and their tracks are even more similar. But only a few species are seasonally common and widespread in the Midwest. These include Forster's Terns (*Sterna forsteri*), Black Terns (*Chlidonias niger*), Ring-Billed Gulls (*Larus delawarensis*), and Herring Gulls (*Larus argentatus*). Several other species have limited ranges or pass through during migration.

TRACKS

Gulls have webbing extending to the tips of toes 2, 3, and 4. The hallux (toe 1) is smaller than in ducks and often does not register. The palm registers roughly half of the time. Gulls walk pigeon-toed. Ring-Billed Gull tracks measure 1⅞"–2¼" long; Herring Gull tracks measure 2½"–2⅞" long.

Terns have an elongated central toe (toe 3) that extends slightly beyond the webbing. The hallux (toe 1) and palm usually register clearly. Smaller than gull tracks, they measure 1"–1¾" long.

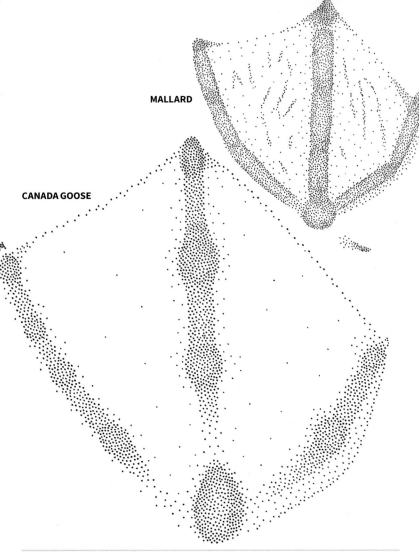

MALLARD

CANADA GOOSE

QUICK ID TIPS

- Three prominent toes connected by webbing.
- The outer toes curve inward.
- The palm usually registers clearly.

Waterfowl
Order Anseriformes: Family Anatidae

Ducks and geese are among the most recognizable birds in the Midwest. More than 40 species live in the Midwest or pass through during migration. All belong to the family Anatidae in the order Anseriformes. The Mallard (*Anas platyrhynchos*) and Canada Goose (*Branta canadensis*) are particularly wide-spread and abundant. Both are prolific track-makers and are common near waterways of all sizes in parks and suburban, exurban, and many rural areas.

TRACKS

Waterfowl tracks show three long toes. Toes are connected by webbing, which causes the outer toes (2 and 4) to curve inward. The palm registers reliably in most species. Geese have a reduced hallux (toe 1) that tends not to register. Knuckles are prominent and often register as lobes along the toes. The central toe (3) and palm often register more deeply than the outer toes (2 and 4). The palm often has a teardrop shape. Canada Goose tracks measure 3⅛"–4¾" long. Ducks have a longer hallux (toe 1) that usually registers. Their slender toes are less distinctly lobed than in geese. The palm tends to appear nearly circular. Track size is roughly, but not exactly, correlated to body size. Mallard tracks measure 2"–2⅞" long. Wood Duck (*Aix sponsa*) tracks are smaller, and Goldeneye and Bufflehead (*Bucephala* spp.) tracks are smaller still.

This section provides detailed information about the track patterns commonly left by mammals in the Midwest, including typical measurements. Each spread includes three to five illustrations of track patterns that are typical for a particular group of animals. On the facing page, you will find ranges of measurements for each species in the group. This layout allows for easy side-by-side comparisons of similar species.

The illustrations in this section are representative examples of track patterns. They are intended to help you interpret tracks and trails you find in the field. Each illustration shows one common arrangement of tracks left by a particular animal moving in a straight line, in a specific gait, and at a constant speed. In the field, you will find many variations on these patterns, as well as irregular patterns left by animals as they twist and turn, stop and start, and sit down and get up again. The illustrations are designed to help familiarize you with common track patterns of different groups of animals, and to provide a foundation for interpreting trails.

The measurements on the facing pages are based on broad collections of data, including my own field measurements, measurements of photographs taken by myself and other certified trackers, and ranges published by other professional trackers. They cover the majority of trails left by adults, and most sub-adults, for each species in this guide. While these data are extensive, they are not definitive or completely comprehensive. If you spend enough time measuring track patterns, you will eventually encounter trails that fall outside of these parameters. And in a few cases, such as the loping and galloping strides of many large hoofed animals, there are too few measurements available for me to offer typical ranges.

Typical track patterns for each group of animals are illustrated across one, two, or three two-page spreads, depending on how much variety is common for each group. Similar track patterns are shown on the same page, when possible. Species are organized into the same groups as the main text, with the exception of the Armadillo. The track patterns and trail measurements for this unusual critter are included together with the flat-footed walkers on pages 322.

MEASURING TRACK PATTERNS

Stride: Measure the stride from any track in a sequence to the next track made by the same foot. To get an accurate measurement, you need to identify which tracks in a pattern were left by the same foot. This is often straightforward but can be tricky when hind tracks register directly on top of fronts. Be sure you can identify the tracks of all four feet in the pattern. Next, make sure you measure from the same part of each track. For some animals, it is easiest to measure from the back edge of the heel on one track to the back edge of the heel on the next. For other animals, it is easier to measure from the front edge of the toe. You can use any part of the two tracks to make your measurement, as long as it is the same.

Trail: Measure trail width perpendicular to the animal's line of travel. For zigzagging track patterns, as well as those left by most lopes and gallops, begin by identifying a section of trail where the animal is moving straight. Next, stretch a string or place a straightedge along the outside edge of two or more consecutive tracks on one side of the trail. Measure the distance between your string and the outside edge of a track on the opposite side of the trail. For most bounds, many side-trots, and Raccoon walks, you can simply measure across the widest portion of the track pattern.

Group: Measure group length from the back edge of the rearmost track in the group to the front edge of the foremost track in the group.

Intergroup Distance: Measure intergroup distance from the front edge of the foremost track in a group and the rear edge of the rearmost track in the next group. The group length plus the intergroup distance is equal to the animal's stride.

For detailed information about interpreting track patterns, please see "Stepping Back: Track Patterns & Gaits," page 18.

A Wolf direct-register trotting gait showing stride and trail width

A Woodchuck bounding gait showing group length, intergroup distance, stride, and trail width

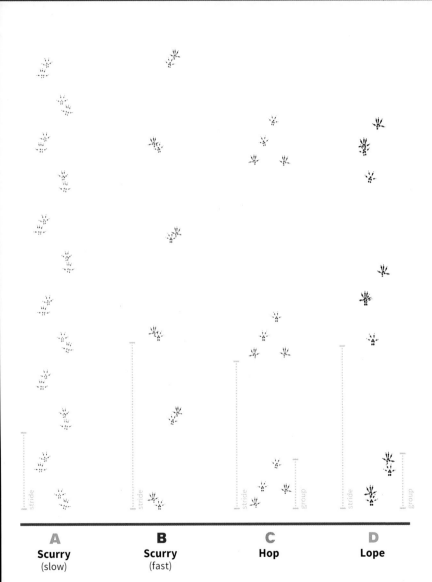

A
Scurry
(slow)

B
Scurry
(fast)

C
Hop

D
Lope

Shrews use a variety of gaits and may leave track patterns like **A**, **B**, **C** or **D**.

Harvest mice and **House Mice** often scurry near cover, leaving patterns like **A** and **B**. **Deer mice** occasionally do.

Voles and **lemmings** use a variety of gaits and may leave track patterns like **A**, **B**, **C** or **D**.

Pocket gophers scurry, leaving patterns like **A** or **B**.

Cotton rats and **rice rats** usually scurry, leaving patterns like **A** or **B**. They may hop in the open, leaving an irregular pattern like **C**.

Woodrats often walk in or near cover, leaving a pattern like **A**.

Old World rats usually scurry when foraging or near cover, leaving patterns like **A** or **B**.

	SCURRY STRIDE	SCURRY TRAIL	HOP/LOPE STRIDE	HOP/LOPE TRAIL	HOP/LOPE GROUP
Shrews	1¾"–4"	½"–1½"	2"–8"	¾"–1½"	½"–2"
Mice	1¾"–4"	1"–1¾"			
Voles	2"–8"	⅞"–1¾"	5½"–10"	1"–1¾"	⅝"–2½"
Pocket Gophers	2¾"–8"	1⅛"–2"			
Cotton & Rice Rats	3¼"–10"	1⅛"–2"	4"–10"	1½"–2¼"	1"–2"
Woodrats	3½"–6¾"	1¾"–2⅜"			
Old World Rats	4"–8"	1½"–2¾"			

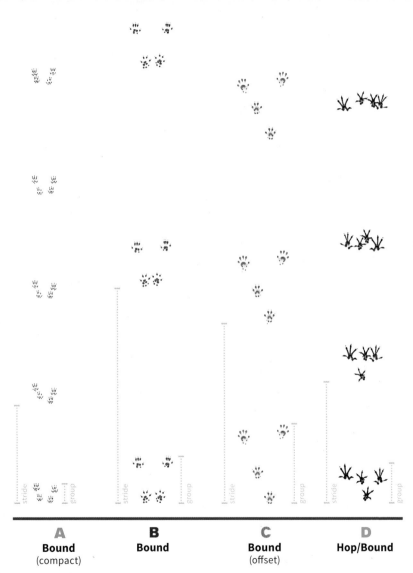

A	**B**	**C**	**D**
Bound	**Bound**	**Bound**	**Hop/Bound**
(compact)		(offset)	

Shrews often bound in snow, leaving compact 2x2 track patterns like **A**.

Pocket mice bound, leaving a pattern similar to **B**, but with their front feet typically turned out and overlapping.

Harvest mice bound, leaving patterns like **B**, **C**, and **D**, which tend to be less regular than those of **house mice** and **deer mice.**

Deer mice and **House Mice** bound, leaving track patterns like **B**. In deep snow (for a mouse), they may leave a compact 2x2 pattern like **A**.

Voles and **lemmings** sometimes bound, leaving compact, irregular patterns like **A** or **D**.

Jumping mice bound, leaving compact, irregular track patterns like **D**. Front feet are usually offset and turned out.

Cotton rats and **rice rats** may bound in the open, leaving irregular track patterns like **C** and **D**.

Woodrats bound in the open, leaving track patterns like **B**, **C**, or sometimes **D**.

Old World rats bound in the open with their front feet offset, leaving patterns like **C** or sometimes **D**.

	BOUND STRIDE	BOUND TRAIL	BOUND GROUP
Shrews	2"–8"	¾"–1½"	½"–2"
Pocket Mice	3"–7½"	¾"–1½"	⅞"–2"
Harvest Mice	4"–9"	1"–1½"	½"–2"
Deer & House Mice	4"–9" (to 24")	1⅛"–1¾"	1"–2½"
Voles	5½"–10"	1"–1¾"	⅝"–2"
Jumping Mice	3"–10" (to 8")	1⅛"–2½"	⅝"–2¼"
Cotton & Rice Rats	4"–10"	1½"–2¼"	1½"–4"
Woodrats	7"–11"	2¼"–3¼"	2"–2½"
Old World Rats	6"–20"	1¾"–3¼"	1½"–4"

Track Patterns: Squirrels

Walking & Bounding

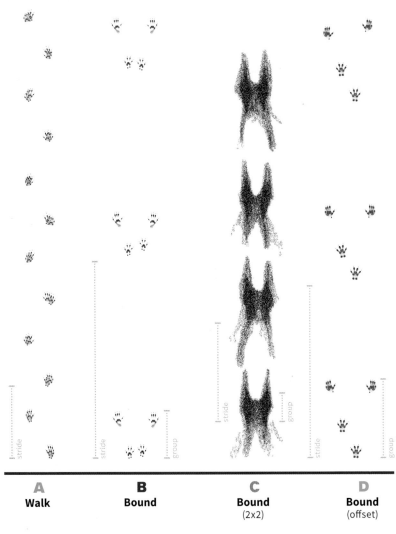

A
Walk

B
Bound

C
Bound
(2x2)

D
Bound
(offset)

Chipmunks bound almost exclusively, leaving track patterns like **B**.

Flying squirrels hop and bound. Hopping patterns resemble **B**, but with the front tracks in front of the hind. Bounding patterns resemble **B**, but with the front feet often placed wider apart.

Red, Gray and **Fox Squirrels** travel in a bound, leaving track patterns like **B**. In deeper snow, they may leave an H-shaped 2x2 pattern like **C**. They occasionally walk short distances, leaving patterns like **A**.

Ground squirrels walk while foraging or near their burrows, leaving patterns like **A**. They often travel in a bound, leaving boxy track patterns similar to **D**.

Prairie dogs usually walk, leaving track patterns like **A**. They may lope across open spaces (see "Track Patterns: Flat-Footed Walkers & Armadillo", page 326. Pattern **B** for an example).

Woodchucks typically walk, leaving track patterns like **A**. They may bound if alarmed, leaving a pattern like **D**.

Long-Tailed Weasels sometimes bound, leaving a squirrel-like track pattern similar to **D**.

	BOUND STRIDE	BOUND TRAIL	BOUND GROUP	WALK STRIDE	TRAIL WIDTH
Chipmunks	4"–20"	2"–3⅛"	1⅛"–4"		
Flying Squirrels	7"–36"	1⅝"–3½"	1½"–5"		
Red Squirrels	8"–48"	2⅞"–4¼"	2"–7"	5½"–10"	2¼"–3¼"
Gray Squirrels	8"–60"	3½"–6"	2"–9"	7"–12"	3½"–5"
Ground Squirrels	12"–34"	2¼"–4½"	2⅝"–8"	5"–10"	2"–3"
Prairie Dogs	20"–36"	3¼"–4¼"	10"–18"	5"–9½"	3"–4½"
Woodchucks	14"–32"	4"–7¾"	4¾"–15"	8"–17"	3¾"–6"
Long-Tailed Weasels	17"–28"	1⅞"–3"	3¾"–10"		

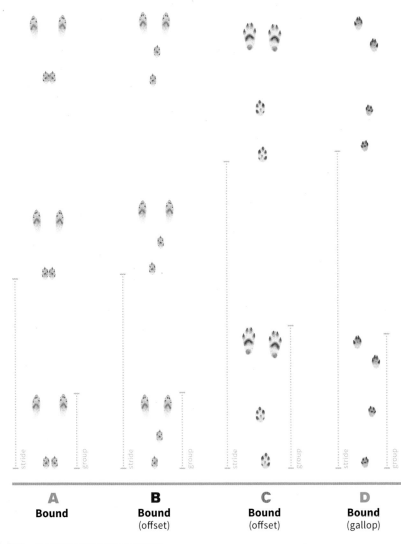

A
Bound

B
Bound
(offset)

C
Bound
(offset)

D
Bound
(gallop)

Cottontails and **Snowshoe Hares** bound almost exclusively, leaving track patterns like **A**, **B**, and **C**.

Jackrabbits travel in a bounding gallop, leaving track patterns like **D**.

	BOUND STRIDE	BOUND TRAIL	BOUND GROUP
Cottontails	10"–66"	2"–5"	5"–18"
Snowshoe Hares	16"–72"	4"–10"	8"–30"
Black-Tailed Jackrabbits	18"–82"+	2½"–5¾"	6½"–35"
White-Tailed Jackrabbits	24"–90"+	3"–8"	10"–46"

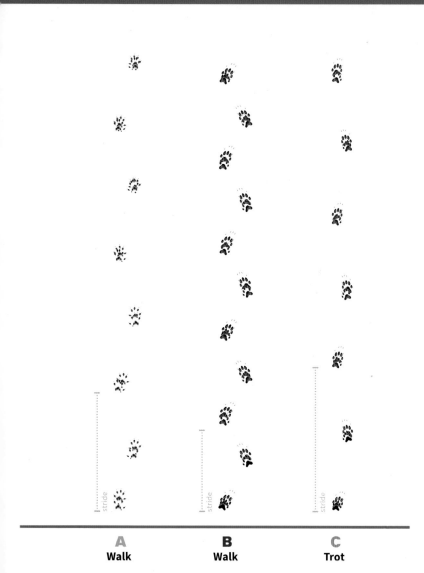

A
Walk

B
Walk

C
Trot

Mink sometimes walk, leaving a track pattern like **A**.

Fishers, particularly larger males, sometimes walk, leaving track patterns like **A**.

River Otters occasionally walk, leaving track patterns like **A**.

Badgers walk and trot with their front feet toed in, leaving patterns such as **B** and **C**.

	WALK STRIDE	WALK TRAIL	TROT STRIDE	TROT TRAIL
Mink	7"–15"	2"–4"		
Fishers	14"–27"	5"–6½"		
River Otters	9"–24"	4½"–7"		
Badgers	11"–21"	4"–7½"	20"–26"	2¾"–5"

Track Patterns: Weasels
Loping & Bounding

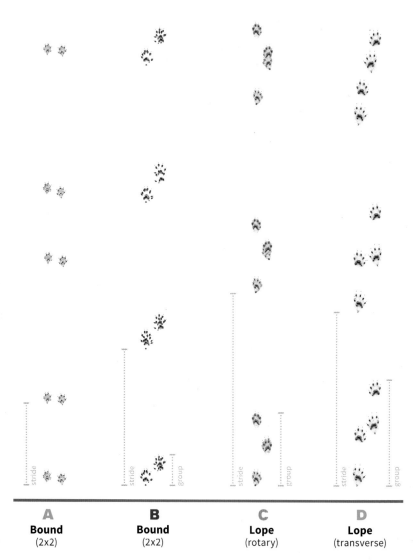

A
Bound
(2x2)

B
Bound
(2x2)

C
Lope
(rotary)

D
Lope
(transverse)

Small weasels lope and bound, often with irregular stride lengths, leaving track patterns like **A** and **B**. **Long-Tailed Weasels** sometimes leave a squirrel-like track pattern (see "Track Patterns: Squirrels," page 314).

Mink bound and lope, leaving a variety of track patterns like **B**, **C**, and **D**, typically with a consistent stride.

Martens bound and lope, leaving track patterns like **B** and **C**.

Fishers bound and lope, leaving track patterns like **B**, **C**, and **D**.

River Otters typically lope, leaving a track pattern like **D**, and sometimes lope or bound, leaving patterns like **B** or **C**.

Badgers may lope when alarmed, leaving a track pattern like **D**.

	LOPE/BOUND STRIDE	2x2 BOUND TRAIL	LOPE GROUP	2x2 BOUND GROUP
Least Weasels	4"–40"	¾"–1⅝"		
Short-Tailed Weasels	4"–40"	⅞"–2⅛"		
Long-Tailed Weasels	4"–40"	1½"–3"		
Mink	10"–36"	1¾"–4"	5"–14"	3½"–6¾"
Martens	14"–40"	2½"–4½"	6"–20"	3"–7"
Fishers	18"–48"	3"–7"	12"–24"	5"–9"
River Otters	18"–40"	4½"–7"	10"–20"	6"–12"
Badgers	24"–36"		16"–20"	

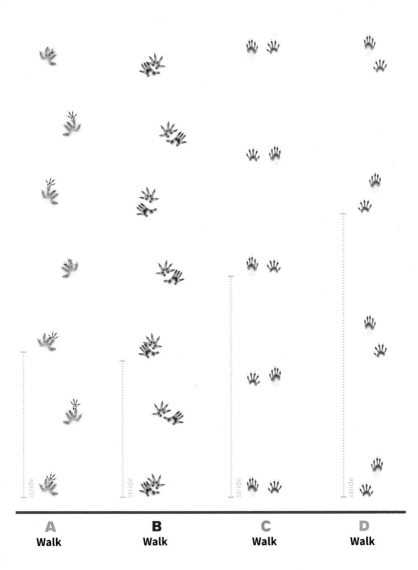

A
Walk

B
Walk

C
Walk

D
Walk

Muskrats usually walk, leaving an indirect-register pattern like **A**.

Opossums often walk, leaving indirect-register patterns like **A** or **B**. Pattern **B** is distinctive for Opossums and may resemble the **Raccoon**'s pattern **C**.

Raccoons walk, leaving distinctive paired track patterns like **C** and **D**. In deep snow, they may leave a pattern similar to **A**.

Beavers usually walk, leaving an indirect-register pattern like **A**. Large hind tracks usually obscure the fronts.

	WALK STRIDE	WALK TRAIL
Muskrats	5"–12"	2⅞"–5¼"
Opossums	9½"–20"	2½"–5½"
Raccoons	18"–44"	3¼"–7"
Beavers	11½"–21"	5½"–10"

Track Patterns: Flat-Footed Walkers & Armadillos
Walking & Trotting

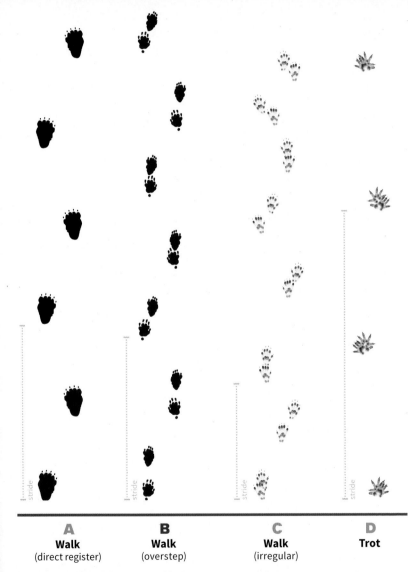

A
Walk
(direct register)

B
Walk
(overstep)

C
Walk
(irregular)

D
Trot

324   TRACK PATTERNS: FLAT-FOOTED WALKERS & ARMADILLO

Armadillos often walk while foraging, leaving track patterns like **B**.

Spotted Skunks walk while foraging, leaving irregular track patterns like **C**.

Striped Skunks often walk, leaving an overstep track pattern like **B** or an irregular pattern like **C**.

Porcupines walk almost exclusively, leaving track patterns like **A** or **B**, with front feet often toed in.

Opossums sometimes trot, leaving patterns like **D**.

Bears usually walk, leaving patterns like **B** or sometimes **A**. They occasionally trot, leaving a pattern like **D**.

	WALK STRIDE	WALK TRAIL	TROT STRIDE	TROT TRAIL
Armadillos	6½"–18"	2¾"–4"		
Spotted Skunks	6"–11"	2"–4"		
Striped Skunks	8"–17"	2½"–4½"		
Porcupines	9"–18"	3¾"–7"		
Opossums	9½"–20"	2½"–5½"	18"–30"	2½"–4"
Black Bears	35"–52"	7"–13"	50"–72"	6"–10"

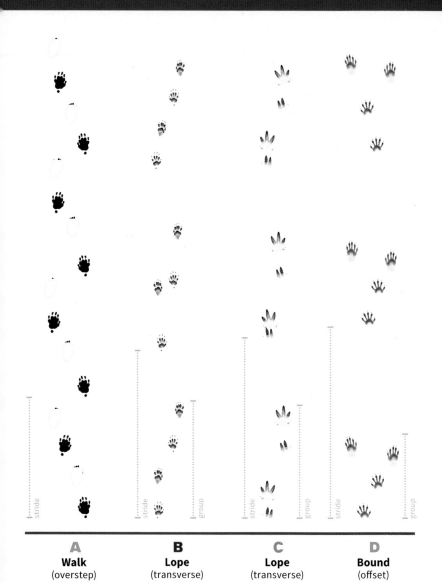

A	**B**	**C**	**D**
Walk (overstep)	**Lope** (transverse)	**Lope** (transverse)	**Bound** (offset)

Armadillos travel in a lope, leaving track patterns like **B** and **C**.

Spotted Skunks travel in a bound, leaving weasel- or squirrel-like track patterns that may resemble **D**.

Striped Skunks often travel in a lope, leaving a pattern like **B**. They also walk, sometimes leaving the similar looking pattern **A**.

Muskrats occasionally lope or bound, leaving patterns like **B**, **C**, or **D**.

Beavers occasionally bound, leaving patterns like **D**.

Raccoons occasionally lope or bound, leaving patterns like **B**, **C**, or **D**.

Black Bears occasionally lope, leaving patterns like **B** or **C**. They sometimes bound, especially on hills, leaving a pattern like **D**.

	LOPE/BOUND STRIDE	LOPE/BOUND TRAIL	LOPE/BOUND GROUP
Armadillos	12"–22"	2¾"–4"	9"–14"
Spotted Skunks	10"–20"	2"–3½"	2½"–8"
Striped Skunks	11"–22"	2"–4¾"	8"–15"
Muskrats	9"–20"	3"–4½"	3½"–9¾"
Beavers	18"–42"	7"–13"	7"–14"
Raccoons	24"–55"	6"–10"	12"–28"
Black Bears	60"–100"+	10"–24"	36"–60"

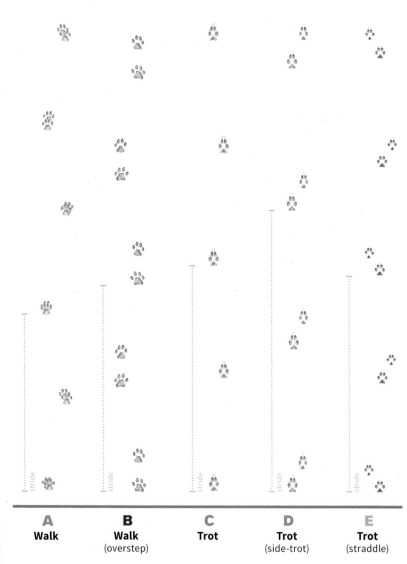

A
Walk

B
Walk
(overstep)

C
Trot

D
Trot
(side-trot)

E
Trot
(straddle)

Cats of all sizes typically walk, leaving an overstep track pattern like **B** or a direct- or indirect-register pattern like **A**. They occasionally trot, leaving a pattern like **C**.

Swift Foxes sometimes trot, leaving a pattern like **C** or **D**. They occasionally walk, leaving a pattern like **A**.

Gray Foxes travel in a trot, leaving patterns like **C** or **E**. They sometimes walk, leaving a pattern like **A**.

Red Foxes commonly trot, leaving patterns like **C**, **D**, and occasionally **E**. They sometimes walk, leaving a pattern like **A**.

Coyote and **Wolves** usually trot but also walk frequently, leaving patterns like **A**, **B**, **C**, and **D**.

Domestic Dogs exhibit a wide range of gaits and may leave track patterns like **A**, **B**, **C**, and **D**.

Fishers sometimes walk, leaving a track pattern like **A**.

	WALK STRIDE	WALK TRAIL	TROT STRIDE	TROT TRAIL
Domestic Cats	12"–24"	2"–4¾"	20"–32"	2"–4"
Bobcats	18"–34"	4"–8"	30"–48"	2½"–4½"
Lynx	18"–36"	4"–10"	36"–50"	4"–6½"
Cougars	25"–48"	4"–12"	58"–76"	3"–5½"
Swift Foxes	9"–14"	1½"–3"	15"–30"	1¼"–3"
Gray Foxes	12"–18"	3"–4¾"	18"–38"	1¾"–5"
Red Foxes	16"–26"	2½"–6"	28"–42"	2"–6"
Coyotes	24"–36"	3"–6"	30"–54"	2¼"–4"
Wolves	33"–48"	6"–10"	44"–80"	4"–9"
Fishers	14"–27"	5"–6½"		

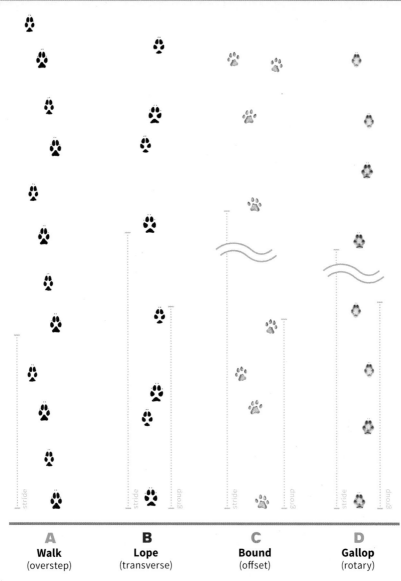

A	**B**	**C**	**D**
Walk	**Lope**	**Bound**	**Gallop**
(overstep)	(transverse)	(offset)	(rotary)

Cats of all sizes speed up into lopes, bounds, and gallops, leaving track patterns like **B**, **C**, and **D**.

Swift Foxes travel in a lope, leaving a track pattern like **B**. They may also gallop, leaving a pattern like **D**.

Gray Foxes speed up into lopes and gallops, leaving patterns like **B** and **D**.

Red Foxes sometimes travel in a lope, leaving a track pattern like **B**. They may also gallop, leaving a pattern like **D**.

Coyotes occasionally walk, leaving pattern **A**, which resembles a lope pattern. They also speed up into lopes and gallops, leaving patterns like **B** and **D**.

Domestic Dogs exhibit a wide range of gaits and may leave track patterns like **A**, **B**, or **D**.

Wolves speed up into lopes and gallops, occasionally while traveling, leaving patterns like **B** and **D**.

	LOPE STRIDE	LOPE GROUP	LOPE TRAIL	GALLOP STRIDE	GALLOP GROUP
Domestic Cats				24"–72"	10"–34"
Bobcats				48"–96"	24"–45"
Lynx				36"–110"	15"–60"
Cougars	85"–105"	40"–50"		84"–180"+	50"–75"
Swift Foxes	20"–30"	15"–20"		36"–72"	24"–45"
Gray Foxes	20"–36"	15"–20"	2"–4"	30"–110"	15"–50"
Red Foxes	30"–48"	20"–36"	2¼"–4"	36"–110"	24"–60"
Coyotes	32"–54"	24"–36"	3"–6"	44"–180"	36"–102"
Wolves	48"–72"	38"–54"		72"–240"	54"–100"

Track Patterns: Hoofed Animals

Walking & Trotting

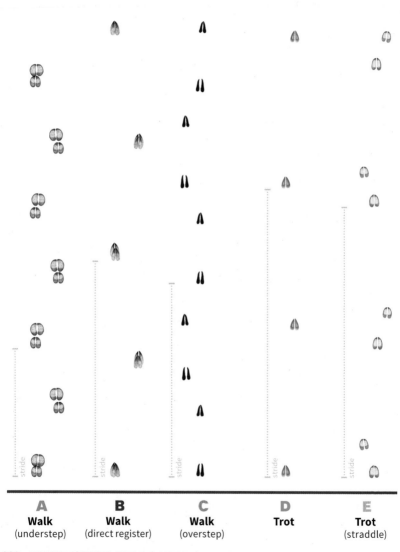

A	B	C	D	E
Walk (understep)	**Walk** (direct register)	**Walk** (overstep)	**Trot**	**Trot** (straddle)

Pigs walk when foraging, leaving patterns like **A** and **B**. They may travel in a trot, leaving a pattern like **D**.

Pronghorn usually walk, often leaving patterns like **B** or, distinctively, an overstep pattern like **C**. They sometimes trot, leaving a pattern like **D**.

Mountain Goats typically walk, leaving a pattern like **B**.

Bighorn Sheep usually walk, leaving patterns like **B** or **C**. They often trot while traveling on level ground, leaving a pattern like **D**.

White-Tailed Deer usually walk, leaving a pattern like **B** or sometimes **A**. They occasionally trot, leaving a pattern like **D**.

Elk and **Moose** typically walk, leaving a pattern like **B**. They speed up into trots, leaving patterns like **D** and **E**.

Bison typically walk, leaving an understep pattern like **A**. They occasionally trot, leaving a pattern like **D**.

Cows typically walk, leaving a pattern like **B**. They may speed up to a trot, leaving a pattern like **D**.

Horses typically walk, leaving a pattern like **C** or sometimes **B**, but they may also trot, leaving a pattern like **D**.

	WALK STRIDE	WALK TRAIL	TROT STRIDE	TROT TRAIL
Feral Pigs	22"–32"	7"–8½"	50"–60"	3"–4½"
Pronghorn	30"–58"	4⅜"–10½"		
White-Tailed Deer	20"–48"	4"–10"	48"–100" (114")*	2"–5" (15")
Elk	36"–70"	5½"–13½"	64"–90" (120")	3½"–7" (15")
Moose	48"–88"	6½"–20"	86"–110" (144")	6½"–15" (22")
Bison	26"–74"	10"–22"	78"–88"	10"–15"
Cows	50"–70"	10"–15"		
Horses	40"–76"	7"–16"	about 200"	

*NUMBERS IN PARENTHESES ARE FOR STRADDLE TROT, **E**.

Track Patterns: Hoofed Animals

Loping, Bounding, Galloping & Pronking

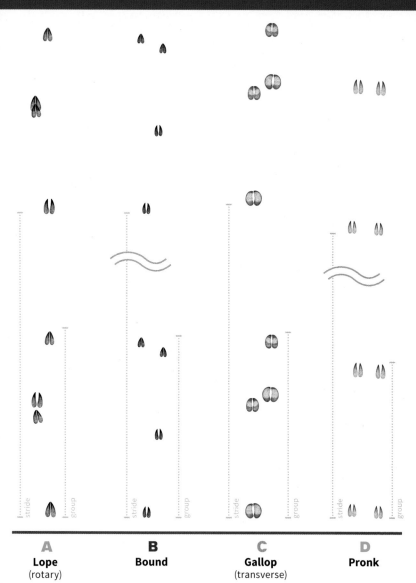

A
Lope
(rotary)

B
Bound

C
Gallop
(transverse)

D
Pronk

Pronghorn speed up into lopes and gallops, leaving patterns like **A** and **C**.

White-Tailed Deer speed up into lopes, bounds, and gallops, leaving patterns like **A**, **B**, and **C**.

Mule Deer speed up into a pronk, nearly unique to this species, leaving a track pattern like **D**.

Elk and **Moose** may speed up into lopes or gallops, leaving patterns like **A** or **C**.

Pigs, Bison, and **cattle** may speed up into lopes and gallops, leaving patterns like **A** or **C**.

Horses may speed up into a lope or gallop, most often leaving track patterns similar to **C**.

Note: There are not enough measurements of the loping or galloping strides of most hoofed animals to offer typical ranges.

	BOUND/ GALLOP STRIDE	BOUND/ GALLOP GROUP	PRONK STRIDE	PRONK GROUP	PRONK TRAIL
Pronghorn	72"–120"+	36"–82"			
White-Tailed Deer	72"–240"	10"–60"			
Moose	110"–240"+	60"–120"			
Mule Deer			74"–200"+	24"–42"	7½"–18"

Quick Reference Size Charts
Range of Track Length

- **BLACK BEAR** and **AMERICAN BEAVER** have hind track maximums beyond the size of this page.

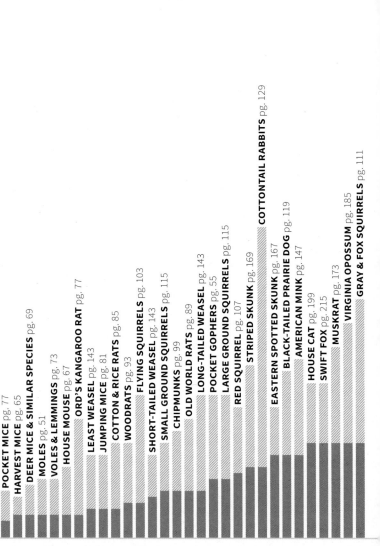

BATS pg. 47
SHREWS pg. 61
POCKET MICE pg. 77
HARVEST MICE pg. 65
DEER MICE & SIMILAR SPECIES pg. 69
MOLES pg. 51
VOLES & LEMMINGS pg. 73
HOUSE MOUSE pg. 67
ORD'S KANGAROO RAT pg. 77
LEAST WEASEL pg. 143
JUMPING MICE pg. 81
COTTON & RICE RATS pg. 85
WOODRATS pg. 93
FLYING SQUIRRELS pg. 103
SHORT-TAILED WEASEL pg. 143
SMALL GROUND SQUIRRELS pg. 115
CHIPMUNKS pg. 99
OLD WORLD RATS pg. 89
LONG-TAILED WEASEL pg. 143
POCKET GOPHERS pg. 55
LARGE GROUND SQUIRRELS pg. 115
RED SQUIRREL pg. 107
STRIPED SKUNK pg. 169
COTTONTAIL RABBITS pg. 129
EASTERN SPOTTED SKUNK pg. 167
BLACK-TAILED PRAIRIE DOG pg. 119
AMERICAN MINK pg. 147
HOUSE CAT pg. 199
SWIFT FOX pg. 215
MUSKRAT pg. 173
VIRGINIA OPOSSUM pg. 185
GRAY & FOX SQUIRRELS pg. 111

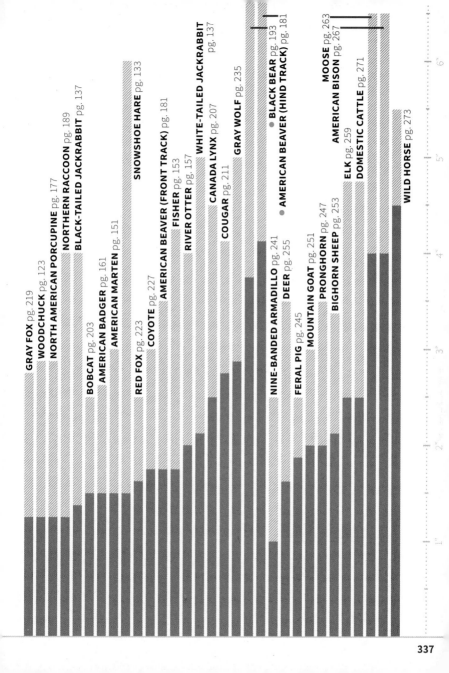

GRAY FOX pg. 219
WOODCHUCK pg. 123
NORTH AMERICAN PORCUPINE pg. 177
NORTHERN RACCOON pg. 189
BLACK-TAILED JACKRABBIT pg. 137
SNOWSHOE HARE pg. 133
BOBCAT pg. 203
AMERICAN BADGER pg. 161
AMERICAN MARTEN pg. 151
RED FOX pg. 223
COYOTE pg. 227
AMERICAN BEAVER (FRONT TRACK) pg. 181
FISHER pg. 153
RIVER OTTER pg. 157
WHITE-TAILED JACKRABBIT pg. 137
CANADA LYNX pg. 207
COUGAR pg. 211
GRAY WOLF pg. 235
● BLACK BEAR pg. 193
● AMERICAN BEAVER (HIND TRACK) pg. 181
NINE-BANDED ARMADILLO pg. 241
DEER pg. 255
FERAL PIG pg. 245
MOUNTAIN GOAT pg. 251
PRONGHORN pg. 247
BIGHORN SHEEP pg. 253
MOOSE pg. 263
AMERICAN BISON pg. 267
ELK pg. 259
DOMESTIC CATTLE pg. 271
WILD HORSE pg. 273

1"   2"   3"   4"   5"   6"

Range of Track Width

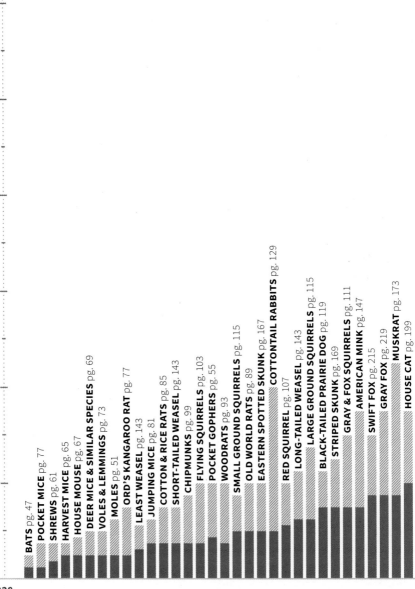

BATS pg. 47
POCKET MICE pg. 77
SHREWS pg. 61
HARVEST MICE pg. 65
HOUSE MOUSE pg. 67
DEER MICE & SIMILAR SPECIES pg. 69
VOLES & LEMMINGS pg. 73
MOLES pg. 51
ORD'S KANGAROO RAT pg. 77
LEAST WEASEL pg. 143
JUMPING MICE pg. 81
COTTON & RICE RATS pg. 85
SHORT-TAILED WEASEL pg. 143
CHIPMUNKS pg. 99
FLYING SQUIRRELS pg. 103
POCKET GOPHERS pg. 55
WOODRATS pg. 93
SMALL GROUND SQUIRRELS pg. 115
OLD WORLD RATS pg. 89
EASTERN SPOTTED SKUNK pg. 167
COTTONTAIL RABBITS pg. 129
RED SQUIRREL pg. 107
LONG-TAILED WEASEL pg. 143
LARGE GROUND SQUIRRELS pg. 115
BLACK-TAILED PRAIRIE DOG pg. 119
STRIPED SKUNK pg. 169
GRAY & FOX SQUIRRELS pg. 111
AMERICAN MINK pg. 147
SWIFT FOX pg. 215
GRAY FOX pg. 219
MUSKRAT pg. 173
HOUSE CAT pg. 199

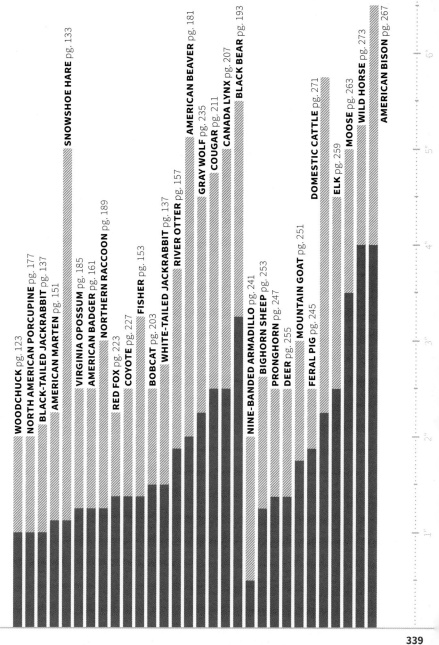

WOODCHUCK pg. 123
NORTH AMERICAN PORCUPINE pg. 177
BLACK-TAILED JACKRABBIT pg. 137
AMERICAN MARTEN pg. 151
SNOWSHOE HARE pg. 133
VIRGINIA OPOSSUM pg. 185
AMERICAN BADGER pg. 161
NORTHERN RACCOON pg. 189
RED FOX pg. 223
COYOTE pg. 227
FISHER pg. 153
BOBCAT pg. 203
WHITE-TAILED JACKRABBIT pg. 137
RIVER OTTER pg. 157
AMERICAN BEAVER pg. 181
GRAY WOLF pg. 235
COUGAR pg. 211
CANADA LYNX pg. 207
BLACK BEAR pg. 193
NINE-BANDED ARMADILLO pg. 241
BIGHORN SHEEP pg. 253
PRONGHORN pg. 247
DEER pg. 255
MOUNTAIN GOAT pg. 251
FERAL PIG pg. 245
DOMESTIC CATTLE pg. 271
ELK pg. 259
MOOSE pg. 263
WILD HORSE pg. 273
AMERICAN BISON pg. 267

1"   2"   3"   4"   5"   6"

Glossary

Arboreal Tree-dwelling.

Asymmetrical gait A gait in which footfalls are spaced unevenly (asymmetrically) in time. Because footfalls are grouped together in time, tracks generally appear grouped together on the ground. In quadrupeds, asymmetrical gaits produce repeating patterns of four tracks. Asymmetrical gaits include bounds and gallops.

Bound An asymmetrical gait in which the hind feet move together as a pair and land side-by-side, or nearly so. Bounds are typically dominated by an extended suspension. The animal is airborne (or nearly so) when its body is in an extended posture after pushing off with its hind feet.

Burrow An excavation in the earth used by an animal for shelter or storage.

Cache A store of food built up by an individual animal for future consumption. Also the act of storing food for later use.

Claws The nails on an animal's foot used for such activities as digging, climbing, and catching prey. In many animals, claws can show in tracks as round holes or narrow triangles in front of the toes.

Clear print A single footprint that shows the major features of the foot, including all of the toe, palm, and heel pads that typically register.

Crepuscular Active during twilight, usually at both dawn and dusk.

Cursorial Adapted for running, either at high speed or at a steady pace for a long distance. Felids, canids, and ungulates are considered cursorial mammals.

Digitigrade Walking on the toes (digits) with the heels high off the ground. Cats and dogs have a digitigrade posture. Contrasts with *plantigrade* and *unguligrade.*

Direct register A symmetrical track pattern in which each hind track is superimposed on top of the front track from the previous step. When only the hind tracks are clearly visible, direct-register patterns resemble bipedal track patterns.

Diurnal Active during the daytime.

Fossorial Having a burrowing lifestyle. Most often applied to animals that live predominantly underground.

Gait The way an animal moves its body for locomotion, including how it coordinates its limbs and the order of its footfalls. Examples of gaits include walks, trots, gallops, and bounds. When tracking, we interpret gaits based on the track patterns an animal leaves behind.

Gallop An asymmetrical gait in which the hind feet move independently and land one ahead of the another. Animals display a wide range of gallops, including stiff-legged "rocking horse" gaits often seen in dogs playing; fluid "Slinky-like" gaits used by weasels; and dramatic whole-body contracting and extending gaits of cats or Greyhounds in all-out sprints. Slow, gentle gallops are often called *lopes* (see below).

Habitat The type of environment where an animal is typically found.

Heel The rearmost portion of the foot. In some animals, the heel is held off the ground and rarely, if ever, registers in the track.

Hibernation A dormant state that some mammals enter into in the winter. It is characterized by a sharp reduction in metabolic activity to conserve energy.

Hoof The tips of the specially adapted toes that bear weight in a deer, horse, or other ungulate.

Hop A bound in which one or both front tracks appear ahead of both hind tracks in the track pattern.

Indirect register A symmetrical track pattern in which each hind track registers partially on top of the front track from the previous step. Similar to a direct register but with some or all features of the front tracks clearly visible.

Intergroup The distance between track groups in an asymmetrical gait. The intergroup distance plus the track group length equals the stride length.

Lead A track that appears farther forward in a track pattern.

Lope A slow, gentle gallop that can be sustained for a long period of time. The distinction between lopes and other gallops is subjective, and it is not always possible to define a lope when watching an animal move, let alone based on the track pattern it leaves behind.

Nest A structure made from leaves, grasses, or similar soft materials that is used by an animal for shelter, especially for giving birth and nursing young.

Nocturnal Active at night.

Overstep A symmetrical track pattern in which each hind track registers in front of the front track from the previous step.

Pad A patch of thick collagen and adipose tissue on the bottom of an animal's foot that cushions the bones.

Palm The area of the foot, especially the pads, located at the base of the toes. These pads are formally named *metacarpal pads* on the front foot and *metatarsal pads* on the hind foot, after the bones they cushion.

Plantigrade Walking on the soles of the feet with the bones of the palm flat to the ground and the heels bearing weight. Humans have a plantigrade posture. Contrasts with *digitigrade* and *unguligrade*.

Raccoon walk A distinctive gait used by Raccoons in which the hind foot lands close to the front foot on the opposite side of the body, creating side-by-side pairs of front and hind tracks.

Range The territory an animal covers in the course of its normal activities. Also the geographic area where a particular species is known to live.

Rotary gallop A galloping gait in which the leading front track is on the opposite side of the body from the leading hind track. The track groups left by a rotary gallop show four tracks arranged in an arc. Sometimes the two middle tracks in the group overlap, creating a group with only three distinct compressions.

Run A symmetrical bipedal (two-legged) gait in which the animal has both feet off the ground mid-stride. The word is sometimes used generically to describe fast quadrupedal locomotion, but does not identify any specific four-legged gait.

Scat Poop. An animal's excrement, which can both aid in identifying the animal and also yield clues about the animal's diet and behavior.

Sign Any indication left behind by an animal that gives a clue about its past activity. Sometimes the word is used to mean every indication left behind that isn't a track. Such indications include scat, scent posts, nests, burrows, digs, scratch marks, and feeding remains.

Step Half of a stride in a symmetrical gait; the movement from one foot contacting the ground until the opposite foot from the same pair contacts the ground. Step length is the distance from one hind track to the next hind track on the opposite side of the body—roughly one half the stride length.

Stride The basic repeating unit of an animal's gait, describing the complete sequence of footfalls from one foot contacting the ground until that same foot contacts the ground again. The length of a stride is the distance from any track in a sequence to the next track made by the same foot.

Substrate The material an animal walks on and on which tracks are made. Substrates include soil, sand, mud, and snow. Different substrates record tracks somewhat differently, and understanding how different substrates behave can help in interpreting tracks and trails, as well as predicting where to find clear tracks to study.

Subunguis The soft material on the underside of an animal's nail. In ungulates (deer, cattle, horses, pigs ,and their relatives), this forms part of the walking surface of the foot, in between the hard hoof wall and the cushioning pad.

Symmetrical gait A gait in which right and left footfalls of each front or hind pair are spaced symmetrically (evenly) in time. Symmetrical gaits produce symmetrical track patterns. Symmetrical gaits include walks and trots.

Toes The digits on the foot of an animal and the impressions left by those digits in the animal's tracks.

Torpor Any extended period of dormancy or inactivity, including hibernation.

Track A footprint left by an animal.

Track group The visual grouping of four tracks left by a single stride of an asymmetrical gait. Although a group always includes four tracks, hind tracks may land on top of fronts, producing groups with only two or three distinct footprints. The length of a track group is measured from the back edge of the rearmost track to the front edge of the foremost track.

Track pattern The repeating arrangement of tracks on the ground left by an animal moving in a particular gait.

Trail The tract an animal followed when it left a set of footprints. Also a well-worn path used repeatedly by an animal or group of animals.

Trail width The total width of an animal's track pattern; the distance from the outermost edge of an animal's left tracks to the outermost edge of the animal's right tracks, measured perpendicular to the animal's line of travel.

Transverse gallop A galloping gait in which the leading front track is on the same side of the body as the leading hind track. The track groups left by a transverse gallop show four tracks in a zigzag or diagonal line.

Trot A symmetrical gait in which diagonally opposite legs move together and there is a moment when the animal has all four feet off the ground. Trotting is similar to bipedal running.

Understep A symmetrical track pattern in which each hind track registers behind the front track from the previous step.

Unguis An animal's nail or claw. In tracking, and wildlife biology in general, the word is used almost exclusively to describe the specially adapted nails that form the horny sheath on an ungulate's hoof.

Ungulate A hoofed animal, such as a deer, cow, horse, or pig. Ungulates are the most abundant large animals in most terrestrial habitats.

Unguligrade Walking on the tips of the toes, including the nail or unguis. Deer and other hoofed animals have an unguligrade posture. Contrasts with *digitigrade* and *plantigrade.*

Walk A symmetrical gait in which the animal has at least one foot of each pair (front and hind) on the ground at all times.

Index

A

Allegheny Woodrat *(Neotoma magister)*, 94, 95
American Badger *(Taxidea taxus)*, 160–163, 319, 321
American Beaver *(Castor canadensis)*, 164–165, 180–183, 323, 327
American Bison *(Bison bison)*, 238–239, 266–269, 333
American Black Bear *(Ursus americanus)*, 164–165, 192–195, 325, 327
American Crow *(Corvus brachyrhynchos)*, 290–291
American Marten *(Martes americana)*, 150–151, 154–155, 321
American Robin, 288–289
American Woodcock, *(Scolopax minor)*, 301
amphibians, 277–280
Appalachian Cottontail *(Sylvilagus obscurus)*, 131
Armadillo, 16–17, 238–239, 240–243, 325, 327

B

Badger, 160–163, 319, 321
Bald Eagle *(Haliaeetus leucocephalus)*, 292–293
Barred Owl *(Strix varia)*, 299
Bat, 44–49
Bear, Black, 164–165, 192–195, 325, 327
Beaver, 164–165, 180–183, 323, 327
Bighorn Sheep *(Ovis canadensis)*, 252–253, 333
birds, 286–307
Bison, 238–239, 266–269, 333
Bitterns *(Botaurus lentiginosus and Ixobrychus exilis)*, 295
Black Bear, 164–165, 192–195, 325, 327

Black-Billed Magpie *(Pica hudsonia)*, 291
Black-Capped Chickadee, 288
Black-Crowned Night Heron *(Nycticorax nycticorax)*, 295
Black Rat *(Rattus rattus)*, 88–91
Black-Tailed Jackrabbit *(Lepus californicus)*, 136–139, 317
Black-Tailed Prairie Dog *(Cynomys ludovicianus)*, 118–121, 315
Black Tern *(Chlidonias niger)*, 305
Blue Jay *(Cyanocitta cristata)*, 290–291
Bobcat *(Lynx rufus)*, 202–205, 329, 331
Bobwhite *(Colinus virginianus)*, 303
Brown Rat *(Rattus norvegicus)*, 88–91
Buffalo, *See* Bison
Bufflehead *(Bucephala* spp.), 307
Bullsnake, 283
Burrowing Owl *(Athene cunicularia)*, 299
Bushy-Tailed Woodrat *(Neotoma cineria)*, 94, 95

C

Canada Goose *(Branta canadensis)*, 306–307
Canada Jay *(Perisoreus canadensis)*, 291
Canada Lynx *(Lynx canadensis)*, 206–209, 329, 331
Cardinals, 288–289
Cats, 16–17, 196–213, 328–331
  Bobcat, 202–205, 329, 331
  Cougar, 210–213, 329, 331
  Domestic, 198–201, 329, 331
  Lynx, 206–209, 329, 331
Chickadee, 288–289

Chipmunks *(Tamias* spp.), 98–101, 315
Common Raven *(Corvus corax)*, 290–291
Corvids, 286–287, 290–291
Cotton Rat *(Sigmodon hispidus)*, 84–87, 311, 313
Cottontail Rabbits *(Sylvilagus* spp.), 128–131, 317
Cougar *(Puma concolor)*, 210–213, 329, 331
Cow, 238–239, 270–271, 333
Coyote *(Canis latrans)*, 226–229, 329, 331
Crow, 290–291

D

Dark-Eyed Junco, 288–289
Deer, 238–239, 254–257, 333, 335
Deer Mice *(Peromyscus* spp.), 68–71, 311, 313
Desert Cottontail *(Sylvilagus audubonii)*, 131
Dogs, 16–17, 196–197, 214–237, 328–331
  Coyote, 226–229, 329, 331
  Domestic, 230–233
  Foxes, 214–225, 329, 331
  Wolf, 234–237, 329, 331
Domestic Cat *(Felis catus)*, 198–201, 329, 331
Domestic Cow *(Bos taurus)*, 238–239, 270–271, 333
Domestic Dog *(Canis familiaris)*, 230–233
Doves, 288–289
Downy Woodpecker *(Picoides pubescens)*, 297
Ducks, 306–307

E

Eagle, 292–293
Eastern Chipmunk *(Tamias minimus)*, 100
Eastern Cottontail *(Sylvilagus floridanus)*, 128–131
Eastern Fox Squirrel *(Sciurus niger)*, 110–113, 315

Eastern Gray Squirrel
(Sciurus carolinensis),
110–113, 315
Eastern Mole (Scalopus
aquaticus), 53
Eastern Newt, 274, 279
Eastern Screech Owl (Otus
asio), 299
Eastern Spotted Skunk
(Spilogale putorius),
164–165, 166–167,
170–171, 325, 327
Eastern Woodrat (Neotoma
floridana), 95
Egret, 295
Elk (Cervus elaphus),
258–261, 333

F
Feral Pig (Sus scrofa),
244–245, 333
Finches, 289
Fisher (Pekania pennanti),
152–155, 319, 321, 329
five-toe walkers, 16–17
flat-footed walkers,
164–195, 322–327
Flicker, Northern, 296–297
Flying Squirrels (Glaucomys
spp.), 102–105, 315
Forster's Tern (Sterna
forsteri), 304–305
Foxes, 214–225, 329, 331
    Gray, 218–221, 329, 331
    Red, 222–225, 329, 331
    Swift, 214–217, 329, 331
Fox Squirrel, 110–113, 315
Franklin's Ground Squirrel
(Poliocitellus franklinii),
116, 117
Frog, 274–275, 276–277

G
Game Birds, 286–287,
302–303
Geese, 306–307
Goat, Mountain,
250–251, 333
Goldeneye (Bucephala
spp.), 307
Golden Mouse (Ochrotomys
nuttalli), 71

Gophers, 44–45, 54–57,
311. See also Ground
Squirrels
Gray Fox (Urocyan cine-
reoargenteus), 218–221,
329, 331
Gray Squirrel, 110–113, 315
Gray Wolf (Canis lupus),
234–237, 329, 331
Great Blue Heron (Ardea
herodias), 294–295
Great Egret (Ardea alba), 295
Great Horned Owl (Bubo
virginianus), 298–299
Green Heron (Butorides
virescens), 295
Green Snake, 283
Groundhog. See
Woodchuck
Ground Squirrels,
114–117, 315
Grouse, 302–303
Gulls, 304–305

H
Hairy-Tailed Mole
(Parascalops breweri), 53
Hares. See Rabbits and Hares
Harvest Mice
(Reithrodontomys spp.),
64–65, 70–71, 311, 313
Hawks, 292–293
Herons, 286–287, 294–295
herps, 274–285
Herring Gull (Larus argenta-
tus), 305
Hispid Cotton Rat
(Sigmodon hispidus),
84–87, 311, 313
Hispid Pocket Mouse
(Chaetodipus hispidus),
78, 79
Hognose Snake, 283
hoofed animals, 16–17,
238–239, 244–273,
332–335
Horse, Wild, 238–239,
272–273, 333
House Mouse (Mus muscu-
lus), 66–67, 70–71, 90–91,
311, 313

J
Jackrabbits, 136–139, 317
Jays (bird), 290–291
Jumping Mice, 80–83, 313
Juncos, 288–289

K
Kangaroo Rat, 76–79
Killdeer (Charadrius
vociferus), 300–301

L
large rodents, 16–17,
172–183
    Beaver, 164–165,
    180–183, 323, 327
    Muskrat, 164–165,
    172–175, 323, 327
    Porcupine, 164–165,
    176–179, 325
Least Chipmunk (Tamias
striatus), 100
Least Shrew (Cryptotis
parva), 63
Least Weasel (Mustela
nivalis), 145, 321
Lemming, 75, 311, 313
Lizard, 274–275, 280–281
Long-Tailed Shrews (Sorex
spp.), 63
Long-Tailed Weasel
(Neogale frenata), 145,
315, 321
Lynx, 206–209, 329, 331

M
Magpie, 291
Mallard (Anas platyrhyn-
chos), 306–307
Marsh Rice Rat (Oryzomys
palustris), 84–87, 311, 313
Marten, American,
150–151, 154–155, 321
Meadow Jumping Mouse
(Zapus hudsonius), 83
Mice, 16–17, 58–59, 64–71,
76–83
    Deer, 68–71, 311, 313
    Harvest, 64–65, 70–71,
    311, 313
    House Mouse, 66–67,
    70–71, 313

Jumping, 80–83, 313
Pocket, 76–79, 313
Mink *(Neogale vision)*,
146–149, 319, 321
Moles, 44–45, 50–54
Moose *(Alces alces)*,
262–265, 333, 335
Mountain Cottontail
(Sylvilagus nuttallii), 131
Mountain Goat *(Oreamnos
americanus)*, 250–251, 333
Mountain Lion. *See* Cougar
Mourning Dove, 288–289
Mouse. *See* Mice
Mule Deer *(Odocoileus
hemionus)*, 254–257, 335
Muskrat *(Ondatra zibethi-
cus)*, 164–165, 172–175,
323, 327

N

Newts, 274, 278–279
Nine-banded Armadillo
(Dasypus novemcinctus),
16–17, 238–239, 240–243,
325, 327
North American Deer
Mouse *(Peromyscus
maniculatus)*, 71
North American Porcupine
(Erethizon dorsatum),
164–165, 176–179, 325
Northern Bobwhite *(Colinus
virginianus)*, 303
Northern Cardinal, 288–289
Northern Flicker *(Colaptes
auratus)*, 296–297
Northern Flying Squirrel
(Glaucomys sabrinus),
104, 105
Northern Grasshopper
Mouse *(Onychomys leuco-
gaster)*, 71
Northern Pocket Gopher
(Thomomys talpoides), 57
Northern Raccoon *(Procyon
lotor)*, 164–165, 188–191,
323, 327
Northern River Otter *(Lontra
canadensis)*, 156–159,
319, 321

Nuthatches, 289

O

Old World Rats, 88–91,
311, 313
Opossum, Virginia, 164–165,
184–187, 323, 325
Ord's Kangaroo Rat
(Dipodomys ordii), 76–79
Otter, River, 156–159,
319, 321
Owls, 286–287, 298–299

P

Packrats. *See* Woodrats
Painted Turtle *(Chrysemys
picta)*, 284–285
Pheasant, 303
Pig, 244–245, 333
Pigeons, 289
Pileated Woodpecker
(Dryocopus pileatus), 297
Pinyon Jay *(Gymnorhinus
cyanocephalus)*, 291
Plains Pocket Gopher
(Geomys bursarius), 57
Plains Pocket Mouse
(Perognathus flavescens),
78, 79
Plains Rattlesnake, 283
Plovers, 301
Pocket Gophers, 44–45,
54–57, 311
Pocket Mice, 76–79, 313
Porcupine, 164–165,
176–179, 325
Prairie Dog, 118–121, 315
Pronghorn *(Antilocapra
americana)*, 238–239,
246–249, 333, 335

R

Rabbits and Hares, 16–17,
126–139, 316–317
Cottontail, 128–131, 317
Jackrabbits, 136–139, 317
Snowshoe Hare,
132–135, 317
Raccoon, 164–165, 188–191,
323, 327
raptors, 286–287, 292–293
Rats, 16–17, 58–59, 84–95,
310–313

Hispid Cotton Rat, 84–87,
311, 313
Marsh Rice Rat, 84–87,
311, 313
Old World, 88–91, 311, 313
Woodrats, 92–95, 311, 313
Raven, 290–291
Redbelly Snake, 283
Red Fox *(Vulpes vulpes)*,
222–225, 329, 331
Red Squirrel *(Tamiasciurus
hudsonicus)*, 106–109, 315
reptiles, 280–285
Rice Rat *(Oryzomys palus-
tris)*, 84–87, 311, 313
Richardson's Ground
Squirrel *(Urocitellus
richardsonii)*, 117
Ring-Billed Gull *(Larus dela-
warensis)*, 304–305
Ring-Necked Pheasant
(Phasianus colchicus), 303
River Otter, 156–159, 319, 321
Robins, 288–289
rodents. *See* large rodents;
Mice; Rats; Squirrels
Ruffed Grouse *(Bonasa
umbellus)*, 302–303

S

Salamander, 274–275,
278–279
Sanderling *(Calidris alba)*, 301
Sandpipers, 301
Seabirds, 286–287, 304–305
Sheep, Bighorn,
252–253, 333
Shorebirds, 286–287,
300–301
Short-Tailed Shrews *(Blarina
spp.)*, 63
Short-Tailed Weasel
(Mustela richardsonii),
145, 321
Shrews, 16–17, 58–63,
310–313
Silky Pocket Mouse
(Perognathus flavus), 79
Skinks *(Eumeces spp.)*,
280–281

Skunks, 16–17, 164–171, 325, 327

Snakes, 274–275, 282–283

Snapping Turtle (Chelydra serpentina), 284–285

Snipe, Wilson's (Gallinago delicata), 301

Snowshoe Hare (Lepus americanus), 132–135, 317

Snowy Owl (Nyctea scandiaca), 299

Songbirds, 286–287, 288–289

Southern Flying Squirrel (Glaucomys volans), 104, 105

Southern Plains Woodrat (Neotoma micropus), 94, 95

Sparrows, 289

Spotted Ground Squirrel (Xerospermophilus spilosoma), 117

Spotted Sandpiper (Actitis macularius), 300–301

Spotted Skunk (Spilogale putorius), 164–165, 166–167, 170–171, 325, 327

Squirrels, 16–17, 96–125, 314–315
  Chipmunks, 98–101, 315
  Eastern Fox, 110–113, 315
  Eastern Gray, 110–113, 315
  Flying, 102–105, 315
  Ground, 114–117, 315
  Prairie Dog, 118–121, 315
  Red, 106–109, 315
  Woodchuck, 122–125, 315

Star-Nosed Mole (Condylura cristata), 53

Striped Skunk (Mephitis mephitis), 164–165, 168–171, 325, 327

Swamp Rabbit (Sylvilagus aquaticus), 131

Swift Fox (Vulpes velox), 214–217, 329, 331

T

Terns, 304–305

Thirteen Lined Ground Squirrel (Ictidomys tridecemlineatus), 116, 117

Tiger Salamander (Ambystoma spp.), 279

tiny track group, 58–95. See also Mice; Voles; Weasels
  Rats, 16–17, 58–59, 84–95, 310–313
  Shrews, 16–17, 58–63, 310–313

Titmouse, 289

Toad, 277

Tree Squirrels, 102–109, 315

Turkey, Wild, 302–303

Turtles, 274–275, 284–285

V

Virginia Opossum (Didelphis virginiana), 164–165, 184–187, 323, 325

Voles, 16–17, 58–59, 72–75, 310–313
  Muskrat, 164–165, 172–175, 323, 327
  Voles and Lemmings, 72–75, 310–313

W

Waterfowl, 286–287, 306–307

Water Snake, 283

Weasels, 16–17, 58, 140–163, 318–321
  Badger, 160–163, 319, 321
  Fisher, 152–155, 319, 321, 329
  Marten, 150–151, 154–155, 321
  Mink, 146–149, 319, 321
  River Otter, 156–159, 319, 321
  Weasels, 142–145, 315, 321

Western Jumping Mouse (Zapus princeps), 83

White-Footed Mouse (Peromyscus leucopus), 71

White-Tailed Deer (Odocoileus virginianus), 238–239, 254–257, 333, 335

White-Tailed Jackrabbit (Lepus townsendii), 136–139, 317

Wild Horse (Equus caballus), 238–239, 272–273, 333

Wild Turkey (Meleagris gallopavo), 302–303

Wilson's Snipe (Gallinago delicata), 300–301

Wolf, Gray, 234–237, 329, 331

Woodchuck (Marmota monax), 122–125, 315

Woodcock, 301

Wood Duck (Aix sponsa), 307

Woodland Jumping Mouse (Napaeozapus insignis), 83

Woodpeckers, 286–287, 296–297

Woodrats (Neotoma spp.), 92–95, 311, 313

Wyoming Pocket Mouse (Perognathus fasciatus), 79

Y

Yellow-Faced Pocket Gopher (Cratogeomys castanops), 57

Photo Credits

Additional Resources

There are a great many resources and references dedicated to tracking and wildlife. Some are excellent, while others can be quite misleading. Below are some of my favorites. You can find many of the books on my curated lists at **www.bookshop.org/shop/poppele.** Bookshop.org donates a percentage of each sale to local, independent bookstores.

GUIDES TO TRACKS & TRACKING

Elbroch, M., Kresky, M., & Evans, J. (2012). *Field Guide to Animal Tracks and Scat of California.* Berkeley: University of California Press.

Evans, J. (2020). *iTrack Wildlife.* App for iOS and Android.

Liebenberg, L., Louw, A., & Elbroch, M. (2010). *Practical Tracking: A Guide to Following Footprints and Finding Animals.* Mechanicsburg, PA: Stackpole Books.

Moskowitz, D. (2010). *Wildlife of the Pacific Northwest: Tracking and Identifying Mammals, Birds, Reptiles, Amphibians, and Invertebrates.* Portland, OR: Timber Press.

Pesaturo, J. (2018). *Camera Trapping Guide: Tracks, Sign, and Behavior of Eastern Wildlife.* Mechanicsburg, PA: Stackpole Books.

Spielman, L. J. (2017). *A Field Guide to Tracking Mammals in the Northeast.* Woodstock, VT: The Countryman Press.

SOCIAL MEDIA SITES

Animals Don't Cover Their Tracks: Animal Track Identification Help Group on Facebook One of the largest and most active social media groups dedicated to animal tracking.

North American Animal Tracks database on iNaturalist This project is one of the most extensive collections of track and sign photos on the web, and a great place to get help with identification. **www.inaturalist.org**

WILDLIFE TRACKER TRAINING, CLUBS & VOLUNTEER OPPORTUNITIES

Tracker Certification North America offers the international standard in wildlife tracker training and certification from world-class instructors. **www.trackercertification.com**

Minnesota Wildlife Tracking Project hosts tracking clubs, study groups, wildlife surveys, and tracker certification opportunities. This is my home organization, and I am active in most of our programs. **www.mntracking.org**

Wisconsin Volunteer Carnivore Tracking Program is a citizen science program organized by the Wisconsin Department of Natural Resources. **dnr.wisconsin.gov**

BOOKS & SCHOLARLY ARTICLES FOR IN-DEPTH STUDY
Comprehensive Reference Guides to Tracks & Sign

Eiseman, C., Charney, N., & Carlson, J. (2010). *Tracks & Sign of Insects & Other Invertebrates: A Guide to North American Species.* Mechanicsburg, PA: Stackpole Books.

Elbroch, M. (2019). *Mammal Tracks & Sign: A Guide to North American Species* (2nd ed.). Mechanicsburg, PA: Stackpole Books.

Elbroch, M., Marks, E., & Boretos, C. D. (2001). *Bird Tracks & Sign: A Guide to North American Species.* Mechanicsburg, PA: Stackpole Books.

Tkaczyk, F. (2015). *Tracks & Sign of Reptiles & Amphibians: A Guide to North American Species.* Mechanicsburg, PA: Stackpole Books.

Mammal Biology, Behavior & Ecology

Elbroch, M., & Rinehart, K. (2011). *Peterson Reference Guide to Behavior of North American Mammals.* New York: Houghton Mifflin Harcourt.

Feldhamer, G. A. (Ed.). (2003). *Wild Mammals of North America: Biology, Management, and Conservation* (2nd ed.). Baltimore, MD: Johns Hopkins University Press.

Hazard, E. B. (1982). *The Mammals of Minnesota.* Minneapolis: University of Minnesota Press.

Schwartz, C. W., & Schwartz, E. R. (2016). *The Wild Mammals of Missouri* (3rd ed.). D. K. Fantz & V. L. Jackson (Eds.). Columbia: University of Missouri Press.

Mammalian Species journal series, published by the American Society of Mammalogists.

Animal Gaits & Locomotion

Dagg, A. I. (1973). Gaits in Mammals. *Mammal Review,* 3(4), 135–154.

Hildebrand, M. (1960). How Animals Run. *Scientific American,* 202(5), 148–160.

Hildebrand, M. (1989). The Quadrupedal Gaits of Vertebrates. *BioScience,* 39(11), 766–775.

Muybridge, E. (1957). *Animals in Motion.* New York: Dover Publications. (Originally published 1887)

About the Author

Jonathan Poppele earned a master's degree in Conservation Biology from the University of Minnesota, studying citizen science, environmental philosophy, and how to cultivate a personal connection to the natural world through animal tracking. He taught for many years at the U of M in both the College of Biological Sciences and the Department of Writing Studies before leaving to focus on his own projects. Jon is the founder and director of the Minnesota Wildlife Tracking Project (www.mntracking.org), where he mentors trackers and coordinates wildlife surveys. Jon is also head instructor for the Minnesota Ki Society, where he teaches meditation, mindfulness, and the peaceful martial art of Ki-Aikido.